Brand for Talent

Eight Essentials to Make Your Talent as Famous as Your Brand

Mark Schumann and Libby Sartain

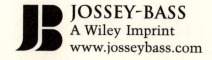
JOSSEY-BASS
A Wiley Imprint
www.josseybass.com

Published by Jossey-Bass
A Wiley Imprint
989 Market Street, San Francisco, CA 94103-1741—www.josseybass.com

Jossey-Bass books and products are available through most bookstores. To contact Jossey-Bass directly call our Customer Care Department within the U.S. at 800-956-7739, outside the U.S. at 317-572-3986, or fax 317-572-4002.

Jossey-Bass also publishes its books in a variety of electronic formats. Some content that appears in print may not be available in electronic books.

Library of Congress Cataloging-in-Publication Data

Schumann, Mark.
  Brand for talent : eight essentials to make your talent as famous as your brand / Mark Schumann and
    Libby Sartain.- 1st ed. p. cm.
  Includes bibliographical references and index.
  ISBN 978-0-470-18268-0 (cloth)
  1. Employees-Recruiting. 2. Human capital-Management. 3. Intellectual capital-Management.
4. Personnel management. I. Sartain, Libby. II. Title.
  HF5549.5.R44S188 2009
  658.3—dc22
                                                                                              2008055667

Printed in the United States of America
FIRST EDITION
HB Printing   10 9 8 7 6 5 4 3 2 1
PB Printing   10 9 8 7 6 5 4 3 2 1

Contents

Introduction   1

Part One: Get Real   11

Essential One: Wake Up   13

Essential Two: Look Ahead   37

Part Two: Get to Work   69

Essential Three: Create   71

Essential Four: Segment   109

Essential Five: Implement   143

Part Three: Get Prepared   175

Essential Six: Sustain   177

Essential Seven: Survive   207

Part Four: What It Means to You   233

Build a Talent Brand Legacy   235

Notes   245

Acknowledgments   253

Index   255

About the Authors   267

To our children, Sarah Sartain and
Jonathan, Matthew, and Garrett Schumann.

Each day you teach us
what it means to authentically deliver
what we promise.

INTRODUCTION

To be a magnet is to lure, to draw, to attract, and, once a connection is made, to engage, to maintain a hold.

Every company, no matter its business, no matter its marketplace, no matter the economic conditions, needs the right people to be engaged in making the right contributions. And every company, no matter its people needs, wants to be a magnet that consistently attracts and engages the best of talent.

To make this happen, a business must first attract the right people to do the right jobs at the right time. Then, after the new workers walk through the door, the business must earn their loyalty and engagement. As many businesses experience, challenging economic conditions can shift the balance of supply and demand for talent, just as with any item in any marketplace. When it comes to people, it can be even more challenging to engage when workers have fewer choices. Nobody likes to feel stuck.

This book tells you how to use your company's brand to attract, retain, and engage the people you need—so you become known, in your industry, as a magnet for the best talent. To make your talent as famous as your brand is to reach beyond what you invest to be known for what you do to be known for who wants to work with you.

When we began to write, in a strong economic environment, we had something important to say about how to differentiate a company as a place to work, and strong beliefs of the importance of being magnet in a vibrant talent market. As we finish, in a different economic environment, we realize our ideas are even more important when times are tough. Becoming a magnet—to secure the best talent in any business—is essential to thrive in any economic time no matter how challenging. Creating brand loyalty—in good times or bad—is critical to engage workers. And the only way business can become a magnet (regardless of economic conditions) is to engage current and future workers in its purpose. That has been the case since the first company used the first recruitment campaign to hire the first worker.

Before any of us commit to sign up for, stay with, or engage in work, we want to know what a company is about, what it does, how secure it is, how well it pays, how to get ahead, who will be the boss, and what kind of people it employs. Because prospective workers can't evaluate a business from the inside, a company must package what it offers so prospects can assess the place much like customers assess a product or service. Once on the inside, workers will test whether the organization authentically delivers what it promises. How companies package these attributes has evolved over time into the concept of employer brand: How a company articulates its value proposition so that current and prospective workers can answer the question, "What's in it for me?"

We pioneered a lot of what is considered standard practice in employer brand in our work at Southwest Airlines, Yahoo!, and other organizations. When we documented our work a few years ago in *Brand from the Inside*, we thought we had thoroughly examined everything about employer brand.

But the world changed. The marketplace for talent turned upside down, workers' expectations intensified, companies' needs to engage workers increased, and the working world became an economic roller coaster. The world of talent has changed so much that *Brand from the Inside* only tells part of the story. Every business is challenged to build a marketing-focused organization that pursues brand loyalty among workers as aggressively as it pursues brand loyalty among customers. That's why we wrote *Brand for Talent*.

A company needs three brands. Its *customer brand* must articulate a compelling reason for customers to buy. Its *employer brand* must articulate what value proposition it offers as a place to work. And its *talent brand*—the focus of this book—must provide a direction to market the company to attract, retain, and engage workers. To *brand for talent* is to aggressively and creatively market the company to continuously fill a pipeline of potential and current workers in various segments of traditional and nontraditional work arrangements.

Five Changes in Talent

As we look at what's happening in talent, and in business, we see five fundamental changes to how business finds and keeps the workers it needs. Added together, they make a strong case to explore what a talent brand can accomplish.

One: Generational Change

Driving change in the search for workers is a new generation that redefines expectations. It's no surprise that business pays a lot of attention to Generation Y. In sheer size, these workers outnumber the Baby Boomers and, in personal habits, they redefine how people work.

From early ages, Generation Y grew up with technology and all things digital. Many learned to use computers before they learned to read. As older children, few knew a television set without a remote control, a family room without a VCR (or, later, a DVD player or TiVo), or a choice of entertainment limited to board games and jigsaw puzzles. As teenagers, few experienced life without the instant message, email, or a cell phone to text or talk. Then, as college students, few had to register for class on paper, turn in an assignment by hand (instead of by email), limit research to what was physically available in a campus library, or call home only once a week from a pay telephone.

Rather than consuming traditional television or the newspaper, Generation Y looks to the web as a gateway to everything from music to fashion to careers. Instead of connecting with friends with two soda cans and a string, they are comfortable collaborating and networking online in open and shared environments. Not willing to consider technology an option, they make it an essential tool to provide entertainment, information, ideas, and connections with friends, strangers, and organizations.

Not only did they learn how to connect, but Generation Y also acquired savvy skills as brand-conscious shoppers. The web taught them to be consumers in a broad marketplace well beyond their immediate reach. Because they absorb so many messages from so many sources about so many products, they rely on brand as a way to cut through the noise. To them, brand is a universal way to simplify, evaluate, and choose.

Two: Consumers of Work

Generation Y comes to work as new consumers of an experience. Not only do they demand online processes as sophisticated as what they experience in the retail world, but they demand brand clarity as they make career choices. They want to fill their resumes with the names of well-branded organizations at the same time as they make a difference, contribute to the world, and balance life and work.

They also bring other expectations carefully created by well-intentioned parents. As young children, when many played on organized sports teams, many were awarded a trophy for any effort—no matter the actual victor. Perhaps parents weren't prepared for how these future workers might react to losing. It's no surprise that, once at work, these consumers feel empowered to demand what they want.

While Generation Y drives much of the change in worker expectations, the shift is not limited to this one demographic. Workers at every age search for experiences that provide fulfillment beyond traditional definitions of task, opportunity, compensation, and security. Savvy marketing has turned prospective workers of all ages into consumers who evaluate professional opportunities with the same skills they use to buy a new car, laptop, or flat screen television. Today's consumers of work are looking for more than work. They are shopping for life.

So while companies struggle to "crack the code" to appeal to the elusive Generation Y, we encourage every business to adjust across the generational lines to meet new expectations. Even older workers now feel they can ask any organization, "What's in it for me?" to work here.

Three: Marketplace for Talent

The new consumers find themselves working in a marketplace that past generations might not recognize. Technology has redefined how workers and business connect. Before the Internet, people actually had to talk with each other to exchange information and perceptions. Because conversations could only happen in real time, a company could easily say anything to any worker because it took so long to check whether the company was telling the truth. Today's consumer can instantly get the scoop on a company on any number of websites and blogs. Workers connect in real time through social networks that have become online water coolers.

Before the Internet, a company's hiring territory was defined by traditional geographic boundaries. This made it easier for a company to focus its message on a finite population that conventional media could easily reach. Today business competes for talent in a free global marketplace with fewer traditional definitions. Fewer companies define their needs in terms of *employees*, while fewer people define their ambitions in terms of *jobs*. Today it's all about the work. Both businesses and workers look for an open exchange in an open marketplace that technology makes possible.

Four: Social Media

Since the first business hired the first worker, companies have carefully communicated messages they could control. But thanks to technology there is very little any company can control any longer. The tools of social media reach beyond corporate transparency to make any business the star of a 24/7 reality show—easily on the air at any time for any current or potential worker to view.

This reality puts great pressure on business to connect with and engage workers. Without traditional message control, it's more difficult for a company to ensure that its messages get through. Without some of the benefits available to past generations—such as the traditions of long-term employment supported by pension benefits—it's more challenging to secure the commitment of workers to give "the something extra" that business needs. Without the classic line of sight between workers and leaders, it's more imperative for the people running a business to authentically deliver what the organization promises.

But it's not easy. The brand-savvy consumer of work—bringing a wide collection of retail skills to the process to *find* work—will keep using those skills when making the choice to *engage* in work. A business that can creatively rely on savvy marketing to lure potential workers must deliver what it promises once recruits walk through the door. Where once a worker could be satisfied in long-term rewards, today's short-attention-spanned worker looks for immediate gratification. Loyalty to any brand, especially an employer brand, must be earned.

In a tight economy, however, even the most retail-oriented consumer of work may have fewer choices. It may be more difficult, when times are tough, for a frustrated worker outside a high-demand field to easily change affiliations. A worker who feels limited opportunity may be less likely to be loyal. That forces an organization to reach deeper into its purpose, and the values for which it stands, to connect with a worker who might be feeling trapped.

Five: Brand Loyalty

With all this change, brand loyalty is essential to an organization's strategy to secure talent. *Brand loyalty*, however, differs from traditional concepts of engagement. While an engaged workforce is critical to business, it focuses on a worker's relationship at a specific moment of time when the worker is doing specific work.

Brand loyalty must last longer. Business must harness the loyalty of workers to its brand as a place to work even after the traditional working relationship may end. And, in a changing marketplace, in a fluctuating economy, brand loyalty becomes a valuable currency for any organization to build. Business must earn worker loyalty to its brand that reaches beyond traditional definitions of employment.

The new consumers of work enter the workforce looking for more and the talent brand must articulate what an organization will deliver. In their careers these workers want meaning and significance. On their resumes they want to list well-branded organizations they can believe in, that will impress their social networks, and that will position them for future opportunities. In their lives they want to make a difference in an experience that is individually personalized.

The talent brand must shortcut what consumers of work want to feel, predict how consumers may use and discard and convey the "big ideas" of hope and ambition. It must communicate to the world what a business is, what it stands for, and what it offers. It must reach the part of a consumer's mind that makes choices about work, just as they choose coffee, a car, or a place to vacation.

The solution is not as simple as looking at an old brand in a new way. It is not about creating a new ad campaign. The consumer of work demands more and buys differently. What retail consumers could once only buy at one store on Main Street can now be easily found from any source without leaving home. The old notions of supply and demand—based on single sources and channels—are replaced by multiple sources with simultaneous marketing. And the consumer relishes the choice.

It's the same with talent. That old, reliable act of placing an advertisement in a newspaper for a candidate is a memory. Just as consumers can search online for products anywhere in the world, they can search for work anywhere in the world from a comfortable home setting. The traditional views of talent supply and demand—rooted in the idea of one employee for one job—are replaced by a free marketplace where a consumer of work uses technology to search the world.

As authors, we bring a new voice that is grounded in the practical, shaded by the human, and rooted in a fundamental belief that business can do what is right for its investors and right for its people. It can brand for talent to attract, retain, and engage the right people for the right jobs to make business succeed.

About This Book

We thought, when we finished *Brand from the Inside*, that we had said everything we had to say about the importance of, development of, and potential of a company's employer brand. But we need to say more.

Every time we give a speech, people ask us what they can do to make their employer brands relevant to the new generation of workers. In our work, people ask us how to balance the brand for the new generation with the reality for the workers currently in place. As businesses face economic challenges, leaders ask us how to engage workers during the turbulence.

As we look at business, we see a need for specialized workers to meet critical business needs in a scarce marketplace for critical talent. That doesn't change in tough times. We see business looking for every way to engage workers. We see consumers of work segmenting into splinters with new habits to understand, new appetites to satisfy, new price points to meet. But we also see tired talent strategies on which business has relied for too long that no longer match new job seekers' habits and tired engagement strategies that do not satisfy what employees hunger for.

While we believe an *employer brand* is essential to any business that wants to compete for people, developing an *employer brand* is no longer enough. The employer brand will only be effective when it is used to aggressively market the business as a place to work. And that effort needs to continue throughout a worker's relationship with the organization. That's why, as we consider the challenges to secure talent, we introduce a new term—the *talent brand*—that we explore in this book. While an *employer brand* articulates an experience, the *talent brand* is a marketing tool to secure and engage workers.

In this book we explore how a talent brand must:

- Appeal to the consumer who has been trained to make decisions by the brand
- Help a business market each touch point of its employee experience
- Position the leadership of the business to be key "poster children" of what the brand stands for
- Shape the products, services, and experience the business offers to workers
- Be a "lens" through which each product and service can be developed as well as marketed
- Be *the* strategic tool for a company to attract and retain people, and
- Survive social media

If you are a business leader, this book can help you turn an organization from being a victim in this new talent marketplace to being a player with a talent brand as famous as your consumer brand and your reputation for work as famous as your consumer experience. You will learn the important link between talented employees and delivering a brand promise. You will learn how to lead your business through this change by creating a brand for talent that will thrive in the new talent marketplace and with the new consumer of work.

Many people ask us, "What's the secret to creating a great employer brand?" Our response is, "What makes a great employer brand is how it serves to attract and retain and engage talent." That's what this book is all about. Together, we describe how to attract, retain and engage the right people in the right work at the right time.

Thank you.
Mark Schumann and Libby Sartain

Part One

GET REAL

1

ESSENTIAL ONE: WAKE UP

He sits, with his earphones playing his favorite downloaded tunes, at a keyboard, staring at a screen filled with multiple pages, conversations, and links. He responds to each of them in a sequenced symphony of communication, as if starting one sentence in one place and ending it in another.

All the while, his eyes never leave the screen, and his focus never leaves the task at hand. He could be shopping for presents, downloading music, talking with friends, or even looking for and applying for a job. No matter the task, he brings a sensibility of a new consumer to his effort, with an attention span that, while short, can certainly multi-task with the best of them.

He is the new *consumer of work* who treats finding work just as he treats ordering a product or service. As the consumer, he is in charge. He sets the timing, dictates the response, and makes sure to be informed. He checks to confirm that the values he holds are in line with the values of the place where he makes his purchase. He knows he can discard the product at any time and find another. Online. In a flash. Being a consumer is being a consumer. It's no different whether he is a consumer of a product or service or whether he is the consumer of work. *What* he consumes is secondary.

To become a magnet for talent, and make your talent as famous as your brand, your business *must* reach this consumer. But it's a challenge to attract, retain, and engage workers with a totally new set of preferences and habits. For a well-branded company like General Mills, Ken Charles, head of recruitment, admits that "it is all about being visible in the channels that the new generation frequents." The web reaches beyond being a minute-by-minute reality for this consumer to be the primary way people connect and choose. Its proliferation alters every stage of a traditional recruitment process. "Now they will meet someone from a company, look them in the eye, listen to what they have to say, and then Google the person, find their LinkedIn profile, and research the company online," Charles says. "They will believe their web experience first, to confirm what they are told, but they will not believe what we tell them simply because we tell them." That's why, according to Charles, General Mills uses a range of new tools such as virtual recruiting and webinars to reinforce what the company says on campus.[1] The comfort with technology is also the reason General Electric uses email to maintain contact with students even after they accept a GE job offer. According to Steve Canale, head of university recruiting at GE, "our monthly 'Keeping in Touch' email reinforces their decision to join GE and builds their enthusiasm, which is critical in the Spring season as competitor employees market their jobs on campus."[2]

So what does this mean to the search for the right workers in the right positions at the right time?

The only way business can hope to find and engage the people it needs is to say hello to the new consumer of work—this new shopper who redefines experience and expectations. While the leaders of this shift are members of Generation Y, the change is too complex to attribute to any one demographic group. The patterns of change are as true of people in their twenties as they are of people in their fifties. Age is less an issue than comfort with and reliance on technology. This is a consumer who, because of technology, is used to controlling a marketplace from a keyboard and sees no reason to adjust when looking for or engaging in work.

This consumer makes every purchase in the shorthand of retail marketing. Each transaction begins with a specific expectation for a return on a purchase or investment; a clear understanding of the money-back guarantee. Each arrangement includes the resources to contact for emergency troubleshooting and the promise of a personalized experience that will lead to bigger things. The new consumer is accustomed to buying familiar brands. It's no surprise that the same sensibility would travel to the marketplace for talent.

This hungry, insightful, savvy consumer quickly looks at what a brand represents. And, according to executive search consultant Janice Ellig, this takes the consumer to the top of an organization. "The worker looks at who is the CEO," according to Ellig, "who is on the leadership team, what they have done to create something in that business."[3] The new consumer will quickly compare the opportunities of Business A and Business B using the consumer skills learned at the mall. And brand will be an easy and familiar way to compare places to work just as it is to compare places to buy.

Are you ready for this change? If so, your business needs to address thirteen basic expectations to begin the discussion. To use your brand to attract and engage you must, first, wake up to say hello to this new consumer.

One of my great pleasures has been to mentor young HR professionals entering the field and to watch them progress and succeed over the years. One such person was a Google HR professional I met at a conference. In his early twenties, he was working at Google, arguably the hottest talent brand of the day. He had been there about a year, and was already feeling antsy about his career progress. He hadn't moved forward fast enough and was exploring the territory at other companies. Shortly, he was offered a promotion and then another, and then an overseas assignment. Yet, he continued to wonder whether such an assignment might derail his forward progress. Gen Y professionals, even at the most well-branded talent organizations, will always have an eye on the next prize and be open for new opportunities inside and outside of their company.

. . . Libby

Wake Up Number 1: Habits

Instead of opening the pages of a daily newspaper and glancing through the classifieds, our new consumer looking for work goes directly to the website of a well-branded employer or to any number of job-hunting websites to find what's available.

Technology makes it easy to find almost any opening that matches consumers' interest in the assignment or the organization. Once on a site, this new consumer—whom we will name Lee—will rely on a search engine to spot key words about responsibilities, experience, and location. Then, with the quick click of the mouse, Lee can submit a resume and, within minutes, quickly scan to the next possible opportunity. If Lee wants to learn more about a company, any number of social network sites make it easy to get "the straight scoop" from current employees or other observers. While preparing for an interview, Lee can easily check everything that anyone has said about the company up to the minute before the first question is asked. Technology makes it possible for this consumer to uncover every possible secret before exchanging the first "hellos."

It's a new world. Thanks to technology, this consumer can apply for work, have initial interviews, perhaps get an offer, and prepare to begin without ever having any actual contact with anyone. Everything can be handled with the speed of an online transaction. With a click of a mouse, it's as easy to "get the dirt" about a company as it is to get a recipe, a sports score, or a headline. Thanks to online fascinations such as YouTube, a corporate reputation—once a sacred commodity any business could manage—is immediately available for anyone to tarnish. Jeanie Mabie, IBM's Recruitment Leader, IBM Global Employment Branding and University, appreciates the significance of this change. "There are major changes in people, preferences, relationships with companies, and expectations for work agreements. With a company as rich in history as IBM, we have to make sure we reeducate people not only about their opportunities, but about our company as well."[4] For any organization, dealing with a new consumer is a challenge they didn't see coming over the horizon.

One reason is that, for the new consumer, the search for work never ends. A range of sites—such as LinkedIn, Plaxo, or Facebook—make it easy to maintain an updated resume or build a career website or link to potential new employers in the hopes to be found. Peppering these resumes are the names of the companies where someone might work. And it's no surprise that company names with cache are better received than the unknown. The employer brand becomes not only a way to tell a company's story but for a consumer of work to illustrate career progress. "Because the loyalty to companies is down—and the number of jobs in a career is so high—the employer brand becomes more of a proxy for one's accomplishments," observes Jim Citrin, executive search consultant for Spencer Stuart. "The employer brand projects the attributes of the brand onto the person. Someone must be cool if at a company with what others consider a cool employer brand."[5] That company logo, once worn only to a summer employee picnic, becomes a way for the consumer to advertise what has been accomplished.

The new consumer of work has become very smart. According to Robert J. Crowder, senior executive recruiter at Aetna, "Potential employees have high expectations and standards for potential employers, and they are willing to talk to several companies before making a decision. Candidates want to know the company's financial outlook, values, and culture. Like generations before them, they are seeking a company where performance is recognized, developed, and rewarded."[6] Technology makes it easy to check a company out. A simple look at any number of corporate reputation sites can generate a quick snapshot of who is saying what about a potential employer.

The change in consumer habits fundamentally alters what an organization must do to connect. No longer is it enough for a company to select one channel to reach current and prospective workers. A company lives in a 360-degree world surrounded by every opportunity to reach, every opportunity to be reached, and every opportunity to be talked about. The consumer of work brings new habits to an open marketplace for talent. A company seeking to attract, retain and engage must adapt.

Wake Up Number 2: Expectations

Technology changes how people look for work. Retail experience may inspire what people look for and aspire to accomplish. Practical experience in a retail market may prepare a consumer of work to be a smart buyer who selectively follows favorite brands. Comfort with technology means this consumer will be online every step of the way.

The retail world taught the consumer what it means to secure "the best buy" for a product. That expectation carries over to a career. The new consumer looks for a company to guarantee an experience and a return on investment just as it would offer a no-surprise promise to a customer. And this consumer won't wait. The validation of work must be as immediate as the confirmation of an online purchase.

Our consumer of work is also a bit self-centered. Lee wants to be recognized and, no matter how electronically connected, looks for real-time attention from real people. Lee craves, and reacts to, the extra effort of a business that pays attention, shows an interest and describes a future path. Lee also wants, at the same time, to feel in control of the work, when to begin and end the day, how much work to take home, and if working on a weekend is necessary. In the end, it's all about Lee.

As we worked through the development of a new college recruitment process and experience with a global organization, we came to many realizations about the new consumer of work. While the legacy process the organization followed had usually resulted in a sufficient number of new hires, the number of "closed deals" had dropped in the past couple of cycles. The closer we looked, the more we realized that the legacy process left considerable gaps in time when the candidate would not hear from the organization. After an on-campus visit to a career fair, the organization might take several days to follow up with interested students. And, once a student expressed interest, and had perhaps even completed an interview, the organization took several days to complete its debrief and selection, which often caused a delay of several weeks before an offer would be extended. We compared this process to our fundamental insight into the talent market and helped the organization realize that it could no longer permit such gaps in communication to occur. The best way to secure these potential workers was to stay in close touch and tighten the gaps in time. The new process has eliminated all of those gaps and significantly increased the communications. Today, a student who emerges as a viable candidate from a career fair receives an invitation to an interview the same day. A student who completes an interview in a one-day experience receives a commitment for an offer or a polite dismissal on the same day. As a student offered a position deliberates his options, he receives regular communications from the organization, to help him realize, day in and day out, just how much he is wanted. The process now fits the consumer reality.

   . . . Mark

Any business that wants to seriously compete for this consumer must gain insight into what Lee wants and how Lee makes choices. Otherwise the brand and marketing messages will fail. Before trying to reach Lee, and others, the business must build a profile of the new consumer of work it seeks so it can effectively tailor its brand and marketing efforts. It must get to know what will disappoint this consumer so it can strategize to please. It must learn what the consumer—as the new ruler of the talent marketplace—expects from the work experience.

This reliance on consumer insight and knowledge is fundamental to any marketing effort for workers. Kristen Weirick, director of Talent Acquisition of the Whirlpool Corporation, believes that a company must learn what is required to appeal to workers. "We have to be flexible with a differentiated approach for different segments," Weirick observes. "For us, the biggest segment difference is between the experienced candidate and the new campus recruit. While we don't veer away from our messaging, we do tweak our messaging to meet the needs of the segment."[7] This awareness of a need for targeted messaging can distinguish messages that are heard from those that are lost.

This insight begins with what consumers expect. According to Steve Canale, "GE's talent acquisition strategies reflect the reality that most entry-level candidates expect to research employment opportunities via the Internet, online job boards, company websites, and even blogs." Canale continues, "This generation is comfortable connecting with potential employers through informal, online forums such as virtual career fairs and WebEx meetings."[8] Certainly an organization that responds to consumer preferences has a better chance to break through the noise.

But insight requires more than knowing a preference for media. The new generation simply looks at work in a different way—either when choosing a place to work or choosing how to work at a current place. The worker who may choose to work today will carefully evaluate how this experience provides background and preparation for tomorrow's opportunity. Recent research shows that 41 percent of Generation Y workers expect to progress rapidly within their existing organization, compared to 20 percent of Generation X.[9] And while many issues may influence this perception, the results say a lot about the expectations consumers bring to work.

Some blame, or thank, the parents. Many companies report that the Generation Y workers enter the workforce with a great deal of parental influence and involvement. Caroline Emmons, University Relations Consultant at Aetna, describes the "infamous 'helicopter parents' who get (or stay) heavily involved in their children's lives well beyond school age." She suggests that, because the new consumers of work grew up with such parental supervision, "this generation has higher expectations that employers and managers will advocate for (or at least cater to) their individual needs or issues." That is one reason, Emmons believes, that new consumers of work look for employers that offer structured development programs that provide formal training, rotational assignments, mentorship and coaching, and frequent feedback and recognition for strong performance.[10] Certainly those organizations that confront complaining parents—such as when a child receives a poor performance appraisal (oh, yes, it happens)—would agree with those who observe a substantial change in consumer behavior.

But it's not as simple as looking at a "one size fits all" approach to this segment of the workforce. Despite the fact that Generation Y will account for sixty-three million members of the American workforce by 2014,[11] many organizations try to look inside this large segment. At General Electric, for example, Steve Canale clarifies that they "try not to paint the Gen Y brush on the entry-level workforce. The entire workforce wants the same kind of flexibility that today's technology has enabled."[12] The changes that Generation Y introduced now characterize many segments of consumers of work.

Wake Up Number 3: Career

The consumer of work looks for a work experience, not a job. Lee may consider a "job" an archaic description by an older generation while "work" is a present experience to build skills and expertise for the next opportunity. To the consumer, "work" must be relevant, meaningful, easy to leverage, and easy to fit into the narrative of a career. Richard Spitz, Chairman, Technology Markets, CEO and Board Services, Korn/Ferry International, observes that "people will respond to the challenge of work, quality of people, and ability to grow."[13] And it's not just about what they actually experience. The value of the "work" is, as well, how the story can be shared.

At the same time, the consumer of work demonstrates a short attention span. Maybe it's because of the media, all the brand messages, experience with a remote control device, or the new approaches to health care and retirement that increase personal financial burden. Regardless of the reasons, this consumer anticipates a career of several stops, adopting a free agent mentality. Any change in what business can offer, or reluctance to be obligated for the long term, gives Lee more freedom to keep looking for new opportunities. Automatic loyalty is not in this consumer's makeup.

As a result this consumer of work will never stop searching for work, even when working. Lee will be just like the eager guest at a party who always looks beyond the current conversation to target the next networking opportunity. Because there is never a finite start or end to the search, Lee will constantly be "out there" with online profiles and active participation in social networks and efforts to survey the marketplace for a better deal. And while Lee may hope to stay at a company as long as it remains relevant, new ways to market accomplishment will always catch this consumer's eye.

Lee will not settle for resumes on 8-1/2 by 11 sheets of paper. A profile on a social network site will be a given. Endorsements from co-workers, bosses, clients, and customers on LinkedIn or other sites will make it easy to check references and background information. This consumer of work will view a career as an ongoing effort to market a personal brand of value. Lee will look at a first job as a pathway to the next, and the next to the next, and perhaps then to grad school, and then to the next. Richard Spitz observes that, today, "everyone has multiple moves," acknowledging that, if someone stays with one company, others may wonder why. "People may ask what's wrong with him" because "moves on a resume will be very important."[14]

Ultimately, new consumers will never stop searching for work. It's just that, sometimes, they may do so while actually working for an organization.

This consumer likes brands on a resume. The reasons are simple. Executive search consultant Jim Bagley of Russell Reynolds observes, "It is easy to go on to the next role if you come successfully from a well-branded company."[15] The practical consumer of work realizes that, when competing for the next job, a resume filled with well-branded companies can make a real impression. Lee shops in terms of appearance: The design of clothing, the type of cell phone, the color of iPod. Lee looks to brands to convey identification and looks to image to make personal statements of identity and beliefs. And Lee knows, as Jim Bagley observes, "that companies look for workers who bring credible references from institutions that are branded."[16] The value of the brand doesn't end at the mall.

Of the changes a new consumer demonstrates, this desire to keep moving may be the most profound. Janice Ellig sees consumers who think, "at most, of what they will do, and what they can accomplish the next five years,"[17] But, to many, five years is an eternity and, in a vibrant economy, many may look to one or two years as the threshold for receiving the appropriate recognition of advancement. Ellig recalls that "most workers will say, 'I will work here two years but unless I am part of the team, have input, am recognized, and feel valued by the company, I will move on.' They do not look for lifetime employment."[18] The search for fulfillment and the online tools make it easy.

In tighter markets, however, the new consumer may not have as many choices. This can frustrate a consumer who fears that staying in one place can be an admission of becoming stale. Someone who believes that moves on a resume indicate ambition—and static means stagnation—may be frustrated when opportunities tighten. While Lee continues the search, stays on the market, and keeps a current resume online, an employer will need to look for many ways to engage this consumer. While Lee may also go as far as to shoot a YouTube resume that will offer insight, a summary of accomplishments, and video endorsements, an employer must use its brand to create a new kind of loyalty.

A client, a global company, was, as many are, rethinking its recruitment process to meet the challenges of a new generation of worker. Of the challenges it found the most troubling, actually, was the realization that people coming to work for the company only planned to stay for a short time. These consumers of work reported that the company had such a strong brand as a place to develop talent that a period of time spent there could be easily leveraged into higher-paying work with a different company. The company realized that, to have any chance to keep these workers, it needed to internally replicate what workers were looking for on the outside. It had to be able to offer workers the chance to move around and advance as much on the inside, both in scope of responsibility and in opportunity for reward, as they could find on the outside. In order to keep the worker, the organization had to satisfy the "itch" the consumer of work gets to move. This realization significantly changed how the company looked at its learning and development efforts, as well as its career management process, and acknowledge that all the talent systems must coordinate to have any hope to retain key workers.

. . . Mark

Wake Up Number 4: Engagement

The consumer of work is not patient. Lee expects any transaction and process to be flawless. This is, after all, a consumer raised on the reliability of systems. The ATM always has enough money to go around. The Internet connection always works or, if not, is quickly repaired. Lee recoils if, during the interview, on-boarding and work experience, everything doesn't go like clockwork.

Lee expects, with the click of a mouse, to learn how a company thinks, who works there, how people work in teams (from a company website), what people say about a company, how it compares to others (from a social network site or blog), what a company offers (back to the company site), and what friends think of the idea to join (back to the social network site). With the convenience of online applications, Lee can easily apply, chat, and listen to music at the same time. After all, this consumer probably applied to college online, selected courses online, and turned in papers online.

During the recruitment process, Lee will not tolerate being forgotten, delayed, or overlooked. Lee spends most waking hours connected to others, seeking the opinions of others, offering suggestions to others, hoping to hear from others. So if a company doesn't show consistent interest, with an occasional email or text message, Lee may quickly feel ignored. This consumer may not understand, nor appreciate, necessary gaps in communication, natural delays in decisions, or issues that may surface in a hiring process. Lee only knows that a period of time in the day is not being filled.

Once work begins, Lee expects to be nurtured and appreciated for arriving with a resume packed with internships, overseas experiences, and serious academic achievements. And because Lee may also arrive with debt from college expenses, look for anticipation of a quick return on the investment. Lee doesn't want to have to wait too long until the loans are paid and the BMW is on the way.

Lee walks into a company expecting to know how a career will develop, knowledge and skills will be acquired, performance will be managed, pay will increase, and work and life will balance. Everything must be spelled in black and white, like the syllabus of a course, without the ambiguity that workers from a previous generation may have tolerated. After growing up in a highly programmed home—where everything was scheduled between play dates and music lessons and sports teams—this consumer wants a clear path to how the experience will unfold.

All of this want is not lost on those who provide. Amy Giglio, senior manager for talent acquisition of Aflac, observes how the new consumers "are equally concerned about what the company can do for them, how they can contribute, advance quicker and demonstrate their skills and knowledge sooner, and the possible career paths and progression after nine to twelve months."[19] The new consumer simply wants to know what will happen on the first day, the names of colleagues, the nature of assignments, and the guidelines for reward and recognition.

This worker is asking, "What can I go do and be involved in?" according to Janice Ellig, "and what experiences will help me to stand out and add to my brand?"[20] Lee will look for everything from the clarity of a career to the karma of a community to the connection with friends to the attention from a supervisor. Now, Lee *is* willing to work just as long as the next opportunity occurs before lunch and recognition begins before dinner. This new consumer simply does not believe that *anything* can't be within reach, including a job, a person, a place, as well as opportunities to step into the spotlight. Plus, there must be time to go to the gym and hang out with friends.

With one client, a global energy company, we had some good laughs about the generation of workers with a viewpoint of excellence skewed by the fact that, as young children, as they participated in their first competitive teams, everyone received a blue ribbon, perhaps because their parents were hesitant to declare any child a winner or loser. Whether or not that experience carried forward, there is an expectation among new consumers of work that they will be recognized and rewarded for achievements that were simply expected in different times. This reality can make it more difficult for one company to differentiate from another when it comes to the experience it delivers simply because the consumer of work expects so much and will only pay attention to a company that actually delivers something different. This company realized that new workers expect to be recognized. This gave it insight into how the career management and development process must be structured. It maintained that unless a worker clearly understands that career advancement is a partnership with the company, he or she may be sitting a long time, frustrated, when movement doesn't automatically occur. The worker must raise the hand, develop the skill, and articulate the ambition. He or she can't simply wait for the ribbon to be presented.

. . . Mark

The new consumer, as well, will expect to be a part of the action at work. Lee won't be satisfied simply observing what the company may be doing. This consumer will come in wanting, expecting, and demanding an experience. Lee will expect, from the start, to be involved in what the business is doing, and, most importantly, to be a voice that is heard.

But Lee also wants to have fun. All the years of programmed experiences create expectations for onsite entertainment. No matter how interesting the work may be, it better not get in the way of going to the gym. Work/life balance is an expectation, not an option, as Lee seeks to seamlessly blend life and work into one experience. But things may change in life and Lee will demand the freedom to leave and re-enter the workforce, as needed, for school, family, and community commitments. Lee will expect flexibility in work schedule, a BlackBerry, perhaps an iPhone, and a commitment to contribute from home, from an office, or at a work site.

This consumer will be looking for, and evaluating, an entire experience at work, from the people to meet to the company's commitment to social causes. While Lee will certainly expect the paycheck to be competitive, and the growth potential to be significant, this consumer will also want to feel good about work and company. The need for image will require that Lee work at a place that people have heard of, in a business that people understand, and doing a job that people look up to.

Wake Up Number 5: Connection

The new consumer will want to connect with colleagues. And that connection may be virtual. Lee will never be without a cell phone, a PDA, an iPod, or an all-in-one smart phone. For this new consumer, a text message or an IM will be a conversation. When considering a company, Lee may actually socialize with workers to learn whether the people are likable.

Technology will make it easy for Lee to hang around the water cooler, and soak it all in, before making a decision about work. Lee can post a message on a social network site or check out www.glassdoor.com to learn how workers rate jobs, bosses, pay, environments, and culture; or www.indeed.com to participate or observe forums where users discuss companies, jobs, career advice, and work stories; or www.experience.com to get free advice about looking for work. This consumer will rely on social media to collect feedback and guidance from all the experts in cyberspace. And connections make a difference when 47 percent of people looking for jobs spend one to three hours a day online searching for work.[21] For the new consumer, the connection defines the experience.

The lesson for the organization is simple: Provide opportunities for connection or be left behind. It's not a matter of potential distinction; it's an issue of a level playing field. The new consumers of work are, simply, "more comfortable searching for employment opportunities via the Internet than using online job boards and company websites," according to Caroline Emmons of Aetna. This generation is more comfortable connecting with potential employers through informal, online forums such as virtual career fairs, and WebEx meetings, and is oftentimes quicker to respond to a text message than to an email.[22] That's not a surprise to the Institute for Corporate Productivity that reports 35 percent of job seekers use social networking as a means to canvass for new jobs. "As a result, the importance of effectively communicating your company brand and values through online media has become increasingly clear over the last several years. Company image on blogs, Web 2.0 media, and social networking sites has become more important in recent years."[23]

Never is this consumer out of touch. Jim Bagley observes how all the opportunities to connect fundamentally change how a candidate can access information, references, and an organization's performance.[24] Ken Charles observes that consumers "believe in the power of their network. They confirm everything through multiple sources of contacts. The lines of privacy are blurred." Specifically, Charles refers to how, at another time, an offer letter was a private document. "Now it is shared openly on the web. Today's candidate sees transparency as an obligation."[25] Technology can make once private information instantly public.

At work this consumer will look for relationships with colleagues. The online world in which Lee lives will redefine the nature of those relationships. Because this consumer lives online and connects online, Lee may look online for connections at work. This consumer, who can multi-task more than one electronic gadget at a time, believes that electronics create personal experiences. Focused on staying connected, Lee will never be out of reach and will expect, when walking in the door, to be connected, engaged, and for the company to be ready.

So Lee will become impatient if the email address isn't ready the first day or if the laptop needs some refresher work. This consumer wants it now. And get ready: This consumer shares everything. That social network, so involved in the decision of where to work, will hear every detail about the work experience. Perhaps Lee will blog or twitter every detail. Or a bored Lee may access old-fashioned tools like email or the instant message.

The reach of consumer connection is staggering. The 2007 Yahoo! HotJobs survey revealed that 21 percent of respondents say they use social networking sites to look for a job, a penetration similar to 25 percent in the Yahoo! HotJobs/Robert Half International Milennials study in 2007 and the Yahoo! HotJobs poll in 2008.[26] Because the new consumer of work defines connection in a new way a company that wants to connect must join in.

With all this connection, consumers of work rarely make decisions alone. They rely on group decision making or, at least, group response to individual decisions. Because technology makes it so easy to ask for feedback, this consumer will seek reaction at every step of a decision, looking to friends for confirmation. Such collective security—well-honed during years of sports teams and group dating—carries to the workplace as the consumer seeks a community of togetherness. As this consumer enters the workforce, well connected from school, other professional experiences, internships, and technology, the network can be nurtured at little or no cost.

For younger consumers—especially those entering the workforce for the first time—parents may be well-trained coaches from the sidelines. Many will take it upon themselves to actively participate in the decision process for work, as some report, by carefully comparing offers, benefit plans, and pay structures. And their involvement will not automatically end when the consumer goes to work. Because many younger workers may live at home when they first go to work, the parent may be there to oversee their homework, or to contact the supervisor if the feedback is less than positive. The Yahoo! HotJobs/Robert Half International survey reports that 25 percent of workers consult their parents when making an employment decision.[27] Those parents who got their helicopter licenses while the consumers-in-training were still in school are not about to give up their roles as controls-in-residence.

A Yahoo! employee was affected by a reduction in force in February 2008. He decided to share the experience with his social network via Twitter and give them a play-by-play account of his last day. He started with an announcement that he had been impacted by the reduction in force. He then reported on packing up his desk and saying goodbye to great co-workers. Waiting for a call from HR to get his paperwork seemed like an eternity. And the biggest downer was that he was going to really miss the free lattes. He then reported on his meeting with HR and his last walk through the cafeteria, fondly remembering his meetings there. He paid tribute to his company-issued BlackBerry, saying goodbye, but let it know that he would have to buy an iPhone on the way home. He got one last latte before HR showed up to collect his laptop. He thanked all his friends for their "tweets" and then faded to black. About three hours later he reported back twittering via his new iPhone while celebrating his unemployment with a giant margarita. For me and all of HR this was a brand new experience - a live account of a layoff. Talk about "transparency"! And it was picked up by the local online gossip rag and published online even as it was twittered. The point here is that nothing is sacred anymore. If you look at the positive side of the story, our process worked as intended, and on the way out, he mentioned many of the best parts of working at the company. Great friends, free latte, a wonderful cafeteria, and the work and environment he would miss. Of course, the negative was that he lost a job he appeared to enjoy.

. . . Libby

Wake Up Number 6: Authenticity

The new consumer will demand authenticity in the work experience. Lee will want to feel good about the world, life, and work. Lee will aspire to be socially aware, sensitive, and responsible, and to work for a place that wants the same. Lee will not be bought—Lee wants to buy. This free agent will not subscribe to a blind oath to stay at a company through thick and thin. Lee will look for greener grass if not getting ahead or if the company does not conform to a sense of values and value. Lee will demand truth, sniff spin, and detest what is not considered transparent.

Because it is so easy for Lee to check a company out an organization's deeds may undermine the authenticity this consumer expects. Janice Ellig observes that "negative press has a negative impact, it can create a sense of unease, what the noise in the market is about the company. It makes a difference to a worker—to his or her reputation."[28] It's impossible, in the 24/7 media world, for any company to hide its news. Savvy consumers can quickly do deep research on a company's actions.

That means a company has to be on its toes. Kristen Weirick of Whirlpool Corporation describes how the organization paints an authentic picture for potential workers. "For the younger candidates, we focus on our commitment to community service, our corporate social responsibility, our relationship with Habitat for Humanity, our Cook for Cure program, and the dollars we donate through our Whirlpool Foundation. At one of our core schools for campus recruiting, we involved the candidates in building a house with us for Habitat, so we could create an experience beyond the career fair."[29] The authenticity the consumer demands frames the commitments the organization makes.

One of my clients strongly believes that the most significant competition they face for new workers is not another company but is, instead, Teach for America, the excellent organization that offers top-level college graduates the opportunity to teach in low-performing school settings. It is known as a first cool job to take while you wait for grad school or decide what you really want to do. What is especially challenging, when competing for talent with a program like Teach for America, is that no commercial enterprise can realistically offer quite the same experience of feeling good at the end of the day for the gifts delivered to others. So my client, rather than try to compete with such a phenomenon, tries to work with it, and structures a flexible approach to some entry-level positions that, essentially, offers someone the chance to spend, say, 50 percent of a work week in a traditional role at the company and 50 percent doing some type of community service. This arrangement recognizes that helping others is a significant part of what makes a new generation special. And rather than look for opportunities on their "spare time," many in this generation expect to find the experience on the job every day.

... Mark

Likewise, at IBM, Jeanne Mabie describes how the company follows a purposeful effort to avoid what she labels "the plastic fantastic," the efforts by some organizations to, perhaps with too much enthusiasm, promote their organizations as a places to work. "We want to tell an authentic story. That's why we ran an employee video contest in our consulting business in the United States." Mabie tells about one entry about career development focusing on a tortoise named Tommy. "It told a completely authentic picture of working life at IBM. And that's what we want. An authentic picture."[30] And it was a picture, because of its authentic roots, that took hold with viewers who would reject a slickly produced episode.

Such authenticity will mean a lot to the new consumer who wants to know what a company stands for. Lee will want to make a difference to the world—or at least work for a company that is trying to do so. A generation ago, a young person might be accused of hugging a tree to avoid going to work. Today's consumer will want to take the tree, feed it, and prune it while doing the work. Lee will couple the search for work with a search for personal meaning, as well as identifying with what a company stands for.

Because of technology, the consumer can also easily and quickly check on how the company reportedly treats people, what its leadership says and does, and what people who work there are saying. Lee will have no patience for companies that do not live a commitment to doing the right things for employees, customers, and the wider world.

Getting to Work

Want to get to know the new consumer of work? Here's how.

First, focus on the *change* that has occurred in your organization in the past couple of years, specifically in how you try to appeal to a new generation of worker. Think about how you reach out to potential workers (experienced as well as on campus), keep your name alive over the months, and try to be different than your competitors. And, once in the door, consider how you are altering the worker experience to appeal to a new type of worker.

Second, think about the potential *experience* you can create for the new consumers of work that may exceed anything they expect. It's one thing to react to a demographic change; it's another to proactively create an experience that will delight.

Third, look at how you tell your company's story, and assess how appealing it may be to the new consumer of work. Is your website fresh? Would consumers consider it a destination? Or has it become, as many have, a place for information to sit rather than for potential workers to dream?

These three steps can help you put the key lessons of this chapter into quick action.

Key Lessons: Chapter One

The first step to brand for talent is to wake up to the new consumer. We begin our journey here because the new consumer defines what that journey entails. No longer can a business dictate how a consumer must react. The consumer of work is now in charge. And business must change.

Ask yourself, are you ready for this new consumer? Is your brand as a place to work positioned to compete for this worker?

Do you focus as closely on what makes you relevant to the new consumer as you do on what you want to say?

- [ ] The new *consumer of work* orders work the same way as ordering a product or service.
- [ ] In a marketplace where knowledge is power, the information a potential worker can seize at his fingertips gives him the upper hand with a potential employer.
- [ ] Employees today simply don't believe they will work for one company for a lifetime. Or two or three. Try seven or eight.
- [ ] While many characteristics of the new consumer can be attributed to younger workers entering the marketplace, the impact reaches every generation at every stage of a relationship with a business.
- [ ] Consumers of work look for a work experience, not a job. They expect the transaction and process to be flawless. They have short attention spans and demand constant attention.
- [ ] The new consumer of work walks into a company with full expectation for a complete program of how a career will develop, performance will be managed, pay will increase, and work and life will balance.

2

ESSENTIAL TWO: LOOK AHEAD

The CEO isn't happy.

He or she wants an answer to simple, straightforward questions, "Why can't we find the people we need to do our work? Why can't we engage the people we have? Why can't we be known as a magnet for talent? And, once a magnet, will we secure the talent we need?"

The questions are fair. And frequent. Today's seemingly impossible pursuit to find, keep, and engage the right workers is beyond anything most organizations have confronted. It simply isn't logical that, no matter the economic conditions, companies with strong reputations can't attract and keep all the good people they need. Even organizations with legendary histories of attracting and engaging the best and the brightest find it challenging to appeal to all the new consumers of work they need. Unaccustomed to the ups and downs of the talent challenge, many a CEO may lose patience and believe, "If this business doesn't meet our objectives, it will be because we don't have the right people doing our work."

We have been there. We have sat in meeting rooms with CEOs who simply want, and certainly deserve, results not excuses, outcomes not processes. We have tried to explain to demanding CEOs that qualified workers don't appear from thin air. We have tried to help CEOs see the realities of competing for quality people at any time, no matter the economy. We have advised CEOs of what they can do to engage people when times are tough. We have tried to educate CEOs that a company's effort to recruit, retain, and engage workers is as demanding and unpredictable as its parallel effort to secure customers. And we have tried to help CEOs discover that, for any organization to secure the workers it needs, it must aggressively, consistently, and creatively market the organization in the talent marketplace with the same discipline and energy as it brings to the retail marketplace.

Over the course of our careers, we have worked with CEOs who get it. Southwest Airlines' Herb Kelleher, with his co-leader Colleen Barrett, consistently demonstrated a legendary instinct about how people make choices about where to buy and where to work. Rick Kelleher (no relation), the once-CEO of Doubletree Hotels, strongly believed that a place to work should be a caring experience that would motivate employees to create an equally caring environment for customers.

Jack Murphy, the standard-bearer of the former oil-field giant Dresser Industries, was frequently humbled by how people choose where they work. As he once remarked to Mark, "Each day our people can vote with their feet, to show or not to show, so we're always running for election."[1] And, more recently, Bernard Claude, the former CEO of Total Petrochemicals USA, said, "The key to any organization's future is to secure the right talent. To do that requires a compelling story of what it means to work here as well as a valuable experience once you get inside the door."[2]

But it's not enough to be a senior leader who recognizes that quality talent leads to business results. Or that leaders need to be as accountable for having great talent as they are for delivering financial results. Today's senior business leader must be as aware of the realities of the talent market as about any market in which the organization competes. It's not as simple as dictating to a staffer what needs to be done. Today's CEO must willingly position the organization at the center of the new battle for worker hearts and minds.

But it's a confusing place to be.

Organizations everywhere seek workers with unparalleled intensity and urgency. It doesn't matter how successful or challenged, driven or passive, compelling or dull an organization may be. All types are challenged to find and engage workers for routine and pivotal roles. Despite a glut of people in many fields, many types of work go underserved; despite economic challenges, many segments of workers refuse to engage.

As a generation of Baby Boomers begins to retire, CEOs fear where and how they will find replacements. And, on the other hand, how long these workers will stay because of personal financial needs. Executive search consultant Janice Ellig observes, "The change in the search for talent creates an imbalance in a company and confusion, noise, and chaos in the senior suite."[3] The CEO accustomed to the delivery of answers may begin to realize that to "get real" about the new talent marketplace may require more direct involvement.

We all remember CEOs who changed their organization's brand for talent. And when a CEO really gets it, the difference can be staggering. A CEO for a major energy company, as it faced a global merger, clearly understood that how he managed the talent issues would have a significant impact on the success of the venture. He realized that retaining key staff was essential to the future so, rather than assume that each of these need-to-keep people would understand their importance, he orchestrated a person-by-person strategy to personally reach out to the key talent he needed the new organization to retain. Rather than rely on a disconnected approach to messaging and messengers, we carefully planned who would reach out to each key staff member and what would be said in each conversation. This CEO instinctively knew that, to keep the best talent, you must reach what is important to a worker, and you must inherently respect that, each day, a worker has the power to make the choice to leave or to stay. And because he approached the key talent in this personalized manner, he retained just about all the people he needed for the future.

. . . Mark

Look in the Rear View Mirror

It wasn't always like this. We remember when it was relatively easy for organizations to find and engage people. A time when all a company needed to fill its rolls was a good reputation and a reliable way to get the word out about available opportunities. A time when employee engagement was a simple matter of keeping people connected and involved. A time when a company had little need to market itself as a place to work; it simply used the brand from its retail consumer advertising.

When we entered the workforce, as part of the Baby Boom, the supply of potential workers so exceeded the demand that most organizations had their pick of the best people. Those of us new to the workforce happily accepted any offers we received. We knew we were lucky to find a job and, once we found it, we followed our parents' advice to do everything we could to keep it, learn from it, and leverage our experience into another position within the organization. We found ourselves surrounded by satisfied senior workers who proudly displayed company logos in their local communities. Changing from one company to another was less frequent than it is today. The stability of associating with one organization for a significant period of a career represented growth and stability—to be labeled a "job hopper" was to risk being considered unsuccessful.

We knew, as Baby Boomers, that a company was in the driver's seat. If it had a job to fill, it advertised in the daily newspaper classifieds (a thick section on Sundays), talked on landline telephones with networks of contacts from professional associations, or staffed booths at job fairs. It waited for resumes and cover letters to arrive through the regular mail. Each day, when the mail room delivered large stacks of responses, its staff read through the letters and resumes that eager candidates had typed on manual typewriters while searching for magic keywords from advertised posts. Eventually, the company would respond—again by regular post—to the candidates it wanted to interview and coordinated the schedules, again, through the mail or by telephone. To help candidates prepare for interviews, it might send a copy of an annual report through the mail. The process to secure people followed the leisurely pace of business with time on its hands.

Rarely, as it looked for candidates to fill jobs, did a business consider that it might need to market itself as a place to work. If applicants had heard of the company, that might help. If the company was known for doing good things in a community, that could be a good thing. But a marketing campaign beyond a classified advertisement was unheard of. Likewise, business rarely—if ever—focused on what it took to engage workers. The paychecks that business offered were the most effective form of feedback a company could provide.

If people came to work, attendance was viewed as engagement. If business issued directives, compliant workers simply followed. By the late 1970s, as business began to discuss "corporate culture" and the emergence of "quality circles," the value of employee involvement was recognized by savvy CEOs. But this was much more about the value added by increased contribution. A foundation of employee engagement was taken for granted.

Sensibilities

As Baby Boomers, we entered the workforce with the sensibilities we inherited from our parents. Their generation traditionally looked to one company as the destination for a lifetime. While we realized, as new employees, that we were not likely to stay at the first company we worked for, we certainly wanted that first or second job to lead to a place where we could stay. We believed we would succeed if we kept the job and pleased the boss. We rarely cared about how late, hard, or long we worked.

Our generation was bred with a need for security. Most of us started to work at times of high interest rates, record inflation, and economic uncertainty. We departed for the first day of work without a cell phone, an iPod, a new car, a gym membership, an expectation of how an employer would support personal priorities, or a safety net of financial support from our parents. We were ecstatic to receive a paycheck and "fringe benefits" and willingly worked hard in return. While that defined benefit retirement plan provided a carrot to stay at a company, we stayed as long as the job provided an opportunity to make ends meet, develop a craft or profession, or offer advancement. We had little reason to look elsewhere. Shopping happened at stores, not the job market.

It's no wonder business could always find the supply of people to meet demand or that engagement was not a challenge. The pool of would-be workers never emptied as steady streams of Baby Boomers entered the workforce during the 1970s and 1980s. Because workers were plentiful, a business could simply plan its needed headcount as part of its annual budget cycle with the well-worn belief that the right people would be found. When a business needed to fill a job, it would open a job requisition, post an advertisement, interview candidates, and make a selection, based on the demand of the moment. Magically, the supply always came through. Business had little need to look beyond its current budget cycle to predict whether supply or demand would change. When it needed more employees, human resources would keep the trail of candidates flowing. At the same time, business could easily keep employees engaged. Workers arrived engaged. Leaders had little need beyond its predictable ways to manage and connect. The job provided an incentive and, between the reliable approaches to recruitment and engagement, talent issues rarely filled agendas in board rooms. Business met its needs at the pace that business required.

Challenges

It's not that these were easy economic times. While we look back at the 1970s and 1980s as periods of major challenges, finding talent was rarely one of them. When industries would suffer—such as aerospace in the 1970s and oil and gas in the 1980s—the talent challenge was to get rid of people, not to find more. In the dark days of the energy bust of the 1980s, in fact, an industry lost a generation of workers jettisoned by employers. As recession spread to other industries, and many companies reduced headcount, employees began to realize they had to watch out. They could not, as their parents had, rely on institutions to provide career stability, They had to take care of themselves. Never again could they permit business to take them for granted. Many who entered the workforce with a fundamental trust of management experienced, for the first time, a sense of abandonment.

Companies, facing struggles, gave themselves more leeway in the hiring and firing of employees. The change in business needs ended a generation's expectations for career employment at a single destination. Technology and lower cost labor replaced longstanding employer-employee relationships as business reduced headcount to respond to competitive challenges. In every industry, business began to spin new descriptions of "the deal" it offered so it could limit employee expectations. Legacy programs that once promised lifetimes of security were replaced with "opportunities" for employees to "take charge" of their careers and finances. Benefits became less proprietary and more portable, more difficult to understand and use, and less easy to value as business began to shift the burden of fundamental security to employees. As organizations became less reliable as providers of long-term employment, those fortunate enough to keep their jobs found companies more explicit about what they would (and would not) offer and expect in return.

Lessons

It could be said that the seeds of today's talent marketplace were planted in this slowdown of the 1980s. Certainly business learned, with changes in demand, it might need to reduce supply despite promises it may have made. Certainly workers learned they could influence the availability of supply by how they engaged in organizations and responded to a company's leaders. The power in the search for talent began to shift from those who provide the work to those who do the work. The reluctance of business to continue to commit initiated the challenge we face today to secure and engage talent. As business challenges intensified, technology progressed, and foreign markets demanded a global view, this shift of power began to stick.

At the same time that leadership influenced a change in worker supply and demand, business began to realize it might need new ways to secure leaders to meet new challenges. For the first time, a business seeking change in executive direction would launch a targeted external search for a specific type of leader from outside the organization. This would require a business to tell its story in a compelling way that would appeal to a specific worker segment who might qualify for such an elite position. Business learned that following a segmented approach to the talent search, rather than rely on traditional techniques of promoting from within, might yield a higher caliber of leader.

The success of this targeted search offered important lessons. When business studied markets, and marketed to targets, it could more effectively close deals with workers. When business studied target candidates, it could more effectively tailor its story. When business engaged partners in marketing, including retained search firms for executive positions, it could upgrade its promotional efforts.

Executive search consultant Jim Citrin remembers that "in the age of specialization, all but a few great companies were forced to get so specialized that it created a thinner pool of general managers at the top."[4] As the demand for high-profile executives increased, candidates discovered the financial benefits of latching on to executive recruiters for a career. Then business, wanting to compete for leaders, upped the marketing and selling efforts. Leaders, wanting to keep themselves visible for high-profile positions, peppered their resumes with positions at well-branded companies. Business, wanting to hire reliable leaders, let the appeal of branded resumes influence their selections. This never-ending spiral solidified the importance of brand to both candidate and business, which ultimately spread to non-leadership roles, too. It came at a pivotal time. Workers once easy to find and engage were now less willing to simply accept what was offered. This opened up the exchange between employer and employee in the talent marketplace.

The freedom of portable employment offered relief to employers and excitement to employees. After decades of ties that bound, employers relished the ease with which they could cast away troublesome segments of workers. Call Center got you down? Send them away. Tired of hiring security detail? Outsource. Looking to make back room operations more efficient? Offshore! With such flexibility, many businesses became shells of the former selves that once promised and delivered more than paychecks.

But they may not have expected workers to grab on to the freedom with so much enthusiasm.

Opportunities

The new talent freedom encouraged smart companies to seize opportunity. Because worker expectations were low, smart companies realized that exceeding diminished expectations might make it easier to attract and engage talent. Southwest emerged from a cluttered airline industry to become a beacon of a new phenomenon labeled "the employee experience." General Electric leveraged its remarkable offerings in learning and development into a distinctive reputation for building careers and leaders. A little-known company known as The Container Store discovered a spotlight in the talent market by focusing its hiring efforts on loyal customers. "Over time," says Jim Citrin, "a company's reputation for handling talent became as important as or more important than any other attribute."[5] From these early reputations emerged the first employer brands that stimulated the talent marketplace.

That excitement—slowed by the impact of corporate scandals and September 11—continued to build until the dismal cloud of the 2008 financial crash. While the market for jobs entered a new era of productivity driven by cost-cutting, outsourcing, and off-shoring, the balance of supply and demand inconsistently changed. Freedom in the labor markets brought cost reductions, while the resulting freedom of trade generated a global redeployment of talent. The balance in talent shifted as supply could no longer keep up with demand in certain fields, while others experienced a surplus. The market for people tightened in specific segments of work where fewer people were available than were needed. Business began to search for workers from new sources as a once static market for jobs evolved into a global marketplace for talent.

Look at the Future

As we look into our crystal ball we see how the new consumer of work—if in a type of work in high demand—will pick and choose opportunities with every retail skill at hand. The less fortunate new consumer—in a type of work in over-supply—may be stuck in one organization, or on the outside, waiting for demand to catch up. Either consumer may be challenging to engage—one because of demand and one because of supply. And an organization's brand may make the difference.

Diane Gherson agrees. As vice president of human resources, IBM GBS and IBM Recruitment, she leads the global giant's daily efforts to compete for talent as it changes its business model from production to consulting. The shift places significant pressure on the brand. "As we bring an employer brand to life for a global marketplace," Gherson says, "our challenge is to balance how we position ourselves globally following our message of 'work for the world,' as we make ourselves compelling and relevant locally, in every corner of the world where we search for people."[6] She describes a world where a company must do more than simply say "we are here" to be noticed and to be believed.

IBM is not alone. Any organization that reaches beyond a single continent must confront—on top of the efforts to recruit, retain, and engage—the challenge to balance what it needs to say globally with what it must express locally. According to GE's Steve Canale, "The biggest challenge for us is competing in a global talent marketplace. We need to be known in new regions to new workers. For example, in the Middle East we are constantly looking for talent, especially in Dubai. In addition to looking locally, we've expanded our search to surrounding Arabic conuntries and other countries such as Canada and the United Kingdom where there are large numbers of Arabic students that may find it interesting to start their GE careers in Dubai."[7] The marketplace for talent is, at one moment, simultaneously global and local.

In our crystal ball, business must find new ways to engage consumers of work. Just like the owner of a successful store who wakes one day to a new competitor stealing customers, business must search and market. This isn't as simple as reacting to demographic changes or as clear as shifting from an industrial to a technological economy or adjusting from work done with hands to work done with minds. Suddenly the balance of supply and demand that we knew—on which business built traditional efforts to source workers—is up for grabs. A new marketplace for talent has emerged, no longer defined by work done in one place or talent supplied from one source.

This is a new marketplace with work done all over the world using people sourced from all over the world and flattened by web-based technology. The market for jobs in which we built careers has become a marketplace for talent. Over time, for high demand positions, it has become what Janice Ellig describes as a seller's market with "not enough talent to meet the needs. Even if a company is downsizing, or in churn companies, there is a need for the best or the brightest or need for great talent."[8]

Susan Johnson, vice president of strategic talent acquisition and diversity management at Pitney Bowes, confirms the challenge: "From a supply perspective it is getting tighter. We are trying to pull people who are already employed but it is harder to get them out. It's a constant challenge to get people excited about different opportunities, especially in tough economic times."[9] In our crystal ball, the challenge to recruit is only exceeded by the challenge to engage.

Business finds itself in a critical position where it must market for talent as aggressively as it markets for customers. But is it ready?

The day I first visited Yahoo!, I couldn't believe the campus and the perks that they provided to employees. It started with the coffee: free latte and specialty coffee 24/7. There was a wonderful cafeteria, subsidized by the company so employees could eat for less than $5 a day. A beautiful workout facility. Basketball, beach volleyball, and bocce ball courts. A walking trail along the southern part of the San Francisco Bay. I wondered what else could be added. Yet, during my tenure there, we added retro-fitted RVs to provide onsite dental, onsite haircuts, along with onsite car wash, oil change, and laundry and cleaning drop-off with delivery to the employees' cubes. Then, along came Google! It started with the food. The Google founders originally hired Jerry Garcia's chef to provide free gourmet meals to all employees and quickly gained a reputation as "the place to eat" in the Silicon Valley. As they expanded they added snack areas on every floor in every building offering granola, M&Ms, nuts, yogurt, fresh fruit and vegetables, along with designer soft drinks and make-your-own cappuccino. It was rumored that the founders believed that no worker should be more than 150 feet from food. Of course, they quickly added everything that Yahoo! offered and, as they grew, they added even more. Their daily scheduled bus transportation to and from San Francisco and other places in the Bay Area was quickly adopted by other companies, including Yahoo! and eBay. Their annual employee ski trips became legendary. On campus, they provided Segways, bicycles, scooters, Toyota Prius loaner cars, and other means to get around the campus or off campus for a meeting or personal business. They provided cash bonuses to employees who bought energy efficient hybrid cars. They added onsite washers and dryers so that employees could do their laundry at work. I once visited their campus for an evening HR event and noticed the washers and dryers going and going at 9:00 p.m. While Google offers one of the most extensive day care programs around it then announced that, with upgrades to the program, they would increase the cost to employees. Employees were allowed to bring dogs to work. And an on-site doctor provides routine healthcare. Engineers can devote 20 percent of their time to projects of their choice. Of course, all of this is designed to keep workers at their desks longer, and it works.

... Libby

Future Issue 1: Work

Business has, since we can remember, thought of its relationship with employees as with people doing "jobs"—defined positions carrying specific responsibilities, tasks, expectations and rewards. When we wanted to work, we applied for a job, with an expectation that we would keep that job—and complete its tasks—until we decided to move on or if we were asked to move on because we weren't making the grade.

As business gradually made traditional jobs more disposable, and traditional workers began to demand more flexibility, the concept of work changed from one of a finite number of jobs to an infinite amount of work a business might need. Organizations began to look at people less in terms of filling spots than doing work; less as lifelong employment than periods of time defined by tasks; less in looking for employees than looking for workers.

The changes of the past decade point to a different environment in which business must search for people. Instead of measuring talent needs by the number of jobs, the forward-thinking business thinks in terms of work—the incremental activities that it must successfully complete for the business to meet its obligations. The measurement of effort as *work* instead of *jobs* enables business to focus on *output* rather than on the *input* of people in specific roles.

Likewise, a worker can look to a business as the source of work for a specific period of time, carefully building a resume filled with accomplishments at well-branded organizations. Without the limitations of traditional benefit programs, this worker can easily move from opportunity to opportunity while a business can freely add or delete workers as the demands change. The result is a free marketplace in which worker and business can make fair and simple transactions.

Realistically, the global world of business is a long way from such an open marketplace. But it's coming. The introduction of online job resources for full-time and project-based work—and the priorities of workers that reach beyond traditional arrangements—pressures business to be flexible about competing for talent. While many businesses will continue to fill their needs in a traditional *market for jobs*, others will explore what a *marketplace for talent* approach can mean. Even organizations that continue to look for workers through traditional jobs must look and sound like organizations that can adjust with the times. The best rarely want to work for the stale. The table below shows how a *market for jobs* and a *marketplace for talent* compare:

	Market for Jobs	Marketplace for Talent
How Business Measures Its Talent Needs	Number of jobs	Number of work opportunities
How Business Fills Its Talent Needs	Hire people for jobs	Hire people for work

	Market for Jobs	*Marketplace for Talent*
How Business Markets Its Opportunities	Market the job, the opportunity, the company	Market the work, the opportunity, the company
How Business Manages the Supply and Demand of Talent	Hire for the jobs based on the numbers of jobs needed	Hire for the work based on the type of work needed
How Workers Respond to Opportunities	Apply for jobs	Transact for work
How People View Opportunities	Jobs for an extended period of time	Work for a short or long term, depending on how long the work is needed and the relationship is deemed to work

Future Issue 2: Pipeline

To manage the supply and demand of talent in a just-in-time manner, business must maintain a pipeline of available, qualified workers. Otherwise it will take too much time to find the workers once a need is identified. Every business has a range of work that it needs to do. Even in a tightening economy, the demand for specific types of people to do specific types of work remains high. Some types of work are, at any given moment, more critical to what the business is trying to accomplish than others; other commodity tasks can be done by anyone as long as they are done well. Some work requires more specialized skills; some can be done by machines; some is easier to fill; some is difficult. It adds up to increased demand by segment of worker.

As a result, business must precisely plan how to meet the demand. To estimate how many workers it will need, business must do more than put a finger in the air to test how the wind blows. Business must carefully plan—segment by segment—how many people it will need to do the work it demands. It must access new disciplines that focus on workforce planning with the mathematical precision once limited to supply chain and yield management. The elusive worker can't be found until business identifies what worker it needs. This will become more evident as Baby Boomers retire and, when they leave, take a great deal of skill and knowledge with them.

But it's not easy to find the right people for the pipeline. When supply simply cannot meet demand, business cannot sit back and passively react. When the best people in the market may not be actively looking for work, business must market for talent. Just as a retailer aggressively approaches a good customer for a competing business, any company interested in securing good talent must inform the otherwise-occupied talent that alternatives exist.

That's where a powerful brand can help. The best people want to work for the best, want to be known for working at a premium employer, and want to capture the bragging rights that come from working for an envied organization. While the best talent look to the highest bidder in the marketplace for talent, they look beyond the immediate paycheck for a long-term return on investment. In addition to monetary growth, they look for career opportunity, training and development, title growth, and a good working environment with an opportunity to connect with others and get things done.

Robert M. Melançon, managing principal of Melançon & Company, observes that "top quality candidates are in greater demand now than they were five years ago. They are far more selective in what they are willing to consider. Companies that want to be able to attract top talent need to begin the 'recruitment process' by building an image as an 'employer of choice' beginning when such candidates are in college, if not earlier."[10] As pipelines become more challenging to fill, the issue of adequate supply reaches beyond a single company's concern to the attention of an entire industry.

Once on the pedestal doesn't mean a stay is permanent, as JetBlue learned in February 2007 when, due to weather challenges, it faced operational problems and customer complaints. Dean Melonas, vice president of recruitment, remembers, "We were an employer of choice. The culture sold people on the company. But our well-publicized operations problems tarnished our brand."[11] To its credit, the company worked hard to return credibility to the operation, reestablish trust with customers, and rebuild bridges with potential workers. "After our challenges on that February 14," Melonas continues, "we believed if we treat our people right, they will do the right thing. We also believed we had to tell a candid story on the recruitment side, to basically say, 'Here's what we have; here is what it can mean coming to work here, here is how you can trust what we are doing,' and we were able to hire great people. We recovered and our culture is stronger."[12] The airline learned the powerful adhesive that brand can be and that, only through hard work and candor, can perception shift. Otherwise, even the best explained and remedied situations can haunt the efforts to attract and engage talent.

The consumer's brand memory is one reason why business must take an aggressive approach to market for talent. Quality is another. While large numbers of resumes may come into an online career source, many business leaders complain they cannot find quality candidates to match business needs. While technology may simplify the selection process, managers complain that it takes too long to identify a limited number of qualified prospects. While business weeds through multitudes of candidates who blast their resumes in response to openings, whether or not they meet the specifications, some managers admit they only hire small percentages after extensive filtering. It's no wonder the patience of business leaders wears thin. If it must settle for less than stellar people, business can't accomplish what it needs. "It has always been intense in our marketplace," says Carol Mahoney, vice president for talent acquisition for Yahoo!. "Finding talent in specific segments is hard. What has changed is the way that we have to reach out to very talented people. On the sourcing side, it is all about reaching passive candidates."[13] A pipeline can't rely on people actively looking for a job. While that may meet today's needs—until these individuals find placement—filling a pipeline represents an ongoing challenge. The only way to keep it full is to stimulate the interest of a wide range of people, many of whom may not think they are looking for a change.

To fill the pipeline, business must acknowledge that supply is no longer bound by location. At one time a company—even a big brand—might go to a local or regional campus to hire employees for nearby openings. It would rely on a local newspaper to carry traditional employment ads to locally market to attract local employees. But business today can't rely on local supply. It must search—virtually—across traditional borders. Because location may be where an employee sits, with 24/7 access, businesses must reach across borders with global voices. But if all the brands use the same tools to market themselves they will, together, create a symphony of noise as they try to appeal to workers. A company's only hope to break through the noise is the strategic, creative use of marketing to reach specific segments of potential workers. A business must differentiate.

To fill the pipeline, a business must also *re-recruit* current workers. This focus on current talent is as critical as the effort to recruit new talent. Just as a business cannot afford to overlook a long-term customer, it cannot forget an experienced worker who may be, at the same time, a target of marketing messages from competing businesses. The value proposition must ring true to current employees so they continue to positively answer the question, "What's in it for me?"

The head of staffing for a global energy company was genuinely frustrated by the challenge to find talent, especially in hard-to-fill positions of engineers and IT. Like most of his colleagues at peer organizations, he looked for traditional sources to fill his open positions. At first he looked at staffing as a recruitment exercise, as he focused on "getting the people in the door," and then relying on others to help people develop. But that view was founded on a traditional notion of filling jobs. When he began to shift his view from one of filling jobs to one of filling a pipeline of available workers to do the work of the business, he began to see the challenge in a broader way. He realized that, to fill a pipeline, the effort cannot end when the work arrangement begins. That is only the beginning. The key to keeping the pipeline full is to constantly nurture the talent doing the work today and develop them so that they are ready for the work that is needed tomorrow. The business must always recruit workers to the pipeline. The effort never ends. This holistic view of the talent challenge, based on filling the pipeline with new and current workers, also helps an organization realize what its employer brand must accomplish to support its recruitment and retention efforts.

... Mark

Future Issue 3: Brand

Ever since merchants began exchanging products with customers, a marketplace has housed consumer transactions. From food to oil to salt, a marketplace sets a price, dictates volume, defines competition, and offers a setting for the exchange of goods and services between parties. In any marketplace, business tries to manage supply and demand by making sure that enough supply is available for an anticipated volume of transactions. If a business can't find enough supply to meet demand, the price rises and a transaction may not happen for those unwilling or unable to pay. This may disrupt the business and cause customers to consider new sources of supply. In the talent marketplace, brand ensures that customers discover the value of offerings.

To attract consumers to that value, however, requires creativity and flexibility. Ken Charles, head of recruitment for General Mills, relates, "In the past we were very attractive to candidates. We followed an organic model. On campus, candidates were attracted to our brands such as the Doughboy and Lucky the Leprechaun. They would meet our people, look them in the eye, and be convinced to join." Charles reports, however, that smaller companies were doing a very effective job telling their stories. The company decided to change its approach. "Now it is all about being in the channels that the new generation frequents," says Charles. "The web is reality for the new generation. They will believe what they learn from the web first or use it confirm what they are told. We now have new tools, virtual recruiting, and webinars that give us a broader reach."[14] The company learned that to compete in the new marketplace it needed to conform its marketing efforts to consumer expectations. And it had to look at the experiences through the new consumer's eyes.

The issues of talent are of top concern to leading executives in a research study conducted for *Brand for Talent* by the Institute for Corporate Productivity in conjunction with HR.com. In the study, titled *Taking the Pulse: Talent Branding*, some 75 percent of HR leaders believe competition for talent is greater than it was five years. And, looking ahead, 84 percent believe that competition will be greater in five years. When these leaders look at Generation Y (born after 1980) some 72 percent say—from a moderate to high extent—that the generation's preferences have changed how they reach out to prospective candidates. The importance of segmentation of market and message is a priority to 55 percent of the respondents, while 97 percent—to some extent—say their organizations have developed employer brands. Encouragingly, some 43 percent believe their corporate cultures support the employer brand—a key factor in worker engagement—while 65 percent believe the employer brand has been effective in engaging current employees and 63 percent cite it as helpful in recruiting the right people to the organization. As we look at these results—compared to other studies over the years—we are encouraged by the progress yet challenged by the opportunity. In the talent marketplace that is changing quickly, we can't wait to a better day to develop the power of brand. The time is now.[15]

... Libby and Mark

The marketplace for business is home to brand. In the marketplace in which we grew up, a drive down any Main Street was a comfortable journey through a local branded economy with stores with people's names on the doors, businesses that were locally owned, and services tailored to the specific needs of buyers in a specific community. But as business owners began to demand more results and consumers began to demand more choice, this simple retail world disappeared. Main Streets were replaced by major thoroughfares filled with the same branded stores from border to border. Strip shopping centers and shopping malls filled themselves with identical brands from coast to coast. The corner coffee shop became one global brand, a hardware store another, and the department store carried the brand of the one name that survived all the mergers and acquisitions. The bookstore is now one of two major global brands, as are the ice cream store, the gas station, and the bank. And the "mom-and-pop" stores that once provided necessary services on the corner have been displaced by the ultimate global brand, a big-box store that takes over any community it invades.

As time passed, consumers discovered they rarely had to leave the comforts of home to access favorite brands. They could simply go online, complete a transaction, and patiently wait for one of the well-branded delivery services to arrive at the door with what they had ordered. This made-to-order mindset spoils a consumer and, in the talent marketplace, challenges organizations to find new ways to appeal. Whirlpool Corporation's Kristen Weirick focuses her efforts on reaching high-quality talent. She believes "it continues to be a candidate marketplace. We are continually challenged to educate hiring managers about change in the talent marketplace." Weirick observes, "There are many systems to find people who are simply looking for a job. The challenge is to find quality talent."[16] The new marketplace can challenge the best-known brands to reach beyond obvious solutions.

While this large, noisy marketplace makes it easier for big brands to market, the scope contributes to the challenge to differentiate. As big brands globally shape buying tastes, all the offerings can begin to look the same with little variety for local taste. Instead of connecting with customers one market at a time, big brands rely on broad connections with less opportunity to differentiate where people are located or where they purchase. It just matters that they purchase. As brands get bigger, they market bigger in order to create bigger networks of loyal customers. The same can happen with talent.

I landed at Yahoo! in the middle of the dot.com bust. There were many challenges in building a talent brand in a rapidly evolving company. Where do you start? How do you brand from the inside out in a young company that has one of the most recognized brands in the world but has never defined the meaning behind the brand nor the promise made to the customer. It took about *three* years to build an employer brand working with our marketing and corporate communications teams as we built the consumer brand. And then we spent another year or two building out our talent brand working the same teams, but also adding our tech group to make sure that the brand was meaningful to our most critical segment, what we called "technical Yahoos!." Then we

created a premium brand and experience to bring in thought leaders whom we called "gurus." But in a rapidly growing business in the Internet space, things change overnight and it was very difficult to define a talent brand and a consumer brand , that would stick. Our brand—Consumer—Employer—Talent—had to evolve with our industry and respond to the most intense competition in our business and for talent the business world has known. Our story, good and bad, was covered day after day by business pundits, analyzed by Wall Street, and studied by academics. Only time will tell whether or not the Yahoo! brand will survive the test of time and become the legend we hoped to create.
. . . Libby

Just as the big brands now compete for mind share on a global stage, many use their customer brand cache to compete for people. Walk into any Starbucks and you will likely see a brochure for potential workers. Step inside McDonald's and notice a promotion for employment on your tray. Go to the website of any global professional services firm to see the calling for workers as front-and-center as the parading of clients. Aetna's Robert J. Crowder relates that "The talent marketplace is highly competitive. We are fortunate to have a strong reputation as a company with continuing growth potential, a sound strategy, and a commitment to fostering employee talent and contributions."[17] Even so, all of the noise makes it challenging for any messages to break through.

The burden is especially strong in the efforts to lure college recruits for in-demand roles. Aetna is one of many organizations that focuses on building a best-in-class employment brand with this demographic. "Our college recruiting strategy is centered on communicating our values and cultural principles that we call The Aetna Way," says Caroline Emmons. "A strong image is helping us recruit and develop the next generation of future leaders." Aetna also reports that, according to the National Association of Colleges and Employers (NACE), companies have increased their college recruiting by 16 percent each year. "As a result, the best students have been reaping the benefits of a market filled with job opportunities and competitive salaries," says Emmons. "Students are interested in working for companies that are performing well financially in the marketplace and committed to making a positive difference in the community. Aetna's culture and public policy positions on health care reform have helped build a distinguishing brand with candidates."[18] Aetna is not the only well-branded company working to make an impression on campus. GE's Steve Canale remarks, "On campus our huge advantage is the fact that we have been around for 130 years and have been recognized globally as having one of the best leadership development programs in the world. Our message to students is that 'you have to build a strong foundation and your own personal brand. We provide the leadership training and the foundation to do that.'"[19] Such a personalized message can reach beyond an organization's reputation to help a student answer fundamental questions about a future.

At first, business reacted to the challenge of noise by publicizing a reputation as a good place to work. Lists of the best employers began to appear everywhere. But in the new marketplace this wasn't always enough. Even the strength of a reputation as a place to work, or the clarity of a value proposition, could not help every quality organization secure the mind share of potential workers. Business realized that a compelling reputation as a place to work is only a start; that reputation must be aggressively marketed to lure and keep workers. Securing the right people is not as simple as offering more money, opportunity, or security. What it takes to win talent today is as personal as what it takes to convince any worker to walk through a company's door.

"In a highly competitive marketplace," according to Jim Citrin, "the employer brand becomes a filter for the strategic planning process. It can drive every big decision to become a magnet for the best."[20] It has also become, to no surprise, a window on how the organization views the global marketplace.

As Paul McKinnon, head of human resources at Citigroup, observes, "What has changed over the last few years is the market demand for our people outside the United States." Like many organizations, Citi relies on its people to understand the subtleties of each target location. "In our global market, we have many people from developing countries," McKinnon says, "who are often the first generation to have an opportunity to make significant wealth, and those people are very ambitious."[21] No matter the global reach, the local impact will define the success of the effort.

At times, it takes an organization a bit of time to fully understand what an employer brand is, how it must evolve into a brand for talent, and what steps it needs to follow to do this work. Some organizations are tempted to simplify the process by focusing only on a clever tagline. They may believe, incorrectly, that a tagline is all that a brand is, and all that is required to brand for talent. That's why, as we begin to work with an organization to brand for talent, we don't begin with "what we want to say." Instead we focus on "what potential and current workers need to hear" and what they may be hungry for. This grounds our brand work in a realistic view of the talent challenge. Then we work through the organization's capability to authentically deliver an experience close to what potential and current workers hunger for. Initially focusing on the realities of the market for talent gives us a much better chance to deliver a brand that is relevant to talent, and that requires much more than a clever tag line.

… Mark

Future Issue 4: Cyberspace

When Mark moved to Houston in 1978, he saw a local Main Street filled with temporary billboards that advertised specific jobs at competitive rates of pay. Each day the billboards filled with new postings in an ever-changing market that could not attract and retain enough people. Years later, when he returned, the billboards were gone. Advertising had moved online as business competed for talent on the Internet. Today, technology fuels the talent marketplace. It's how companies market, collect applications, source and select, and even onboard successful candidates.

The most formidable change the Internet created was how business looks for workers and workers look for work. It has become a lot like buying anything in a marketplace. Craigslist, the Internet phenomenon, is no longer just a place to find a cheap sofa or a place to live: it has replaced newspaper classifieds as a primary channel for people looking for work or business looking for workers. At the same time, online job boards such as Monster, Yahoo! HotJobs, or CareerBuilder—while no longer the new kids on the virtual block—remain key placement opportunities in lieu of traditional newspaper classifieds. Niche websites like www.theLadders.com and www.Dice.com target certain segments for specific types of hires while the new sites www.simplyhired.com and www.indeed.com can display all the jobs listed on the Internet, including company sites, to a candidate in one place.

But that's not all. Social networking sites are no longer merely places to meet people. They are primary channels for people looking for work to share experiences. The Facebook application OfficeBook enables the sixty million Facebook "friends" to rate company cultures and values. It offers any user the opportunity to anonymously observe what's happening inside a company and give potential workers a chance to check out the culture in advance. Many college graduates also post resumes on Facebook that make it easy to keep up as a friend, as a professional, or as a prospect. The website www.glassdoor.com is a career and workplace community where anyone can find and anonymously share real-time reviews, ratings, and salary details about specific jobs for specific employers. And, because information is posted by people who work for the company, many view the content as more reliable than a recruiter's sales pitch.

Savvy employers have picked up on the new consumer's habits. At Pitney Bowes, Susan Johnson says that "doing some things with social networking on Facebook and LinkedIn enables us to reach out to key talent segments who are more savvy on line. Our LinkedIn page for IT and engineering tells potential candidates about our company as an interesting place to work."[22] Many many job seekers—including people who currently have jobs—use LinkedIn profiles to connect with potential opportunities. This online network of more than twenty-four million experienced professionals from around the world helps professionals open doors to opportunities using existing relationships. For many, it has replaced the business card file to maintain networks of prospective connections. Aflac's Amy Giglo believes that Facebook and LinkedIn are efficient ways to maintain relationships with prospective candidates. The sites "open doors that could not be opened before," she says. "LinkedIn helps us with passive recruiting in that we can protect our brand and connect with candidates who may be working for other employers within the same industry." This is especially important as business prepares for a new generation. "The most sophisticated, accomplished, entitled graduates ever produced by American colleges are heading into the workplace. And employers are falling all over themselves to vie for their talents."[23] Clearly, the new social world creates new forms of conversation.

With a click of a mouse social networks redefine how to reach potential supply to meet demand. To find candidates who may not be looking for work, aggressive recruiters search profiles on social network sites. They reach out to passive candidates who may not be looking for work. Employers use social network sites to get more personal perspectives on candidates who post experience and insight that may appeal. In fact, more than 80 percent of executive recruiters use search engines, like Google, to learn more about candidates, according to ExecuNet, the executive networking firm.[24] At the same time, 68 percent of respondents to a Yahoo! college senior survey reported that company reputation is important when considering a job opportunity.[25] No wonder that websites like www.ReputationDefender.com are now available to help potential worker protect their online reputations.

Future Issue 5: Human Resources

As we look in our crystal ball for future sources and trends, we see a marketplace that will become an ultimate open exchange for talent. In this marketplace, workers will more likely to be found than to be looking for work, business will be more deliberate in looking for workers, deals will be cut, and work will begin. Business, no longer able to rely on candidates responding to online posts for jobs, will search for candidates on social media sites or online marketplaces where, as on eBay, talent may go to a highest bidder. Start-up companies like www.Jobvite.com will find unique ways for employers to ask employees to refer qualified candidates. Filling the new marketplace will be an aggressive consumer who will hunger for each work opportunity to earn a livelihood and attain aspirations for career and lifestyle. This new consumer will no longer view a career as a series of jobs but as a series of resume-building work experiences.

All of this change will fundamentally alter how human resources will support the business hunger for talent. As Bob Melançon observes, "The days of gearing up a recruitment effort only after the need is already there are behind us. HR should view recruitment as an ongoing, image-building and image-maintaining process, with a view toward the long term."[26] This requires HR to look at what they do in a different way. According to Amy Giglio of Aflac, "Our function as recruiters has moved from pushing paper and filling jobs to a more strategic role. The recruiting team can add value to any business unit. We pay attention to the total employee and his or her career needs and desires, coupled with the business need, versus just putting a candidate in a role. Now it is about the entire experience, and recruiters are prepared to discuss and fill those business needs."[27] No longer can HR claim success because processes are efficient. Now it must be measured by the success of the marketing effort.

In this marketplace for talent, speed will be everything. With increasing pressure to balance supply and demand, organizations that can identify the needs for work first, and source the candidates to do the work first, will have the best chance to get and keep people before their competition identifies a need. This is especially true on competitive college campuses. As Ted Hoff vice president, Center for Learning and Development at IBM, observes, "No matter how global our message may be, it is a local challenge on every campus. That's why, across the world, we develop longstanding, deep relationships with universities. We know the faculty, the curriculum, and what we can influence. That's a key way for us to efficiently localize a global effort."[28] The pressure is on human resources to fill the internal and external pipelines of people available to work. The organization that uses its talent brand to create demand as a place to work will be first in line to become a magnet for workers.

Today, many organizations are struggling with how to build a talent acquisition capability that is prepared for the new talent marketplace. In our work with a global energy company, we discovered, initially, that the talent function was split among several different fiefdoms. There was the silo for recruitment, the silo for learning and development, the silo for employee engagement, and the silo for workforce planning. And, living up to the definition of silos, they rarely connected with each other in a meaningful way, and they certainly did not look at the acquisition of talent as a collaborative challenge. When they stepped back, with out help, and viewed how their various functions had to connect to create a reasonably consistent experience for the worker as well as a reasonably sound process for the organization, they realized that only when they work together as "connected dots" could they hope to support the talent needs the organization must confront. And that can happen only when they move away from the concept of filling a requisition for a job to the realization that filling the pipeline for talent needs requires a consistent experience at each touch point in a worker's relationship with the organization. This requires human resources, marketing, and corporate communications to commit to a common purpose.

... Mark

Getting to Work

Want your business—and your brand—to be relevant in the new talent marketplace? Here's how.

First, focus on how the changes in the marketplace impact your business. Is it more difficult for you to find and engage workers? Do the workers you seek focus on *work* more than they focus on *jobs*? Is there, among the workers you seek, a move to a marketplace of exchange where worker and employer can freely negotiate terms of agreement?

Second, look at your competitors and how they may be reacting to changes in the talent marketplace. Are you alone in looking ahead to what the marketplace may mean to your business—or is it common among companies in your space? How can you differentiate your business as an employer that understands the consumer and the marketplace—and uses this insight to create a definitive experience?

Third, what must your brand as a place to work say to the marketplace for your business to be noticed? How must your brand appeal to the consumer of work *and* authentically compete for talent? And what steps should you begin to take today to make sure you are ready?

Taking a moment to answer these questions will help you put what you learned in this chapter to work.

Key Lessons: Chapter Two

The next step in the journey to brand is to look ahead to the new talent marketplace. Embracing this future is essential to your efforts to create a talent brand. And that brand is essential to attract, retain and engage the new consumer of work.

Are you ready for this change? As we will explore in the following pages, you must prepare your business today, or be left behind as the new marketplace for talent moves on.

☐ Business once experienced a balance in supply and demand. When it needed to fill a job, it would simply open a job requisition, post an advertisement, interview the candidates, and make a selection, based on the demand of the moment.

☐ The market for people has tightened and, in many segments of work, fewer people are available than are needed to do the necessary work. Supply no longer can keep up with demand. Like a business looking for customers in new places, business must search for workers from new sources.

☐ The concept of "jobs" is gradually shifting to a concept of "work." Many an organization looks less at filling spots than at people to do work; less at lifelong employment than at defined assignments; less of looking for employees than looking for workers.

☐ The "market for jobs" differs from a "marketplace for work." In a marketplace, managing the talent supply is all about managing a pipeline of available workers. The Internet shifts the balance of power in this marketplace to the candidates who finds new ways to consider, evaluate, and select where they work. The Internet places more pressure on a business to brand itself to create demand.

☐ Filling the new marketplace is an aggressive consumer who hungers for each and every work opportunity to earn a livelihood and attain aspirations for career experience and lifestyle. Today's marketplace for talent is home to people who use technology to shop for work, just as they shop for everything else.

Part Two

GET TO WORK

3

ESSENTIAL THREE: CREATE

We sit in rooms cluttered with ideas as we search for just the right way to tell a company's story to potential workers. We know the company well enough to immediately seize upon what is authentic. We know the competition well enough to quickly identify what is unique. We know the talent marketplace well enough to thoroughly consider what prospective workers will consider compelling. This setting reminds us of another time with another daunting challenge.

The year was 1997. At the height of the dot.com boom when the economy in California was strong, Southwest Airlines struggled to hire the entry-level people it needed to meet its rapid expansion. The effort was difficult because retail stores and fast-food outlets paid higher hourly rates in some markets and, with national labor contracts in place, Southwest could not easily raise its entry salaries to compete in these higher-paying areas. As the people expected to deliver the people, we had no choice but to market the Southwest culture as a fun, freeing place to work that also provided stability and career progression.

In those trying, competitive days, we discovered the potential power of building a company's reputation as a place to work—what we now call an employer brand—to become known as a magnet for talent. We focused on building the Southwest image without realizing we were building what would become a legendary employer brand. We effectively capitalized on Southwest's retail image as a fun way to fly by marketing the company as a fun place to work. But we never suggested that people would not have to work hard. We simply emphasized that hard work delivered an opportunity to build a career in a stable, people-friendly environment that stood out from other companies in the industry. We marketed a reputation that was grounded in customer and employee quality, reliability, and safety. And we discovered how a company's brand as a place to work can influence how employees anticipate, perceive, and choose a work experience. Even though we may not have called this effort "branding" in those early years, we learned the initial "how-to's" of marketing an employer's reputation as a place to work.

We knew that the key to marketing the Southwest brand as an employer was to focus on the same reliability, intimacy, ingenuity, and sense of humor that defined Southwest as an airline. After viewing these early marketing materials, we wanted employees to say, "I work for a smart company that truly values its people. That is what's in it for me to be here." We imagined the employee as a customer for what the company offered on the inside, much as the company considered its external customers for what it delivered on the outside. We discovered, through creative trial and error, that by talking about Southwest as a place to work—and applying the same level of creative effort that Southwest brought to its external marketing—we could create an emotional connection between what happened inside the company and what it delivered outside. Without realizing it, we originated many of the concepts that, in the years since, are widely recognized as the origins for employer brand. We had no idea we had uncovered a powerful tool that a company could use to recruit, retain, and motivate employees. We just thought we came up with some good ideas. As Jeff Lamb, vice president of people at Southwest, remarks today, "We are pretty simple in our approach. We have not tried to establish different brands. Our employer brand is the same as our company brand."[1] Years after originating so many strong ideas, Southwest continues to thrive.

We also learned that the potential impact of creating a reputation as a legendary employer is not limited to marketing to potential and current employees. It can, as well, become a foundation to connect the customer experience to the employee experience. By focusing on this experience, Southwest became known as the first real magnet for talent in an industry where the battle for good people had been raging for years. It topped every "best places to work" list and prompted business leaders around the world to ask for "the recipe" to consistently and effectively recruit, retain, and motivate employees to deliver a customer brand. The initial enthusiasm of companies to develop employer brands—to articulate their value propositions for employees—led many to believe that developing the brand was the only required step to make a business a magnet for talent. Many believed that, if they had the words, the actions would automatically follow, and the people would join, stay, and engage.

As early as 1988, Southwest developed a mission statement that has been core to its philosophies for more than twenty years. The mission statement does not mention flying airplanes, creating shareholder value, or even turning a profit. As Herb and Colleen constantly reminded us, Southwest Airlines is, first and foremost, a Customer Service company. If, perhaps, someday airline travel went the way of the buggy whip, they would evolve to a new service with the same dedication. The mission statement starts with a pledge to Customers. To serve with a "sense of warmth, friendliness, individual pride, and Company Spirit." Southwest was a pioneer in realizing that the Customer Service pledge is totally dependent upon Employees (always spelled with a capital "E"). So the second part of the mission is a pledge or commitment to those employees, who are considered Internal Customers, to provide job stability and personal and professional growth. Living this mission is what has made Southwest so successful for the last twenty years.

... Libby

From Employer to Talent Brand

It was a different time when a simple message could reach all potential and current workers. But in today's noisy marketplace, a creative, clear employer brand is not enough to successfully compete. A company must creatively market its employer brand to each segment of worker it needs to secure. Being known as a great place to work is not enough. Today a company must be known for its talent, too.

This becomes more important in a talent battle that fluctuates with the ups and downs of the marketplace. As Dean Melonas of JetBlue remarks, "We always keep our employer brand in line with our customer brand—nice, smart, fresh (innovative), witty, stylish."[2] When supply becomes scarce, the solution is not simply to look harder for talent. It must *always* search for and nurture talent in more places, in more ways, through more channels. That's why business needs a compelling employer brand as a place to work.

But no employer brand—no matter how creative and strategic—can reach all the segments of workers a business may need. No business can rely on the old ways to generically talk about itself as a place to work. It can't simply say, "Come work here and you'll have a good life." First of all, it may not seek lifetime employees at the same time that workers may hesitate to make long-term commitments. To compete for workers, business must aggressively tailor its *employer brand* to reach each segment of potential worker. This shift to a retail-based approach is what a *talent brand* is all about. As Bob Melançon observes, "The best-known companies all do a terrific job of branding so candidates are already 'pre-sold' on the company when we contact them."[3] A phrase, tagline, or artwork is only part of the work; the key is how a business will market its brand to create demand for talent.

As we look at the talent marketplace, we view an *employer brand* as a company's brand as a place to work. A *talent brand* is, beyond this, a company's brand for the talent is attracts, retains, and engages. If an *employer brand* is all about the company, the *talent brand* is, as the name describes, all about the talent. If an *employer brand* is all about the experience, the *talent brand* is all about the reputation as a magnet for talent. For example, at Southwest Airlines, the *employer brand* tells the story of the company as a place to work. The *talent brand* tells the story of what it can mean to the lives and careers of the airline's 35,000 workers to be there every day.

The best talent brands, to be noticed and remembered, tap the curiosity in those they reach. They reveal as much as they sell, live in each layer of a company's fabric, and celebrate real life without trying to hide. "By implementing a well-aligned employment brand, organizations can increase their likelihood of attracting and retaining employees that best 'fit' their culture," according to Tim Brown of the Society for Human Resource Management."[4] The best talent brands never let themselves get cute because they look at themselves through the consumer's eye. They market with humility. They best give an organization its voice and provide evidence of authenticity. They make the right person want to do the right job for the right company at the right time or wait until the right work is available. They best talent brands create demand.

Until I joined Yahoo! I had never been a big fan of employment contracts, except maybe for the CEO or a few top executives. As we began to develop our media business, we hired people from the entertainment industry. As we tried to recruit, I learned about the prevalence of employment contracts in the entertainment world. In Hollywood, people are hired for a term, usually three years, and renegotiate as the end of the term approaches. While most lawyers advise that these contracts won't hold up in court, the system works because it is a mutual agreement and an accepted practice in the industry. We found that we needed to find a way

to mirror this approach to bring in the talent we needed. We used new grants of stock options and restricted stock units that vested over three years. It was an effective retention program that gave us flexibility if we decided not to retain a person beyond a specified time period. While this system won't hold up in other industries, the concept of "rehiring your employees" every few years really works. It is unfortunate that most employers don't put the intensity into the retention that they put into recruiting. Negotiating every two to three years—re-recruiting employees with a mutual agreement as to what they will achieve and contribute and what the company will do for them, getting a time-bound commitment—is a great way to retain critical talent.
... Libby

Brand for Talent

This new approach to market the employer brand is the creative effort to *brand for talent*—how a business markets itself as a place for talent to the segments of workers it needs to reach. The *talent brand* is the logical extension of the *value proposition* a business may adopt and the *employer brand* it may create. The *talent brand* is the effort to market these promises to secure and engage workers. (See Figure 3.1.)

An organization looks at its talent needs and determines what story it needs to tell the marketplace. Chances are it has already labeled its various programs and may use a tagline to describe its offerings. But it has never actually developed an employer brand, much less a talent brand. So it begins by focusing on the value that current and potential workers need to experience—to motivate the worker's choice—which the organization can authentically deliver. That statement of value becomes the *value proposition*.

Because that statement is too wordy to be used in marketing, the organization shortens it into a snappy *employer brand*. But that employer brand—generally describing the company as a place to

Figure 3.1

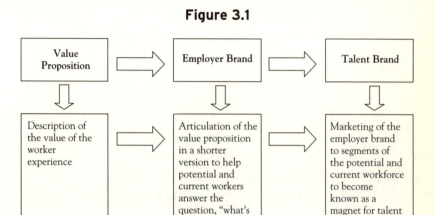

work—is intended to mean the same thing to everyone. It is too general to target specific segments of workers. The *talent brand*, however, is designed to create the reputation as a magnet for talent—to reach the segments of talent a business needs most. So the business targets its message to reach its needed segments by evolving its *employer brand* into its *talent brand*. If the employer brand is based on who the business *is*, the talent brand is based on who the business *needs*. The business must listen closely to what people need to hear to choose a place to work. The talent brand is how the business markets its employer brand.

The potential impact of this branding effort is revealed in a compelling survey of HR professionals conducted by the Society for Human Resources Management (SHRM). The study reports that 61 percent of respondents say their companies now have an employer brand, while 25 percent either recently developed their employer brand or are planning to do so within the next twelve months. Eighty-one percent of HR professionals said their organizations have either a formal or informal HR strategy to use their employer brands to attract talent, and 69 percent use their brands to retain talent. Sixty-three percent of HR professionals report their organizations create communications to make the brand understandable to potential and current employees. Of those organizations with recognized employer brands in place, 55 percent indicate using the employer brand helps them "hire the right people" followed by "a greater number of qualified candidates" (49 percent), "reputation as an employer of choice" (45 percent), and "increased number of employer referrals of qualified candidates" (41 percent).[5] The insight from this study supports the importance of an employer brand as a fundamental business strategy. It also reveals there is more work to do.

To many organizations, the shift from employer brand to talent brand requires a personal appeal to workers that is tailored for various segments. Whirlpool, in its general website message, invites prospective workers to consider what it's like "to create something that touches the lives of millions of people," which helps the company express its promise for "building a better world." But it doesn't stop with a general statement; the site targets its message to potential segments of talent. To Finance, it explains that, "It's more than crunching numbers." For Brand Marketing, it says, "You help build brands and innovative products that win the hearts of our customers, improving their lives." And, for Sales, it exclaims, "You are the face of Whirlpool."[6] The company evolves its promise from the broad to the specific to enable potential workers to picture themselves on the inside and consider whether they want to learn more.

Finding this right fit is especially important when an organization changes its brand message as it repositions itself in the market. Diane Gherson of IBM remembers when the company had a brand as a PC company. She explains how that "limited view would not help us attract the kind of people we need going forward." Instead IBM has used its brand to expand its base of potential workers by telling a compelling story about how the company has changed. "We need people attracted to the service industry, who see us for what we are, as the largest consulting firm in the world," she says. "We need our brand to help them stop thinking of IBM as a big box. It is a place to build career as a professional, an information architect, a technology specialist."[7]

By reaching beyond the traditional use of the employer brand, IBM demonstrates what a talent brand can be by showcasing the aspiration that a company and a candidate can share.

> To brand for talent is to market an organization as a place to work to create demand—as a magnet for talent—to attract, retain, and engage the right people to do the right work at the right time with the right results. The impact is a company as famous for talent as for its products and services.

The talent brand is *not* the same as the employer brand. The talent brand is all about how an organization markets its employer brand to draw in, engage, and retain the right talent—to create a reputation as a magnet for talent. While an employer brand may be broad, general and lasting, a talent brand can change as the needs change. The employer uses its talent brand to precisely appeal to specific segments of workers the organization needs at a moment in time.

This means that a company needs three brands. To attract customers, the *customer brand* articulates a place to buy. To generally engage employees, the *employer brand* packages a place to work. And to recruit and re-recruit workers in specific segments, the *talent brand* markets a place to work. To *brand for talent* is to aggressively and creatively market the organization as a magnet for talent that fills its pipeline from the inside and outside. But it's not as simple as thinking up new words. Before a business can effectively brand for talent, it must complete four essential steps.

Many times an organization will look into how its three brands—customer, employer, and talent—must connect and support each other, especially if it is a company with either a very visible customer brand, an invisible customer brand, or multiple customer brands within one holding company structure. Rather than try to immediately reconcile the distinctions between the customer brand or brands, we work with these organizations to start with the worker experience they need to recruit and retain the right workers. By starting with a focus on the talent need, the emerging talent brand can be grounded in the reality of what it takes to attract and keep people. We first identify what the people in the various talent segments need to hear and experience. Then we identify how the company can authentically provide that experience and what that experience can be. Next we look at the common elements of the various experiences the company must deliver. Finally, we see how those common experiences can be packaged into a brand message that will resonate across the company's brand family. In other words, from the real expectations of people, we develop a talent brand that articulates what we need to say today to get the workers today and tomorrow. We develop an employer brand that, in a less time-specific manner, articulates the value proposition the company will offer to ultimately show how the workers support the delivery of the brand promise to customers. No matter how the brands connect, it's not enough to simply rely on an employer brand to tell all the stories. Segmentation of message is key to brand for talent.

... Mark

Step 1: Identify a Talent Strategy

To brand for talent, a business must regularly study its crystal ball of what work it will need—the demand—and what workers it can find—the supply. But it can't wait, as in the past, for someone in the business to express a need for a worker. Instead, the business must calculate its need for *work* long before the *workers* are actually needed. It can't wait for *jobs* to be requisitioned.

This means that a business must identify a strategy to attract the workers it needs from the inside and the outside. It must manage this strategy with the same precision as it manages any supply chain. Just as "supply chain management" covers the raw materials that the business may acquire, the business must adopt an efficient process to manage the supply of talent in order to meet the demand. Only when it plans ahead can it effectively use its brand to secure the right talent. "If company doesn't cull—or self-select—the good people will go first," observes Richard Spitz of Korn/Ferry International. "It must use the brand to reassure the best talent."[8] To brand for talent is to proactively market to specific segments of candidates to satisfy the demand for *work* rather than wait to identify candidates for immediate *jobs*.

A business knows what sales it must generate to meet its revenue targets. And it knows what expenses it must manage to generate profit from that revenue. To brand for talent requires an organization to proactively plan for the work it needs to complete based on sales, revenue, and profit targets. The organization must look into the future at the cost of talent, just as it looks into the future cost of any raw material it may use, and make plans to manage that expense in a proactive manner.

Integral to this strategy is the talent brand. But it's not simply a matter of "getting the word out" as a place to work. As HR observer Tom Janz asks, "Is the best brand the one that maximizes the number of candidates who express interest per position opening, or the one that attracts only highly qualified and suitable candidates for each opening? Optimal brand messaging would attract only those persons willing to accept an offer whose performance would create the most value for the organization."[9] Smart organizations use the talent brand not only to market what the worker experience can be but also to challenge the worker if this is the right step to take.

As we began to grow and change our business model, Yahoo! realized we needed to hire a very special new segment of employee. Internally, we began to call these hires "gurus." We needed experts in social networking to help us move forward with our Web 2.0

strategy, economists to help us create value from advertising on the web, experts who were developing new strategies in mobile web, designers with interactive experience, and the foremost thinkers on data mining to help drive our advertising strategy. To hire just a few people with these areas of expertise required us to rethink our recruiting. We called together a task force that included members of our HR team, as well as lawyers, technical experts, and corporate communications and marketing specialists. We assigned one of our best recruiting leaders to oversee the project. We identified a dozen specialty areas and went after the world's most influential thought leaders in each field. Some of the folks were academics; some were working at other companies, or NASA, or the government. Some were still in college working on advanced degrees or as researchers. Some were entrepreneurial heads of start-ups and bloggers. The most interesting, perhaps, were the gurus we already had on board. How did we use them more effectively to lead in new areas? Our strategies included opening satellite offices adjacent to college campuses, buying small companies to acquire their talent, hiring academics on sabbatical, and creating special innovation and research labs inside of the company. Within eighteen months we had hired two dozen gurus and they were attracting like-minded talent.

. . . Libby

Step 2: Fill the Talent Pipeline

To brand for talent, an organization must identify the *work* to be done, create the *pipeline* of available talent inside and outside of the organization to potentially fill the need, and fill the pipeline *before* the need for work is identified. Then, when the work is identified, the effort to reach into the pipeline can be targeted and quick. Just as raw materials are made ready at various times in a manufacturing process, talent will be "made ready" through development programs, on-the-job experience, and mentoring for future roles. The business that foresees what talent it will need—and fills the talent pipeline for this work *before* the work is needed—will be a step ahead because it can market to all the possible sources of talent without waiting for actual jobs to materialize.

This requires a business to look beyond what it takes to hire the next worker and to consistently and precisely market to fill its pipeline—not only with talent it sources from the outside but with talent it develops on the inside, too. In fact, it may no longer consider the recruitment effort complete when a new worker walks through the door. To brand for talent, as soon as someone starts to work, he or she should become a part of the talent pipeline for future opportunities.

This forward thinking approach doesn't just focus on hiring and retaining people—it builds capability in the organization. That's why it must start with recruitment and continue through on-boarding, training and development, rewards, ongoing re-recruitment and, ultimately, departure. "Companies need to ask, 'Who do we need to rehire all over again?'," observes Korn/Ferry International's Richard Spitz. "They should rehire the most valuable talent every year."[10] And, as Tom Janz observes, "To the extent that the brand messages include both positive components that appeal to top performers and a realistic picture of frustrating and discouraging components that serve to deflect the interests of poor performers, the value of a strong talent brand is increased if it selectively attracts top talent."[11] Companies that develop a talent brand strategy to fill a pipeline for talent are a step ahead to secure the talent they need and become known for the talent they develop.

Kristen Weirick of Whirlpool Corporation believes employee referral is a key to keeping the pipeline full. "The best way to find quality talent is through referrals and relationships. Our employee referral program provides us with our most successful source of hire. We ultimately hire more than 30 percent of our employee referrals." To maximize this opportunity to fill a pipeline—and help the business manage the aspirations of the candidate in the pipeline—a talent brand can achieve more than good marketing. It can help a business succeed. "We try to build a talent mindset,"

Weirick says. "by valuing talent in the organization and focusing on engagement and development."[12] By expanding the efforts to fill the pipeline—supported by the talent brand—a company can position itself to weather any potential talent or economic storm.

To brand for talent requires more than one approach to fill the pipeline. Like marketers who analyze and segment customers according to what they buy, to brand for talent requires a precise approach to segment workers. Some may be identified based on the essential nature of the work, and others by the demand in the marketplace; a search for pivotal workers will likely differ from the search for workers completing predictable tasks. How a business will address *brand segmentation* is pivotal to how it brands for talent, as we will explore later in this book.

Step 3: Create a Talent Brand

An organization that wants to market to workers needs both an employer brand and a talent brand. A quick look at how the employer and talent brands compare and connect is shown in the chart below.

	Employer Brand	*Talent Brand*
How Used by the Business	Articulation of the value proposition for current and potential workers	Foundation for how the company markets to segments of needed current and potential workers
How Developed by the Business	The organization's external (or customer) brand; mission statement; values clarification	The organization's talent strategy, workforce plan, business strategy, and its external brand and employer brand

	Employer Brand	*Talent Brand*
What Results for the Business	Current and potential workers can answer the question, "What's in it for me to work here?"	Potential workers want to ask the question, "How do I engage with this organization to work there?" and current workers want to ask, "What do I do to make sure my career progresses here?"
What Impact on the Worker	"I understand what the company believes, and how it believes in me, and what I will experience if I work here."	"I understand why I must work for this company, the experience I will have working here, the rewards and benefits I will earn, the reputation I will carry forward because I was here."
What Action the Worker Must Take (for the Brand to Succeed)	Understanding of, and belief in, the value of a relationship with the company	Understanding of, and belief in, the value of the relationship, in addition to the compelling urgency to join the company as soon as possible
How Connected to the Value Proposition	Articulation of the value proposition to engage employees	Marketing of the value proposition to attract workers
How Long It May Last	As long as the company believes in what it says	As long as it is useful to the marketing for workers

If an employer brand effectively captures the essence of the organization, the talent brand creatively captures the attention of the prospective worker. An employer brand tells the story of what it means to work inside the organization. A talent brand, however, tells the story of what working for an organization can mean to precise segments of workers—so that the right people in the right talent segments decide to explore the opportunity for work. If the employer brand is the description of the experience; the talent brand is the sales pitch. "The employer brand does play a big part in people's thinking," observes Jim Bagley. "People look at a company's curb appeal."[13] To help make the company as appealing and relevant as possible, organizations treat the talent brand in different ways for different talent segments.

On its website, for example, a well-branded Aetna welcomes potential workers by saying, "We're looking for smart, energized people who are ready to make a difference in the working world" [at a company] "where the work is real and the results really matter." But it doesn't stop with generally describing what the company can do. Instead it challenges the worker to make a choice. "You provide the knowledge and passion to make a difference," the site continues, "and we'll provide the opportunity to see your ideas put into action." The message moves to a specific promise that, for experienced workers, declares, "We're looking for leaders to join a leader," while to workers returning to the workforce it offers "flexible work arrangements and real opportunities to do what you do best," and for recent college graduates, it asks, "Ready to find your place in the world? Aetna is a company dedicated to helping people manage what matters most in their lives—their health and financial well-being. Join our team to start to make a real difference in the world."[14] By openly targeting its value to specific segments of workers, Aetna capitalizes on a talent brand that can mean different things to different people.

Of course, the best marketing approach will only succeed if the organization actually delivers what the advertising promises. To ensure authenticity, talent brand marketing must be based on the value proposition the company commits to deliver to workers. "Consumers look for the name on the hat, the name on the t-shirt, the name on the resume," observes Korn/Ferry International's Richard Spitz. "They want to build great brand equity on their resumes. Everyone knows a great brand, what it does, what it is, what permission it has to tell its story. It's no different with talent than with any product or service. Great brands stand for something."[15] To brand for talent is not about words. It must be more than a tag line. The talent brand must come to life in the feel of the experience it offers as it shapes the available programs and products.

Yahoo! started as a web directory, edited by humans. To make this happen we hired a group of diverse employees with backgrounds ranging from artificial intelligence to librarians to media editors, and we called them "surfers." It was a truly unique new job. While we created this new kind of worker, sometimes called "cyber-surfer," other Internet businesses quickly followed suit. We became the source for the most talented people in this business. Eventually, as the algorithmic search took hold, the function was automated to some extent and the editorial function evolved.

… Libby

If an employer brand is about clarity and authenticity, a talent brand is about energy. It is the organization's strategic way to be known in the market for the talent it attracts. Any organization that wants to be a required destination among workers must have a talent brand. If done right, it can create the buzz that will be virally transmitted to the targeted audiences. The talent brand makes the right person want to do the right work for this organization at the right time that will create the right result. Or wait until a job is available.

General Mills creates this pull with a simple description, "a great place to start, a great place to stay." It continues to declare, "We are highly committed to an environment that supports the varying needs of all our employees inside and outside of work." In a few words, it moves beyond the images of its consumer products to paint a picture of the life it offers, "in the environment we create at work" and the programs "to help you balance the demands of work and your life outside of work."[16] The message works for the consumer because it is so personal. It works, at the same time, for the talent because it is so targeted. The very people who will warm to the message are the people the company clearly wants to reach.

If an employer brand is about the values and principles that last in an organization, the talent brand is about the messages the organization must send today to secure the workers it needs today. That's how an organization can keep an employer brand for several years and, during these years, develop specific talent branding campaigns for specific periods of time to reach specific audiences. A talent brand is based on short-term goals—who we need to bring into roles right now—to support a view of what our brand says about our talent, the talent we are known for, and what we want to be known for over time.

Step 4: Apply the Talent Brand

Organizations develop employer brands for many reasons. Some want to enhance how employees perceive the value of the work experience. Some want to motivate employees to deliver the brand promise to customers. Some want to label specific programs and benefits. This mixture of objectives for an employer brand leads to a range of approaches to its development and use. But a talent brand has only one purpose—to market to workers, those to be hired and those already on board, so they choose to work for the company.

So if an employer brand can serve many purposes—to articulate a value proposition and motivate employees to deliver an experience—the talent brand only exists to lure workers to an organization and to keep the right talent on board. As HR observer Peter Nguyen notes, "I see many companies jump on the bandwagon too soon and launch a premature 'employer branding strategy' to attract talent when the word 'talent' is not properly defined, or when employers have not yet fully grasped the concept of a talent-based career."[17] Such confusion can impact the creative process and cloud a consumer's reaction. Only when a company knows what its talent brand must achieve can it work to bring it to life.

Many an employer brand is considered successful if it tells a story, frames a message, and provides a consistency in packaging. But it's difficult to measure its results because few organizations employ consistent metrics. A talent brand only succeeds when the business secures the people it needs to do the work. It isn't enough that a talent brand can differentiate the organization as a place to work or "create buzz" for the organization as a magnet for talent. It must actually deliver workers. The metrics of hiring and retention will define success.

It was a long time ago, but we once believed that the dawning of the year 2000 would bring down the tech world. Organizations across the world were hiring computer programmers and coders until there were none left to have. Organizations tried many innovative hiring tactics, including hiring music majors and training them to code. Southwest Airlines was in need of hundreds of programmers. One of our tactics was to host a contest among Rapid Rewards members, our frequent flyers. So in our newsletter we offered a drawing for a free computer (donated by one of our vendors) to any Rapid Reward member who sent us a valid resume. We received over two thousand resumes, but only hired two of those referred to us. You might think this was a failed exercise, but due to unintended consequences, it wasn't. We didn't think about the possibility that many of our frequent flyers were business writers and reporters. We were contacted by *The Arizona Republic*, the *L.A. Times*, and *The Dallas Morning News*, who did stories on our hiring initiatives and gave us a chance to highlight the many cool technologies behind the scenes at Southwest. Then, after the local newspaper story ran, a local Dallas TV station came out to our Dispatch Center and filmed a package on our technology and hiring needs. Thanks to the media coverage, we hired many more programmers.

   . . . Libby

Result 1: Magnet for Talent

To be a magnet for talent is to, simply, be a company that can successfully compete for any worker it needs. To become a magnet for talent is the objective of any talent brand. To succeed in the talent marketplace, a company must market what it offers to talent just as, in the retail marketplace, it must market what it offers to customers.

Even so, most businesses handle efforts to secure workers much differently than to secure customers. While a business willingly spends money and creative energy to lure customers, some take a different approach to the acquisition of workers. Some believe the elusive customer demands the most creative approaches, while the easy-to-find worker can be reached with less marketing effort. While some businesses segment efforts to attract new customers, retain old customers, and reward the best customers, many overlook similar segmentation to lure workers. While some marketing masterminds use extensive research to segment populations of elusive customers, many in human resources continue to look at the worker base as one pool.

To brand for talent, business must translate its general value proposition into targeted messages that will appeal to each specific segment of worker it needs to secure. The best marketers instinctively know how to keep a message to customers fresh and differentiated as they work within customers' short attention spans to differentiate products. To brand for talent, a business must speak directly to a consumer's sense of choice. A talent brand is not designed to entertain or inform. It needs to create demand. And, to create demand, the talent brand must show how the organization offers something that a worker simply can't find anywhere else.

Many a well-branded company will be as careful in the pitch of a talent brand as with a customer brand. eBay's message to potential workers is as direct as its pleas to customers. "You can find a lot of cool things on eBay," the company says, "but you won't find anything cooler than our jobs." The company continues with, "We enjoy our work and we'll be the first to admit it," and promises, "So as we grow (and we are) we'll try our darnedest to retain the fun, community feeling that makes eBay so unique." The company tailors this message to potential segments, such as college graduates, where it welcomes potential workers to its University Community. "Where did you go when you needed that new taxidermy moose head for the frat house or the rattan tiki bar for the living room? Hunt through our career collection. Who knows? You might just find what you're looking for."[18] Such a welcome declaration of the value of an experience reflects an organization that is not only self-aware but is consumer aware, too. Becoming a magnet for the right talent requires such clarity.

Our work with a major retailer brings to mind the essence of what a talent brand can be. An effective talent brand is not only a compelling marketing tool, it is also the lens through which an organization nurtures its culture. This organization enjoys success in the marketplace and a distinctive reputation. And, as a retailer, it looks to its customers as a key source of entry-level talent. But much of its work is less than glamorous, and, despite the upbeat nature of its people, it was experiencing too much turnover within the first six months that a new worker joined. After doing some research, we concluded that the culture was simply bypassing the newer workers who were leaving before they could connect with the positive cultural experience the company offers. This insight resulted in a more extensive on-boarding process for new workers so they could experience the cultural experience sooner; so the culture would "stick" with the new workers; all of which was articulated in a new talent brand that articulated the importance of people to the organization. At the same time, we developed a recruitment marketing strategy to highlight the stories of actual worker experience, and to use the talent brand to create demand for the organization as a place to work. As a result, the pipeline for new workers has significantly increased, as the retention rates have also stabilized.

. . . Mark

Result 2: A Clear Company Story

Most workers considering organizations look for clarity in what different places have to say. That's why, when many companies develop employer brands, they take a close look at their mission and values, so that they offer a clear story. They want the employer brand to capture, in a broad sense, the "big idea" that the company seeks to achieve. While many general statements of beliefs and values may be lasting, they may lack precision and specificity.

The talent brand, however, gives the organization a chance to articulate what it stands for in a way that is relevant to the workers it seeks to lure. The talent brand can put the employer brand in a marketing language that a would-be worker will instantly grasp and internalize. "A company has to understand what is the value proposition in the consumers' minds when they hear your company's name," according to Korn/Ferry International's

Richard Spitz. "What is special? What are the values they want me to demonstrate? What is important to them?"[19] Jeanie Mabie of IBM believes, "It all starts with the values. And we spent a lot of time working through what our values must be globally, to be relevant locally."[20] That relevance can only occur when the internal view is made with 20/20 accuracy and candor. This is not the time for an organization to paint a picture of what is wished for. The talent brand must reveal what is.

Sometimes the hunger for authenticity can stimulate a new dimension of creativity and engagement. IBM's Ted Hoff describes how the global giant engaged all employees, around the world, in an online discussion about its values and aspirations for the next fifty years. This online experience made history inside and outside. Hoff remembers, "We invited our employees to participate in the online 'values jam' where they could tell us what they think the values of IBM are and should be. Over a two-week period, we heard from more than 200,000 employees." Leaders organized the ideas and suggestions into themes and threads that ultimately led to the clarification of the company's values. Involvement and commitment started at the top. "Our CEO became very involved and listened to employees," Hoff recalls, "as they 'jammed' with thoughts of 'What can we aspire to? How can we stretch? How do we reach beyond being a technology company? How do we sustain client success? How do we nurture a remarkable culture? and How do we earn trust every day?' It became very personal and lasting."[21] By reaching beyond the walls of corporate headquarters, and involving the people it sought to engage, IBM reinforced the value of participation as a key business strategy. And it reminded everyone that two heads can be better than one. Or 200,000.

A global financial services organization that had gone through a great deal of change needed a new way to reach out to potential workers for hard-to-fill positions in specific talent segments.

Previously, it had focused its messages to potential workers based on "what the company could offer to a worker" rather than "how the company could provide what a worker needs." By making this subtle, yet essential, shift in its talent brand approach, the organization succeeded at increasing the flow of potential candidates into its pipeline. How did this happen? First, we talked with workers in the hard-to-fill segments about what could differentiate this organization from other places they could work. By engaging workers in the challenge to find other workers, we reached beyond superficial impressions of a work experience to practical things a company can deliver to satisfy. We learned from these discussions that, for this specific segment, the company could differentiate itself by focusing on innovative ways for workers to balance their work and their personal obligations. Through such programs as flexible hours and scheduling, remote worker access, variable hours, and flexible approaches to development programs, the organization could successfully deliver a work experience that met and exceeded worker expectations. Then we helped the organization summarize this point of view into a value proposition to effectively describe the experience it offered to the people in exchange for the work they delivered. We then summarized this value proposition into a memorable tagline, sometimes accompanied by a visual representation, that the company now uses to label various elements of the worker experience. And it all began, successfully, with learning what workers want and need, and what they will choose a place to work for.

 . . . Mark

Result 3: A Differentiated Brand

Every time a consumer prepares to make a choice, the range of options can be overwhelming. A consumer of work often confronts the same challenge. To add to the confusion, while many companies focus their general employer brands on what happens on the inside, the messages are so general they may not resonate with anyone who does not yet know the organization. The specificity required by a talent brand can help any business differentiate its value proposition. This comes from the picture the company paints about what the work experience can mean to various segments of workers.

In the summer of 2004 a mysterious billboard appeared on Highway 101 in the Silicon Valley near Yahoo! headquarters and another near Microsoft headquarters in Washington State. The billboard was a math problem on a white background with no other information: {first 10-digit prime found in consecutive digits of e}.com From what I understand, few would be capable of solving that problem on their morning commute, but many software engineers quickly devised codes and programs to solve the problem, which gave them the ten digits that led to an URL linked to the Google website. The site congratulated their brilliance and invited them to complete more quizzes and jump more hurdles to apply for a job at Google. I had to admit that it was a clever way to recruit talent. Within a few hours bloggers were blogging and business writers were writing about Google's hiring needs and the very smart people they targeted for hire.

... Libby

How does this happen? By marrying what consumers look for with what the company offers, the talent brand—expanding what may be included in an employer brand—can clearly express the difference the company can make to a worker. It can capture the personal and professional satisfaction that an individual joining the company can experience as a career progresses. And with social responsibility such a priority for workers, the talent brand can also crystallize the ultimate good the organization seeks to create and how a worker can contribute.

So it's no accident that many organizations see their talent brands as opportunities to invite people to participate in a mission. Accenture, for example, proclaims itself as home to "some of the most creative, forward-thinking people in the business world ... from a wide range of cultural, educational and geographic backgrounds ... able to work in a dynamic and professional environment that values each person's perspective."[22] Such a personal, yet social appeal may be compelling to consumers who share similar perspectives. These appeals are joined by others, including eBay, which celebrates "the growth of communities where people can share interests about things they have or want"[23] or JetBlue's promise "to bring humanity back to air travel"[24] or The Container Store origins to help "people simplify their lives."[25] While each may encounter its challenges to authentically deliver the promises, the missions define the environments in which workers can potentially thrive. And the talent brand can invite people to join in the journey.

Result 4: Reasons to Engage

Every company looks for ways to engage its people. Clear employer brands help many companies articulate the reasons a company is in business and the contributions that would be lost if, for some reason, it went away.

The talent brand—with its focus on the consumer of work— can make the organization's reasons to exist, and the potential contributions that workers can make, a fundamental part of a message to engage specific segments. While the message to an engineer may be entirely different from the message to a marketer, the talent brand can help each worker believe in the ultimate contribution the organization makes.

The family favorite Heinz, for example, leverages its familiar brand names to describe its opportunities for workers. As consumers, we know this brand well. So it's no surprise that, as workers, we would be heartened by its invitation to "bring us your appetite for success. You already know that Heinz is home to some of the world's great brands. But we're also a place to find extraordinary careers that have the potential to touch lives all over the globe."[26] Its talent brand offers an opportunity to engage.

While Google, on the other hand, is a consumer brand known to millions, its talent brand creatively makes the message less about itself and more about the workers the company tries to reach. The appeal to workers parallels its appeal to customers when it says, "Chances are you have a good idea of where you want to go in life. At Google, we've designed a culture that helps you get there." The message continues by asking workers, "Into being challenged? Into having fun? Want to change the world? If the answer is yes, then you've come to the right place."[27] By appealing to a consumer's hopes, the company offers an immediate reason to engage.

The employer brand, for many companies, is a statement of purpose or perception. It is not a call to action, nor does it need to be. It's an expression of value, not a motivation for choice. That permits the employer brand to make a definitive statement without asking the recipient to take action. But the talent brand exists to get people to want to work for the business. That's why it must paint the picture to the prospective worker of why he or she must work at an organization. It must create a sense of urgency to make the prospect think, "I can't let anything get in the way of my working there." It must differentiate the organization as a magnet where people simply must work.

But a talent brand can't simply be an empty promise. As HR observer Chris Warrender notes, "Branding to attract talent is really about real treatment of the employee rather than the veneer of treatment and the 'cool' factor."[28] No matter the appeal of the introductory message. The real proof is in what the company delivers. So while Google focuses on "cool" as it promises "that every employee has something important to say and every employee is integral to our success,"[29] the real test is when it must bring the promise to life. What happens on the inside happens on the inside, but the brand creates the perception.

At Yahoo!, creating values was the first step in our branding work. Five years later, we changed our business model, articulated a new purpose and strategy, outlined the change in culture that would be needed to deliver, and articulated new behaviors for leaders and employees. A review of our values reinforced that they were as relevant as they were the day we implemented them. The moral of this story is that, while business models, strategies, and missions change, values should stay the same for the long haul.

... Libby

Result 5: A Call to Action

An employer brand succeeds when workers understand and believe in the value an organization delivers. A talent brand succeeds when people decide to join, stay with, and advocate—when the talent brand creates a call to action.

This can only happen if the talent brand is marketed with a commitment to specificity, urgency, immediacy, and targeting. Even the most compelling talent brand will not be effective if not strategically marketed. To brand for talent is to develop a precise, results-oriented marketing strategy designed to reach specific segments of potential workers.

At the core of this strategy must be a specific call to action for workers to follow—an ultimate expression of the organization's employer brand, value proposition, employee experience, and products and services. *Brand for Talent* means that you look at everything your business can do to market your employer brand to secure the talent you need. But this effort can't be just an "HR thing" or a "communications thing," according to Kristen Weirick of Whirlpool. "You must engage corporate communications and marketing, if you have a branding organization, so the effort isn't minimized before it starts."[30] This is a strategy based in the reality of the change to a marketplace for talent, recognizing the emergence of a consumer of work, and appreciating the power of brand to influence how people choose where to work.

It's more difficult than it may seem. We meet people every day who think marketing a business as a place to work is as easy as getting named on a "best places to work" list, coming up with a catchy slogan or tagline, or posting some compelling advertisements. Imagine, for a moment, your business as a "place to work" product. Developing your brand as a place for talent to soar involves much more than simply making an announcement. As Peter Nguyen observes, "Generic lists of 'best employers to work for' provide benefits that most people would like in an employer, but this doesn't necessarily translate into a super-charged environment or culture that attracts, motivates, and earns the loyalty of talent."[31] The challenge of getting caught up in what works at another company is to avoid the temptation to copy rather than invest the effort and time it takes to get to know the consumer. There's no such thing as a talent brand that you can lift off a shelf. To brand for talent requires intimate knowledge of what the consumer of work wants.

To make sure the call to action is relevant and realistic, a marketer must test any product to make sure it actually works. At the same time it must put the marketing strategy through testing, too, to make sure potential customers respond. Then, when everything seems to be working, the product is ready to go to market. It's the same with the talent brand. You don't go to market one time only. You keep the product in front of the customer—through a range of creative promotional strategies—so that the customer never thinks twice about a purchase without thinking about your brand and value proposition, your product, and new messages you introduce as circumstances change. This way you can adjust your brand to emphasize different aspects as needs change.

The organization that brands for talent knows that, if it can't find the workers it needs, it won't matter what it promises to customers, because it may not be able to deliver. The commitment an organization makes to brand for talent is a commitment to apply as much discipline, process, and resource to the marketing to workers as to the marketing to customers. The organization that brands for talent realizes that, to secure the workers it needs, it must actually market; it can't simply communicate and expect people to show up. And it realizes that one message won't reach every type of worker; it must segment its workforce according to the receptivity to the brand message.

The organization that brands for talent realizes the talent brand must live in every aspect of the employee experience. It must be real. It must create real results. It can't just feel good. It must guide behaviors and actions. At Hewlett-Packard, human resources works to drive a "high performance culture" in the midst of its integration of the EDS. According to Paul Rogers, who heads up the employer branding initiatives, "We have defined our 'people promise' as our employee value proposition. Our goal now is to make it real through our approach to compensation, employee development, our career framework, and employee behaviors."[32] The talent brand creates a call to action when it makes a worker feel working for a company can be a life changing experience. That's why Amazon reaches out to potential workers with a plea to be part of its corporate mission. "We believe that every day is still Day One," the company says, "your day to make your ideas come to life ... in a company that redefines itself every day."[33] The talent brand reflects the personality of the organization, the style of the leadership, and the organization's voice.

As an organization develops advertising to market its talent brand, however, it can't simply reach for old solutions. As JetBlue's Dean Melonas observes, "We have learned that traditional advertising methods don't reach the people we are looking for. The new generation doesn't read print ads. If we want to stay ahead of the curve, we have to look at new advertising methods. We can't get stuck in the traditional ways." That's why the organization works so hard to keep its brand fresh. "We do a lot of polling of crewmembers on what it is like to work here so we know what experience we are delivering and how we can work on it," Melonas says."[34]

This company, like others, recognizes the limitations of words. As Aetna's Robert J. Crowder remarks, "Our strategy is based on the premise that an employer brand is not what *we say about ourselves* as an employer, it is what *other people say about us* that is our employer brand."[35] The company knows that workers must be able to see through the brand. Its talent brand celebrates who it is without trying to hide. It is welcoming. It is easy to get to know. And it never pushes its message too hard. Instead, it uses the brand as a pull to lure the worker, never indulging itself in words that are too gimmicky, ideas too silly, and thoughts over the top. It simply gets the job done.

One morning in the late nineties, as I arrived at work at Southwest, my phone rang before I could even sit down at the desk. Apparently there was a young man dressed in a suit and sitting in a lawn chair, holding up a handmade sign at the front entrance to our parking lot (I had gone in the back entrance) with a sign that said "Will Work for Peanuts." I found a recruiter to go over and talk to him about his goals. He wanted to work in P.R. or Marketing so we put him through a series of interviews that day and made an offer before he left. As a college student in Utah, he had heard a Southwest recruiter speak about the employee experience at Southwest. He had sent resumes, but hadn't been invited for an interview, so he drove from Utah to Dallas to get our attention. Interestingly, he ultimately turned down our offer for another that paid a higher salary, so we joked that his sign should have said "Will Work for Chocolate Covered Macadamia Nuts."

... Libby

Result 6: A Lasting Commitment

A talent brand is not designed for a one-time use. The overall description is so true in its message and so distinct in its appeal that it becomes impossible to forget. It makes a worker curious. It taps into the worker's self-directed aspiration to experience and accomplish. It motivates the worker to take action to satisfy questions and interest. Over time the company with a strong talent brand becomes as well known for the talent inside as it does for its products and services.

That's how grocery store Trader Joe's sees it. The company simply says, "If you love great food, are ambitious and adventuresome, enjoy smiling and have a strong sense of value" [the company may be for you] "if you've ever thought about working for a casual, upbeat, challenging people-oriented company." Its reach to less traditional workers continues with, "We encourage laughter and fun at work and we offer flexible schedules perfect for students, retirees, stay-at-home parents, and anyone else looking for something other than 9 to 5."[36] Anyone who steps into one of their stores immediately knows the claim is real. The workers bring the brand to life. This talent brand gets to the core. This sense of discovery can help endear the organization to the worker. A talent brand expresses what *this* organization can express that no other organization may claim.

Sometimes an organization developing a talent brand isn't sure where to start. That's why we start with the talent and what they need to experience to choose the company as a place to work. We started out with a global financial company by asking, "What is the most challenging worker for you to hire right now?" For each of the most popular responses in the room, we asked, "What about your organization, and your employer brand, should appeal to this worker?" and "What about your organization, and your employer brand, should make this worker curious to learn more?" We then asked, "What about your organization would differentiate in a positive way from other places that worker could be?" followed by, "What about your organization could create demand among other, similar workers?" From these responses, we were able to

articulate what the talent brand could say about the organization that was *new*. One trap that brand work can fall into is when the brand sounds the same as every other brand. Just as serious is if it sounds the same today as it may have sounded many years ago. While the essence of the experience a company offers may not change over time, certainly not the values on which it is built, how it is packaged and marketed—through the talent—must be flexible enough to change with each day and each talent segment while remaining authentic to the actual worker experience.
... Mark

To brand for talent requires that an organization take a different look at what it takes to secure workers. And that means the organization may need to stop doing things the same old way. Here are a few.

Stop thinking about filling jobs—*start thinking about finding people for work that will be required now and in the future.* Instead of thinking about a finite number of jobs, think about an infinite amount of work a business needs to do. It's a matter of filling the need for people to do the work instead of waiting for specific jobs to fill, moving from a world of requisition to a world of sourcing.

Stop thinking about talent pools—*think about a talent pipeline.* To brand for talent is about constantly replenishing a pipeline of qualified workers—from inside and outside—to be the available supply when the demand increases. If you connect this effort to how you train and develop your people, you can ensure your internally generated pipeline is filled with viable candidates as well as keep your people interested in working for your business.

Stop thinking of marketing for talent as a media effort only. Every worker who joins your business can become a candidate in your talent pipeline and a recruiter of new talent. Anyone who works for your company can support your face-to-face referral efforts.

Stop thinking about employees. Start thinking about consumers. The person doing the work may not be an employee. She may be a vendor, a contractor, a contingent worker, or she may work independently at home or from a remote location or in a remote talent center across borders. No matter the status, she or he is a consumer of work to whom your brand must appeal. The new brand-for-talent strategy must give the consumer a reason to buy. This is not a retail environment in which you can rely on a big sale to drive customer traffic, succeed because you have a monopoly, or rely on a convenient location. You must differentiate at every turn.

Stop thinking about describing. Start thinking about marketing. In the retail world, a marketing strategy is designed to create demand. Those customers are attracted to the *magnet* because the marketing strategy effectively differentiates the company and the work among its competitors. The company becomes this magnet by differentiating its value proposition. It's the same in the new talent world. The marketing strategy must create demand.

Stop thinking you are ever finished. To brand for talent never ends, even in an economic downturn. The retail world knows that no matter how successful today may have been, it will all be a memory when the store opens tomorrow. As a company competing in this new retail world, you must give the consumer of work—the prospective or current employee—a reason to buy more. Give the consumer a reason to buy from you instead of across the street. Do something different or better to create demand. Employ the same insight to secure your employees in the talent market as you do for your customers in the retail market. Use the same degree of analysis and the same emphasis on creativity. And remember that the consumer is always right.

Stop thinking transactions. Think relationships. A traditional talent strategy focused on processes to source and screen candidates. It assumed that a viable candidate would be interested in a specific job simply by reading the specs. It assumed that the company would sell itself and that the customer would want to buy. In a new strategy, a company develops relationships on the inside to forecast the work needed and to source current employees as potential candidates to do this work. The company must constantly nurture relationships on the outside to source the best candidates all the time, never waiting for actual jobs to be identified.

Stop thinking of communicating facts. Think branding. It's not as simple as communicating a job opening. When everyone competes for the same talent, a company must differentiate itself. A company must constantly market itself as a place to work. It must be in the market even if the openings aren't yet listed. It must create demand so that the best candidates in the market constantly present themselves to the company, so that they are there when the company has a need. The new retailer of the employment experience realizes a customer is fickle, always susceptible to the latest fads, always influenced by other buyers, always open to possible changes. So the new retailer should place as much effort on re-selling to current customers as on luring new customers. It must spend as much time nurturing its current employees as key potentials for new work as it does looking on the outside.

Getting to Work

Want to create a compelling talent brand? Here's how.

First, focus on the *value proposition* your business offers to the workers you need. This is the description of experience you offer to the people who work at your organization in exchange for the work they deliver to your organization.

Second, articulate your *employer brand*. This is the creative application of the value proposition into a catchy, pithy, memorable phrase or tagline, sometimes accompanied by a visual representation, and used to label various elements of the employee experience. Usually, the employer brand is a general statement, not specific to a particular time or place or audience. If you're not sure what this could be for your organization, answer this simple question, "How would your employees answer the question, 'What's in it for me to work here?'"

Third, imagine your *talent brand*. Your talent brand is how you strategically market your organization to establish it as a magnet for the segments of talent that you need to engage. Think about how you can use your employer brand as you message and market to the segments of workers you need to attract. What this means, in a practical way, is how you can convert your employer brand—that describes what your organization is and what offers—into a talent brand—that attracts worker attention to what their lives can be if they connect with the organization.

Fourth, to help you imagine your talent brand, answer these questions. What is the most challenging worker for you to hire right now? What about your organization, and your employer brand, should appeal to this worker? What about your organization, and your employer brand, should make this worker curious to learn more? What about your organization, and your employer brand, would differentiate in a positive way from other places that worker could be? What about your organization, and your employer brand, could create demand among other, similar workers?

These steps can help you put the key lessons of this chapter into action—to be on your way to be a magnet for talent.

Key Lessons: Chapter Three

To brand for talent requires a practical plan based on real knowledge of the worker market. This has to be a product of your talent strategy or else your brand, no matter how creative, will not have a chance to succeed. Is your business ready to brand for talent? Are you ready to create and position a brand to help candidates self-assess whether they "have what it takes" to thrive in your business? Just as a commercial brand creates a clear picture?

☐ A creative, clear employer brand is not enough for a company to successfully compete in the new marketplace for talent. A company must creatively market its employer brand to each segment of worker it needs to get the work done to deliver what the business promises.

☐ To *brand for talent* is how a business markets its brand as a place to work to the segments of consumers of work it needs to reach.

☐ A *talent brand* is the logical extension of the *value proposition* a business may adopt and the *employer brand* it may create.

☐ To brand for talent is the discipline to market an organization as a place to work to create demand—as a magnet for talent—in order to find, keep, and engage people to do the right work at the right time with the right results.

☐ To brand for talent is to develop—based on the talent brand—a precise, results-oriented marketing strategy to reach specific segments of potential workers that parallels the precise, results-oriented marketing strategy to reach potential customers.

4

ESSENTIAL FOUR: SEGMENT

As we delivered our presentation at an annual conference of human resources and communication professionals, a man in the second row captured our attention. He displayed a corporate confidence that seemed to express, with each idea we offered, "You aren't telling me anything new, we did the same thing at our company." He nodded in agreement as we continued to explain that, for any business trying to find workers, simply developing an employer brand is not enough. As we led the participants through the steps to brand for talent, he checked his watch. When we asked him what recruiting challenges he was facing at his organization, he responded, "Actually, none. We ran a successful recruitment advertisement campaign a few years ago and hired more people than we need. Now we are not hiring but, when we do, we can just dust off the old employer brand and run it again."

We hate to disagree, but it's not that simple. As important as developing an employer brand can be for a business, that alone is not enough. Once a business could ride the momentum created by its reputation as a place to work. Once a general "shotgun" approach could suffice. But the new marketplace for talent, filled with new consumers of work, requires more. To brand for talent requires a business to refresh, rethink, recharge, and sometimes reinvent. The marketplace for talent doesn't stand still.

I started to work with a client who arrived at the first meeting with her underlined and notated copy of our first book, *Brand from the Inside*. She started the meeting by saying, "You, know, I think we can skip over the preliminaries because, well, I have read the book and I think we can accomplish what we need very quickly." I thanked her for taking the content so seriously and tried to remind her that a fundamental message of our approach to brand is that no two approaches can be the same because no two organizations face the same challenges. It's impossible to lift what may work at one place and apply it to another. I asked her, after suggesting she put down the copy of the book, to list the five most challenging segments of talent for her business to reach. I then asked her, for each of these talent segments, "What are these people hungry to receive from a business where they might work?" Then I worked with her to estimate the pressure the talent brand would face to deliver the messages to appeal to these workers. It didn't take long for her to realize that, to brand for talent, you have to look at what each segment needs to hear, how those messages can connect, and what the business can authentically offer.

. . . Mark

Segmented Marketing

Like any brand, a talent brand is a promise—a statement of commitment of what a business will provide in exchange for what a worker will contribute. Like any brand, a talent brand is a reflection of what a business stands for and believes in. And, like any brand, a talent brand seeks to differentiate this business from the others competing for the consumer's mind share. Only this time the consumer is a consumer of work.

All consumers of work, no matter how they may share behaviors, differ in what work they do, what aspirations they carry, and what experience they seek. Because these consumers differ, one expression of a talent brand can't possibly mean the same thing to all of them or motivate all of them to do the same thing. A business has no choice but to target its talent brand message to the distinct segments of workers it seeks to internally and externally add to its pipeline. How the business targets its talent brand in its marketing to specific types of workers is the essence of branding for talent. The talent brand is what an organization needs to say today to get the talent today. That may be different tomorrow.

So it's no surprise when a brand-conscious company like American Apparel describes itself as "a company concerned with human factors" in its effort to be relevant to potential workers and promises. "Rather than exploit cheap labor, we leverage art, design, and technology to advance our business."[1] At the core of its talent brand is its value proposition that may mean different things to different people. And in marketing a business to different types of workers, that value proposition may *need* to mean different things and be interpreted in different ways. No single statement, no one talent brand, can reach all the people a business may need unless it is creatively tailored to what each segment needs to hear. Those segments do not stand still. It's not enough to develop a talent brand once and expect the results to automatically repeat. Success only comes in how a business markets that talent brand to specific segments of workers. The chart below shows the essence of branding for talent.

How Marketing an Employer Brand Compares to Marketing a Talent Brand

	Traditional Employer Brand Marketing	*New Talent Brand Marketing*
Brand Promise	One for all	Tailored to each segment
Recruitment Media	Traditional mix of media used to recruit workers – primarily print, radio, and television	Tailored approach to media based on the priorities of each segment

	Traditional Employer Brand Marketing	*New Talent Brand Marketing*
Marketing Plan	One for all	Tailored to each segment based on knowledge of the needs and wants of the segment
Interview Experience	Tailored for segments by types of work	Tailored to each segment based on knowledge of the needs and wants of the segment
Worker Segmentation	One approach to marketing the brand; distinctive approaches to interviewing by segment of worker	Distinctive approaches to marketing the brand based on the *brand for talent* approach to worker demand and brand readiness

Yahoo!'s answer to innovation was our "Hack Day," which was designed to encourage small teams to build innovative and cool solutions to a particular problem or need. Held quarterly at our headquarters and at other locations across the globe, this contest allowed employees to develop their "hack" within a twenty-four-hour period and showcase it in less than two minutes. The prize, of course, was not just a trophy or t-shirt, but the right to be considered as a future new Yahoo! product. As this event grew in popularity, we expanded it to outsiders and to university hackers. Of course, it attracted new talent, but also got coders interested in innovation using Yahoo! products and tools.

. . . Libby

How to Segment Talent

Segmentation is at the core of *any* effective marketing program. With customers, segmentation enables a business to focus on subsets of prospects that are most likely to purchase what a business offers. With talent, segmentation can yield a higher "close rate" among potential workers because the brand message has a better chance to get through. A business can deliberately adjust the message for each segment, which can eliminate unnecessary noise. The talent brand can move beyond generic messaging to express what will truly make the difference to a worker. For some, the brand may instigate a choice and for others reinforce a choice.

But segmentation doesn't mean creating a separate talent brand for each segment. It simply means adapting the talent brand message for each segment based on insight into audience needs and preferences. According to Ken Charles of General Mills, "We developed our own brand architecture tool, which allows us to gather insights from each segment. We built one for campus hires, MBAs, experienced hires, and international employees. We realized that we were getting a spread, so we created one unifying brand."[2]

Nor does segmentation mean creating a separate talent brand for each part of a business. Instead, one talent brand can reach across traditional boundaries. "The differentiator for us is our portfolio of world icon brands," according to Ken Charles. "As an employer, General Mills has prestige, no matter where in the business people may work, and they want to add that to their resumes. If we can get them here, we can keep them here. Our brands are the platform where someone has the opportunity to build a legacy. We are a company of brands, not a branded company. Over time, we have been shy about lifting the story of General Mills to the broader public. The key design element of our branding is a matrix that shows the breadth and depth of our brands."[3] It's the same with a talent brand. Only when segmented can it accomplish what is expected.

Segmentation of the marketing message, however, requires more than simply listing the different types of work the business needs to fill. Identifying specific roles is not the same as preparing how to reach potential workers for each role. That requires a subtlety of planning as precise as how external marketers reach for pockets of product consumers. And while a business may likely segment according to a few fundamental demographic dynamics, to brand for talent requires a more complex view of the needs, aspirations, and priorities of workers—balanced with the demand for the work they can contribute.

While it can be tempting to simply segment workers by traditional demographics or standard definitions of tasks, dividing the market by type of work fails to consider all the factors that may influence if a brand motivates a worker to join. For each segment, the talent brand must address the barriers to receive the message. Is it noise? Cynicism? The company's reputation? A worker's experience? An organization needs to know how a potential worker will make choices about where to work. It's like soap. Some people buy it to wash their hair, some for the smell, some for the experience. A business needs to know why people buy.

John Boudreau, professor of management and organization at the Marshall School of Business at the University of Southern California, reinforces the need for a segmented approach to talent. He advocates that an organization identify its pivot points and its pivotal talent. Boudreau suggests that organizations can begin by looking for the work that provides the best leverage, to look for areas where there are gaps or bottlenecks that slow growth or productivity. Identifying the pivot points directs where an organization should invest. "Whether that gap is the result of an inadequate pipeline from within or an external shortage due to market competition, this specific talent suddenly becomes pivotal to your organization and you understand it as something you must obtain to move forward," Boudreau says.[4] Such a segmented approach reaches beyond the formation of a talent strategy or development of a talent plan to the creating of a talent brand.

> To compete in the most intense job market ever, and against competitors such as Google and Microsoft, Yahoo! knew it had to do something really unique with our talent brand. As part of our preparation, we asked the marketing research specialists affiliated with our advertising agency to survey the technology world to get the perspectives on Yahoo!, our Tech Talent, and our work. The results were not as easy to hear as we would have liked. They found among recent grads and others looking for work that Yahoo! had lost its "cool factor," especially when compared to Google. We realized that we hadn't told our story. We hadn't highlighted our brilliant technologists. We hadn't highlighted our work. We asked our recruiters to survey people who recently signed on to work for the company to find out why they chose Yahoo! over the competition. We found that they chose Yahoo! because the work matched their career goals, while the competitors may have been less specific about the opportunity. This research informed our talent brand work. To successfully conduct this research, you may have to compensate those who turned down the offer with a coupon for a free product or a little cash to get their participation. Then you might want to ask people, in segments, why they would or wouldn't apply.
> . . . Libby

A business can segment workers by the value they deliver, the impact on results, and the specialty or function they bring. This proven approach can help a business estimate the number of workers it may need by the types of work they may do. But to brand for talent requires more than slotting workers into categories based on function. Instead, a business must realistically assess the demand for the work and the pressure for a brand for each segment. As Kristen Weirick of Whirlpool Corporation observes, "We break down our talent needs by function, and then based on what we can tell about each function, we set priorities for each segment."[5] This approach enables a business to plan the *intensity* with which it will tailor, package, and market its talent brand to each segment. It will identify how much pressure the brand must apply to secure a worker based on the need and the knowledge of the consumer's aspirations, habits and priorities.

To segment your workers to brand for talent, consider how difficult it will be to secure the workers as well as the responsiveness they may demonstrate to your message.

Step 1: Assign Priorities

Look at what the business needs, the type of work the business does, and the specific types of workers the business must secure. This may be based on which workers create, sell, or deliver the product or service. Look across all the types of work your business does and identify which segments are the most important. Arrange these in the order of the value they add to the business, the impact they create, or how dramatically they move the needle.

The type of worker that a business labels as most important may be *critical for operations*: a worker a business simply can't live without. In an airline this may be a pilot or a mechanic; in a bank it may be an economist; in an oil company it may be a petroleum engineer; for pharma it may be the chemist; in healthcare a nurse; for high-tech firms it is almost always the software engineer. Without these workers, a business would screech to a grinding halt. And they are the most important to populate in a pipeline for talent.

No two contributions to any business are equal in value. No matter what work you may do, some segments of work will produce value-enhancing results, as measured by yield or return on investment, while other segments will be necessary but will not move any needles. Many companies are reluctant to admit that certain types of work are more valuable than others, as if making such a declaration makes the people doing one type of work more important than others. But acknowledging that a type of work adds more value is a simple demonstration that you understand what the business does and what resources it needs to do its work. This doesn't mean the business values the people in one type of work over another. It simply means the business is grounded in a reality of what type of worker is essential for its pipeline. Certain workers will, in any business, add more value than others, such as a new executive selected to run a new area of business or thought leaders who drive what a business pursues.

As you prepare to list the segments, think about the types of work your business can't live without. Is it the work to deliver a product or service? Is it the work to develop new product with a focus on innovation? What pivotal work, when done well, makes the biggest impact on results? What is most important to the growth of the business? What is essential to "moving the needle" in how the business performs? What is the *core work* that, without it, you would not be able to open the doors? What *investment work* is essential for the company to grow? And what *game changing work* is needed to push the company to reinvent itself in a current or new space or to differentiate from the competition?

Segmenting is not as simple as saying the top three types of *core work* will be at the top of your list, the top *investment* work next, and the top *game changing* work next. It depends on what is most important to your business at a specific period of time. It may be that, today, and in the future, if you don't get the work done to *game change* then you won't be able to focus on anything else. Or if you don't stick to the *core* work you can't expect the market to look at your efforts to *game change* with any credibility or trust.

This one comes under the category of "your talent brand is out there whether you know it our not." A couple of years ago I was forwarded an email from one of my co-workers that had been forwarded to him by his wife. It seems a mom who was a member of the Parents Club of Palo Alto and Menlo Park (in the heart of the Silicon Valley) was considering a job offer from Yahoo!. She sent a note out to her network and asked about the boss, the role, the job, and the company. Within a few hours she had answers from current and former employees, spouses of employees, and candidates who had turned down offers. Surprisingly, her information was as accurate as she could have received from any Yahoo! insider, including the good, the bad, and the ugly. She even got advice about which bosses were friendly to working parents and which were not. She based her decision on what she found out from her network versus what the company told her. The network is the most trusted and, perhaps, accurate source of information.

. . . Libby

Step 2: Evaluate Demand

After you identify the segments of work, take a close look at how much demand you face for each. Are other businesses in your industry looking for the same worker and trying to steal some of yours? How does the demand for the workers compare to the volume you may need? What is the supply and demand in the marketplace? Are the most essential jobs the most in demand? As you look ahead, how many of these workers are available now? How many will be available in the future? Are there people you can bring in and develop inside? If so, how available are these people?

It may be that, even though one type of work is more essential than another, the demand may actually be less because the business needs fewer of them. Think about whether a type of work can be completed by a full-time worker or a part-time worker, or whether there are other, less traditional ways to complete the work. Assess whether there could be an overabundant supply of workers for the type of work that you need. Is this a segment for which demand exceeds supply or a type of work where demand is diminished?

> When we developed our careers site at Yahoo!, we realized we needed to highlight two experiences—one for technical folks and one for non-technical and creative types. The site has separate entry points. For the Left Brainiacs: Tech running through your veins? We've got all kinds of opportunities for you to put your passion to work. And for the Right Brainiacs: Big ideas. Passion. Creativity. A hankering for fun. Just a few of the requirements for the roles below.
> . . . Libby

Step 3: Compare to Competition

Who does your business compete with for workers in each segment? Who are the competitors, beyond the "usual suspects" for talent? Are any of these companies actively recruiting your workers? How intense is the competition? How do the competitors market their brands as places to work? Keep in mind the efforts of your competition as you plan how to market your brand for talent. Determine—based on your working knowledge of the marketplace—how intensely others compete for workers in the marketplace. As IBM's Diane Gherson observes, "We face intense competition from companies we may not be accustomed to competing with. That demands that we take a different approach, to make sure the story we tell is compelling."[6] Some competitors may be less aggressive simply because they continue to ride the momentum of strong reputations as places to work. Others may be as hungry as you.

For each segment, consider how well-known you are as a magnet for talent. What is your reputation? How much potential worker traffic do you attract simply because of who you are and what others say about you? What is your talent market share? Depending on the dominance of your brand, you may experience less pressure to secure talent. The less the general public knows you as a company, the more pressure your brand may have to confront. Ask yourself:

How You Differentiate from the Competition. How clear are the competitors' value propositions? How aggressive is their marketing? How compelling is their pitch? How successful are their efforts? How does your business appeal and what will it take to get a candidate interested? What may you need to clarify in your marketing so a target will look at your business differently?

How Well You Know the Segments. Get to know what each segment you need to reach thinks about your business. Identify what messages may appeal and if the workers you seek prefer one type of message over another. Find out what someone will listen to, what message will successfully motivate action, what balance of brand and marketing will be trusted and believed, and how you must differentiate your message in comparison to the competition. Consider doing some market research into talent similar to, in external marketing, when a business studies the buying patterns of segments of the population. This is no different when marketing a company as a place to work. As with all marketing, the best way to learn is to ask.

Sometimes you just have to jump through hoops to get the right talent. When I first got to Yahoo!, we had to recruit and hire new leadership teams over most business units. One candidate was particularly difficult to land. He had many objections. Not to the job or the role, but to relocation and the offer. My strategy was to overcome each objection one by one. At the end of the negotiation, I had to ask Lloyd's of London to underwrite three separate insurance policies to address his concern that he might die or become disabled during his transition and move and before his benefits kicked in. It cost a little bit to do this, but the candidate was so impressed that every one of his personal concerns had been addressed creatively that he happily accepted his new leadership role.

. . . Libby

What Resistance Your Messages May Receive. How receptive will workers be to your marketing message? What resistance may they demonstrate? Is there something about the reputation of your business that may get in the way of your messages? Has your business been the subject of negative press? Do you suffer reputation challenges? You need to know when the workers you seek fundamentally oppose working for you. Identify any specific reasons why someone you need will not consider listening to what you have to say.

Whether Your Business Is a Magnet for Talent. Are you already considered a magnet for talent for the workers you need? What is your current experience hiring for this segment? Do workers think of your business as a place they might want to work? How much effort will you have to expend to reach each segment? What do you learn about the company's reputation as a place to work from new people working for your business? How did this reputation influence their work decision? What feedback do your internal and external recruiters provide? What about those who declined your offers? All together, how much does your reputation and your brand attract people. The degree to which you already draw talent will influence how you begin to market your brand.

Step 4: Assess Brand Intensity

Next, establish whether the segment of workers demands a high-intensity or low-maintenance approach to talent brand marketing. A *high-intensity* approach means this worker segment is at the top of your list of people to reach with a broad marketing of the value proposition as well as the specific attributes of potential work. A *low-intensity* approach, on the other hand, means this worker segment is important but you can "get by" with a less tailored approach to marketing the value proposition as well as the attributes of the work.

Workers who demand *high-intensity marketing* may receive an overabundance of marketing messages because they sit at the top at similar lists at every company. If so, your messaging must be precise, relevant, and authentic to break through the noise. Workers who require *low-intensity marketing* may, however, be contingent workers to whom you do not need to tailor your talent brand.

Now and then someone we work with will comment that developing the talent brand can be a lot of work and take a lot of time. We admit that it does take a lot of careful effort to work through the segments and the messages, but it doesn't have to take a lot of time. A global energy company didn't have a lot of time. They needed a new talent brand yesterday. In three weeks, we interviewed employees in six locations around the world and summarized the value propositions that needed to be explored with the global HR leadership. Turns out they were all in one place for a four-day meeting, so we walked in at the start of Day One with our research findings and draft value propositions in hand. Over a four-hour session, we worked through the brand priorities to reach each of these segments around the world to create a talent brand that would work globally as well as one that would be relevant locally. Over the next two days, we developed a range of brand ideas, which we returned to discuss with them at the end of their four-day session. We emerged two hours later with a global employer brand, specific talent brands to appeal to each segment in each location, as well as an engagement strategy and an implementation plan.

. . . Mark

To help you assess the brand intensity, consider how workers in each segment choose where they work. If the workers you seek do not make choices about work in ways you can predict, you may need to adjust how you use your brand to enhance your appeal. You need to know what it means when a potential worker may itch so you know, through your brand and marketing efforts, how to apply the most meaningful scratch. You need to find their work patterns, when they join an organization, for how long, and what motivates them to make a change. While past behavior is not a foolproof way to predict the future, it can give you important insight into what balance of brand and marketing may appeal.

You also need to consider how potential workers connect. There may be, for example, large groups of workers you may want to hire. Some may hold regular conferences and seminars around the world. Many may have created strategic sourcing units in their talent acquisition groups. Others may be virtually connected around the clock. And others may connect with people who currently work for your organization—your most effective recruiters.

It's no surprise that, in a tight talent market, employee referral programs are again popular. Some organizations use social networks as an employee referral source. New technology allows employers to mine their own social networks. Companies like www.Jobvite.com, www.BountyJobs, and www.Bluechipexpert .com make it easy for employers to pay anyone who refers a candidate hired by the company for specific jobs or roles via social networks.

As a company works through each of its segments—and assesses the demand for talent and pressure on the brand—we hear the question about how all of this ties together into one brand. A food company faced this issue as it struggled to provide one employee experience to a range of satellite operations. It needed the brand to be relevant to each locality, to each segment, and to each talent challenge. Also contributing to those relevant brand messages as well would be the constants that define the overall value proposition. We developed—from the insight we gained talking with employees—distinct value propositions for each key talent segment. While these propositions differed in many ways, they overlapped in the fundamental experience delivered to a worker. From these distinct value propositions, we developed an overall value proposition for the entire organization from which we developed the overall employer brand. And from this overall employer brand, we developed specific talent brand messages to appeal to each talent segment. We came full circle from the segments to the talent segments with a cohesive value proposition and employer brand connecting the messages.

. . . Mark

At the same time, any business that markets to segments finds it valuable to keep track of what customers want and need. As airline travelers, we might look at frequent flyer programs as a way to fly extra trips. To the airline it's also a great way to mine the data of the best customers for the airline. Grocery stores do the same with discount cards. Financial services businesses study and segment customers so they know which are more likely to buy other products they offer.

It's no surprise that the same type of knowledge is a necessary step for the talent marketplace. Ultimately, it will be easy to gather data on available workers in a pipeline without advertising. In an open marketplace for talent, every worker will keep some type of resume online and will participate in an online social network. Many will create their own websites to highlight their professional accomplishments to which potential employers will be flooded with links. Also, colleagues and associates may endorse or recommend the work of someone in a network, which will offer a potential employer an easy way to learn a lot about a potential worker. Sites like www.howsthatjob.com and www.glassdoor.com already offer opportunities for workers to anonymously share reviews of jobs and organizations.

To accurately assess brand intensity, ask yourself what it is about your story that will align with what potential workers want and need. What will hit home or turn them off? To what degree is your brand—in the external market—revered, respected, or tarnished? One reason that this is so important is that your brand doesn't need to motivate *all* potential workers to apply. It needs to motivate the *right* workers to apply—those who will have the best chance to succeed. It's much like when an airline or financial services organization, marketing a specific service to a specific segment of buyer, can learn from its data that a buyer is likely to make a purchase, enjoy a trip, and recommend a service to others. A business needs the same insight to know how to target brand and marketing messages so that, in turn, workers will self-select before they apply for work.

Marcy Lawless, VP of personnel, who hired me at Southwest, shared this story with me. When Herb Kelleher promoted Marcy from a sales and marketing position to head of HR (called "Personnel" then) he told her he wanted to make it an imperative that all new hires possessed a good sense of humor. Marcy asked Herb: "How shall we determine this? Maybe we should put a whoopee cushion on the seats of our interview chairs. If candidates laugh after hearing the sound . . . then we will hire them!" We did devise many ways of assessing a sense of humor over the years, and well, yes, every now and then we used a whoopee cushion."

. . . Libby

Step 5: Assign Brand Pressure

The assessment of brand intensity will come from the demand for workers, the legacy and reach of the brand. Next, your business should assess the demand for workers for each segment you need as shown on the left axis of the chart in Figure 4.1. This is based, as we have discussed in this chapter, on its uniqueness, essence to the business, and competitive threat.

To assign the pressure to be placed on the talent brand, take a close look at how your competitors market, how much of a magnet your company may be, and how your talent brand must resonate with workers. The outcome is the *pressure* placed on the *brand* to make a difference to secure people. This can give you a roadmap to identify the segments of talent you need to reach—by demand—and the pressure on the brand to secure those segments.

In practical terms, the varying degree of brand pressure mean, simply, where the talent brand has to perform. It means that, as you develop a creative approach, you need to begin with the workers in *high demand* and with *high brand pressure*—while paying less attention to those in less critical categories. This effort to segment the pressure on the brand is what separates a talent

Figure 4.1

High Worker Demand		
Low Worker Demand		
	Low Brand Pressure	High Brand Pressure

brand from an employer brand. The steps below give you an easy way to work through this process without getting bogged down.

High Brand Pressure/High Worker Demand. Workers in this segment should be the highest priority for your talent brand. A segment in this category is in high demand with workers who are difficult to find and may be bombarded with marketing messages from competing organizations. A segment in this category will require the most creative and consistent attention, from the careful tailoring of the message to the consistency of the worker experience.

In a high-tech company, the hard-to-find technical architects would be in high demand and, as a result of a degree of skepticism, may be in the _high brand pressure_ category, a nice way of saying, "prove it to me." In the energy sector, the dearth of engineers places them in the _high worker demand_ category and all the noise in the industry—as every company makes its plea for the same workers—adds pressure to the brand. As you begin to brand for talent, begin with the segments in high demand and with high brand pressure. This will set both a creative and strategic tone for your brand messaging.

Ask yourself which segments of workers are in high demand for your organization. Then, of these workers, identify which segments will require high brand pressure—because of competing messages and potential immunity—and segments that require a less intensive effort. This can be the foundation for how you creatively approach your talent brand message.

The only way for a talent brand to make a difference is for the brand to help the company attract the most difficult-to-reach segments of talent. In my work with a global energy company, this segmentation became as specific as the same type of worker in one location differentiated from a colleague in another location. By talking with workers in both locations, we were able to determine what the segmented brand messages must be and the degree of pressure the brand would be under to secure workers at each location. It turned out that, in one location, the brand message would be under much more pressure than the other, simply because the reputation of the company influenced how potential workers viewed the value proposition. With this insight, we developed an overall brand message—appropriate for all locations—that we could effectively localize according to the local challenges and conditions. Recruitment advertising in each location focused on targeted, differentiating factors, while competing companies stayed with generic employer brands. The strong improvement in securing workers was credited to the locally focused message based on segmentation.

. . . Mark

High Brand Pressure/Low Worker Demand. Workers in this category may be challenging. The high brand pressure may make the efforts to reach them complex and time-consuming. Yet, because these workers are in low demand, the results may be less than defining for your business. As a result, you will face a balancing act—to give these worker segments enough attention without allocating too much of your time and resources. Carefully consider how to streamline your efforts. Airline mechanics may find themselves in low demand during staff cuts, but the cynicism many bring to the job may require—when demand increases—a focus on the brand. At Peet's Coffee, however, someone is groomed for many years to be a *master coffee roaster*. While the company may not hire many of them, when they do, they need to be the best, and that can pressure the brand.[7]

Ask yourself, as you develop your talent brand messages, if what you are saying to appeal to the high demand/high pressure segments can resonate with these workers as well. For example, any talent brand may include messages related to the *company*, the *work*, and the *life* that association with the organization can create. As you move from one level of pressure to another, the essence of the brand message may not fundamentally change, but its emphasis may shift from one topic to another. In an organization with high demand for IT workers, a talent brand emphasis on the *work* may appeal while, in the same organization, an emphasis on the quality of *life* may be appropriate for less pressured segments. The brand is the same—but how it is used may vary according to the pressure of the segments.

As we worked with a retail organization, they believed they only needed "a little brand tweaking" because they had little trouble finding people and because their brand was well-known in the marketplace. They believed that their brand momentum would carry them through any challenging time. When we talked with their people, we learned that a competing retail organization would soon be arriving in the area and that workers were excited to hear what the new company would have to say. The employees actually felt a bit ignored and taken for granted by the company and welcomed hearing what the competing company would say. Fortunately, the company refocused its efforts on current workers before the competitors came into town. And leadership learned an important lesson that no worker can be ignored because any worker may listen to the competition.

. . . Mark

Low Brand Pressure/High Worker Demand. Workers may be in this category because the brand may already have a high degree of recognition or these workers may be predisposed to work for the business. Airline pilots prepare for years for their careers, and by the time they meet the requirements in hours flown and type-ratings, they have a target company or two in sight.

While the result is less pressure on the brand, the brand message must be consistent to attract the right candidates. Otherwise potential workers in these segments could inadvertently become immune to brand messages and, as a result, begin to demand more attention. In almost any industry, for example, there is a constant demand for finance and accounting professionals, even as many positions move offshore. But they may experience less marketplace noise and higher degrees of employee loyalty, which, when combined, will lower the pressure on the brand to lure workers.

What this means to your talent brand is that, even though the workers may be in high demand, there is little need for a creative brand message. Either you already have a degree of brand equity with this segment—or they are less difficult to reach—giving you the flexibility to adapt brand messages for more challenging segments.

Low Brand Pressure/Low Worker Demand. The worker segments in this category need the least tailored brand attention. General messages about the brand—the type that fill most traditional recruitment efforts—may be all that is needed. Because demand for these workers is lower, the risks are lower, which leaves you more time to focus on the other categories. In the airline industry, for example, there is less demand today—as companies cut flights and staff—for flight attendants. But when an airline needs them, it doesn't have to ask for long, because there is always an available supply. Because of that supply, there is less pressure on the brand.

These segments, actually, are the most appropriate for general messages about the organization's value proposition—what might have been, in a different time, suitable for the marketing of an employer brand. All the talent brand has to accomplish, for these segments, is to reinforce what they already believe. No persuasion is needed.

A healthcare organization did not have more demand for people than it could meet through its traditional recruitment efforts. But this savvy company was not satisfied to wait for the next crisis to spring into action. They realized that, even though everything was under control today, that was no guarantee the pressure might not increase to fill certain types of work. And, when it did, because they would likely experience high brand pressure, they would have to get ready quickly. Because this organization, by its nature, believed in preventive medicine, it decided to embark upon some preventive branding, and created a series of marketing messages and advertisements to "have on hand" for the next talent crisis. They now are ready, no matter what they face next.

    . . . Mark

Step 6: Prepare to Market

You have learned a great deal about how workers make decisions about where to work, what messages may attract them, those that may offend them, and those they may ignore. You have used this insight to assign the pressure and priority for your talent brand. Now you can use what you know to market your talent brand.

How you market depends on what you need your talent brand to accomplish. Coca-Cola, for example, builds upon the strength of its customer brand when it promises that "A career at The Coca-Cola Company is truly a one-of-a-kind experience. It's more than working for the global beverage leader. It's an opportunity to be a part of something that impacts the world. We offer you not only the chance to build a successful career— we offer you an opportunity to make a difference in the world."[8] This is the appeal to someone who is aware of the company's external brand image and links that perception to a potential work arrangement.

Others, however, appeal to potential segments of workers. Apple, for example, deliberately reaches out to its high-pressure worker segments when it exclaims, "Seasoned pro or fresh out of school, you'll find a career at Apple challenging and inspiring." In its targeted search for engineers, the company invites "ingenious engineering minds that design and develop Apple's revolutionary products," while its search for salespeople calls for "the right combination of passion and product knowledge to deliver the Apple experience worldwide." It even speaks directly to the recent college graduate: "If you have limited or no on-the-job experience—but a sharp intellect, a top-notch educational background, and the energy to move the industry forward—Apple would like to talk to you."[9] By carefully considering what the talent brand must accomplish—and what pressure it must confront—the marketer can create a message that appeals to the consumer.

As you prepare to market your talent brand, select which type of talent brand will accomplish what your organization needs. Figure 4.2 shows how different types of talent brands will appeal to different segments of workers. Now that you know the pressure your brand will be under, and the segments you need to reach, consider which type of talent brand is right for you.

Aspiration. This approach to a talent brand can express what an organization wants to be. It can market a "work in progress" that an organization may undertake, with the "sale" being what the organization can be in the future. This type of talent brand is usually considered by an organization that is going through a period of change. A business may reason that a current change

Figure 4.2

Aspiration	Value	Timing	Beliefs	Experience	Action
What the organization realistically aspires to deliver	What a worker can value in the experience the organization currently delivers	What is unique about this particular moment in time for the organization	What the organization fundamentally believes in and stands for	What a worker will experience at the organization today	What action a business needs a worker to take

experience may deter some workers from signing on. So, instead of reasoning its way through all the current issues, the talent brand can focus on what the outcome may be. The catch will be whether or not the aspiration can be believed. That's why this talent brand must balance what can be created and what must be overcome. This approach is most effective to reach worker segments in the *high brand* and *low brand pressure* categories.

High Brand Pressure	Low Brand Pressure
The *aspiration* approach to the talent brand can emotionally appeal to a worker who wants to be part of an organization with a mission	The *aspiration* approach to the talent brand can emotionally recommit a worker who is familiar with the mission and wants to be a part of it

Many companies market *aspiration* in a talent brand. Intel, for example, offers the opportunity to "unleash your potential" in a company that, according to the talent brand, thrives on big thinking. It promises to "put brilliant minds together and give them the tools to succeed."[10] The retail giant IKEA, as well, taps into people's dreams. The company salutes its corporate success as it openly declares "It takes a dream to create a successful business idea. It takes people to make dreams a reality. Could you be one of those people?" By connecting its brand to the company's mission to "improve everyday life" it simplifies the hopes of a worker "to grow, both as individuals and in their professional roles, so that together we are strongly committed to creating a better everyday life for ourselves and our customers."[11] The simplicity of the message delivers its power.

Other well-branded organizations capitalize on familiar aspirations. The talent and consumer brands almost become one. The magic of the Disney customer brand comes to life when the company says "the bottom line is imagination, our culture is magic and wonder, and required previous work experience: childhood dreams."[12] Meanwhile, McDonald's says, "It's not just a job. It's a career." But it doesn't stop here. In an open appeal to diverse segments of workers, the company makes its case for people who may not be looking for careers. "If you're not looking for a career, rest easy. McDonald's has the flexibility to work with you, too. Fact is, for countless employees McDonald's is the perfect way to earn additional income."[13]

While some brands focus on the work environment (Nokia: "Our goal is to create an environment in which all employees can fulfill their potential"[14]), others invite workers to look in the mirror (Microsoft: "We're working toward a future where everyone's potential can be fulfilled. What about yours?"[15]). Some, like IBM, simply help a worker focus on what it takes to succeed: "If you could see the future, and then look back on your success at IBM, you'd see this: You were open to gaining new experiences and increasing your knowledge and expertise; you thrived in a stimulating, fast-changing environment; and you were rewarded for exceptional performance through increased responsibility and visibility."[16] In each case, effective talent brands balance personal and corporate aspiration.

Value. This approach to a talent brand expresses how a worker can realistically value what an organization offers today. It can market how the various dimensions of the current experience "add up" to create value for the worker. This type of talent brand is usually considered by an organization that does not believe it "gets enough credit" for what it offers to workers or may be frustrated when workers leave for what they believe is "greener grass" somewhere else.

As a result, this talent brand may be more appropriate for an organization facing retention issues or a highly competitive marketplace for workers. A business may reason that, by extolling the value it offers, workers will make the correct choice. But the organization must deliver evidence that the promise is true and it must package the message from the perspective of the worker, not the business.

High Brand Pressure	Low Brand Pressure
The *value* approach to the talent brand can emotionally appeal to a worker who searches for more than simply the work	The *value* approach to the talent brand can emotionally recommit a worker who is familiar with–and wants to experience–the value offered

One example of a value brand, Starbucks, offers a proposition that is all about providing its partners with "opportunities to develop your skills, further your career, and achieve your goals." It uses its brand to describe the partners it wants to hire. "We look for people who are adaptable, self-motivated, passionate, creative team players. If that sounds like you, why not bring your talents and skills to Starbucks?" Among its training offerings are Coffee Education—a course focusing on a passion for coffee—and a series of courses including basic computer skills, conflict resolution, and management training.[17] The message—directly tied to the customer experience the company offers—draws a picture of what the organization considers important.

The same holds true for American Express, which directly ties the values for the employee and customer. The company expresses its commitment to make "a positive contribution to our customers' lives, and to the lives of our employees as well."[18] Hewlett-Packard, however, candidly links a great place to work with an ease to attract top talent. "For us, being a great place to work is good business. HP people live for the big idea. The next great discovery. The new way of being. To us, 'Invent' is more than a word. It's who we are. The very soul of our organization."[19] Still others, like Honda, simply believe that "the best people produce the best products," as the company declares it is "constantly on the lookout for bright, ambitious team players who have a strong commitment to improving society, the environment, even themselves."[20] No matter the articulation, the focus on value—to the worker and the consumer—can differentiate the message from the competition for talent.

Timing. This talent brand captures a particular moment in time that the organization is experiencing and how "being here right now" can offer a situation that no competitor can match. This type of talent brand is usually considered by organizations going through a period of change. But rather than focusing on the end result—as with the *aspiration* approach to talent brand—the organization focuses on the change experience itself.

A business may reason that to attract bold workers of determination it can make the most of the fact that the experience of working for a business at such a "defining moment" in its evolution can yield great results for a worker's personal brand. At the same time the organization can't neglect the fundamental things that any worker, no matter how bold, will likely be seeking.

High Brand Pressure	Low Brand Pressure
The *timing* approach to the talent brand can emotionally challenge a worker to boldly claim part of a moment in the organization's history	The *timing* approach to the talent brand can emotionally recommit a worker who is familiar with the history and wants to commit to the moment

This type of talent brand capitalizes on a moment in time. A company known for speed, such as Oracle, describes that its "recruiters are always searching for brilliant employees with an entrepreneurial spirit, looking for a work culture where innovation is the goal, hard work is expected, and creativity is rewarded."

While many organizations could say such things, what distinguishes the Oracle message is how specific it quickly becomes: "What are the work hours? There are none. Working at Oracle is like eating at a buffet—choose what suits you. In other words, if you want to arrive at noon and leave at 8 p.m., that's fine. If you're a programmer and you want to wear your beach shorts and

Oracle T-shirt to the office at 6 a.m., that's fine. Even if you want to set up a home PC and work from home two days a week, you won't be the first."[21] By showing such intimacy with the worker, the company may establish a credibility—as if a brand could read a consumer's mind.

Beliefs. This approach to talent brand articulates something absolutely fundamental to the business and the people. It markets a dimension of the corporate responsibility that will be meaningful to workers and can be supported by actions the organization takes.

This type of talent brand is usually considered by an organization that believes its sense of commitment—whether to its workers, its communities, or its customers—significantly differentiates it as a place to work. A business may reason that, by defining the experience by the beliefs on which it stands, the worker will join to be a part of something larger than a work experience. But the business must deliver on the beliefs because, as we learn many times, actions speak louder than words.

High Brand Pressure	Low Brand Pressure
The *beliefs* approach to the talent brand can emotionally appeal to a worker searching for aligned beliefs so the worker can feel at home	The *beliefs* approach to the talent brand can emotionally recommit a worker who is familiar with the beliefs and wants to feel at home

When it comes to brand icons, few can compare with Tony the Tiger from days long gone by. Tony's parent, Kellogg's, brings such classic beliefs to life in its brand. Kellogg's invites workers "to be a part of something special and touch a couple billion lives" as it invites prospects to get "come on in and see what we mean." There is, to the supports of this brand, no other company like Kellogg."[22] The brand is, simply, a bit sacred.

The same can be said for Harley-Davidson, presumably, for a different segment of the market. Interestingly enough, when marketing for talent, the organization sounds much more like a cultural dream than a recreational provider. "The H-D culture provides employees with continued opportunities for growth and professional development because we believe that people are our only long-term competitive advantage." The messages continue to describe, in detail, how the company provides high customer satisfaction by supplying products and services that "delight customers and offer value. And our culture values and promote employee development, diversity, and leadership excellence."[23] The strong expression of an internal culture only makes the products that much more intriguing.

Experience. This approach to talent brand packages what a worker will experience every day from the first moment he or she walks through the door. Marketing "the ride" and "the destination" is usually considered by organizations that are well known for, and duly proud of, their reputations for delivering a positive experience for workers, and who believe that experience is a key differentiator. A business may reason that, if all other competitive issues are equal, the worker will vote for the experience. The challenge for the business is that, over time, it must make sure it continues to deliver that experience, or its workers may begin a new search for what they fear they have lost.

High Brand Pressure	Low Brand Pressure
The *experience* approach to the talent brand can emotionally appeal to a worker who places high value on the work experience—the "karma" of the place	The *experience* approach to the talent brand can emotionally recommit a worker who is comfortable and secure with the experience

Sometimes the focus on experience is a direct challenge to a potential worker. PepsiCo openly discusses its need for strong workers: "Our ability to grow year after year is driven by our ability to attract, develop, and retain world-class people who will thrive in our environment. This is why we are committed to making PepsiCo the best consumer products company in the world in every aspect of our business."[24] The popularity of the brand as a place to work is no surprise to anyone who has observed the company acquire its strong reputation as a place that develops strong people. The talent brand reaches beyond this image "to match great talent with important opportunities to build our business." as this legendary company, like many others, looks for ways to engage its workforce.

When Yahoo! celebrated our ten-year anniversary, we also decided to add a service award program into the employee experience. I dispatched a task force to select the awards. My guidance was that it had to be uniquely Yahoo!, in keeping with our culture, and be the kind of memento that people would keep in their homes, perhaps to tell their grandchildren about. Well, the task force originally considered the typical service awards such as Plexiglas paperweights and logo watches or other jewelry. But none of it was right. Finally, one of the events crew suggested the gumball machine. It was perfect. It reflected the fact that every Yahoo! lobby had a supply of gum and breath mints available to visitors and employees and the main lobby had a huge gumball machine used as part of a past promotion. What was more special was the blog by one of Yahoo!'s five-year employees who received it. He told the story better than we could so here: http://blog.unitedheroes.net/archives/p/2224/
. . . Libby

Action. This approach to talent brand is all about what a business needs a worker to *do*—the action that is needed at the moment. This may be as simple as a decision to join, stay, engage, commit, or as complex as to support an organization during a period of serious change. Whatever the situation, the brand must support a strategy the business pursues.

This type of talent brand may be used by a business that needs a specific behavior from workers and wants to motivate the action to begin now. A business may reason that using the brand to clearly frame the action offers the best opportunity for the action to occur. But the business must, in the brand message, clearly state what the worker will receive in return.

High Brand Pressure	Low Brand Pressure
The *action* approach to the talent brand can emotionally appeal to a worker who wants to make things happen	The *experience* approach to the talent brand can emotionally recommit a worker who wants to get things done

The retail-branded L'Oréal gets right to work when a new worker joins. L'Oréal makes the most of a worker's first day. "Excitement and enthusiasm, nerves and expectations. . . . Whatever your level of experience, the first day in a new job is full of challenge, with the promise of more to come. At L'Oréal, providing the right introduction to our organization is a key priority. That means making everyone feel welcome—from Day One."[25] Without focusing on too many thoughts, or a range of ideas, the brand simply reveals what a life inside can create.

It is possible for a brand to reach across more than one type depending on the overall situation the business faces. As we worked with a global energy company going through a merger, we started with all six types of brands. And as we worked through the value proposition we deliberated whether or not potential workers would be more moved by a message about the "company," a message about "the type of work," or a message about "the type of life" a worker could lead, including the balance of work and life. Our reactions to those questions helped us realize that we might need different segments for the brand ideas. We developed our brand ideas according to four of the six categories we mention here as well as two other categories that, based on our value proposition work, were more relevant to this situation. It's important to adjust any process to the realities of the given situation. No process can be applied from one challenge to another without some degree of adjustment. Otherwise all the brands in all the companies might start to look a bit the same.

. . . Mark

Getting to Work

Want to segment your talent brand message? Here's how.

First, identify the top segments of worker you need to attract. That can be as simple as a brainstorming discussion or a detailed workforce analysis. No matter the approach, the outcome should be precise: A careful look at what types of workers your business needs most so you can direct your talent brand marketing efforts.

Second, assign the pressure on the brand to lure each worker—from low brand pressure to high brand pressure. That's a matter of looking, segment by segment, at what your brand must accomplish in order for your pipeline for workers to be healthy.

Third, consider which type of talent brand will most effectively address this pressure—from aspiration to timing to action. In any brand discussion, depending on the priorities of a worker segment, the emphasis of the brand may need to adjust. Your employer brand needs to be broad enough so that—as you take it to market—you can emphasize different specifics for different specific populations.

Fourth, begin to develop how to message the talent brand to reach each of the top worker segments. This is the creative work—how to shape the message to create that magnet status. An effective talent brand is a combination of what consumers of work may be hungry for and how effectively you provide that nutrition.

Get ready to follow these steps to capitalize on the key lessons of the chapter.

Key Lessons: Chapter Four

We can't say enough about the importance of segmentation as you brand for talent. We have seen too many companies develop marvelous *generic* talent brands that sound great for the masses but never reach the specific segments. And, as a result, they don't contribute to the business.

Are you ready to segment your talent market? And consider the "pressure" the talent brand will face to reach these segments? Are you ready to move beyond one simple expression of value to carefully developed expressions that are compelling and relevant to the talent segments you seek to reach?

☐ An organization must market its talent brand to the specific segments it seeks to attract and retain.

☐ In the Brand for Talent Segmentation Framework (Figure 4.1) you assess the demand and opportunity for each segment of worker you seek to reach with your talent brand. By identifying in which of the four categories to place a segment of your workforce, you can more clearly determine how to shape messages and how much effort to commit.

☐ *High worker demand, high brand pressure* workers are difficult to find, and workers may be bombarded with marketing messages from competing organizations; with *high worker demand, low brand pressure* workers, the pressure on the brand is less so, perhaps because the brand already has a high degree of recognition among this group; *low worker demand, low brand pressure* workers demand less focus, while *low worker demand, high brand pressure* workers can eat up a lot of time without significant result.

5

ESSENTIAL FIVE: IMPLEMENT

A brand is a compelling dimension of the retail landscape that marketers can use to influence, motivate, remind, nudge, inspire, and drive a consumer to take action. A memorable brand effectively connects what a consumer wants to what a product or service can offer. We never doubt whether we need a Kleenex when we sneeze, want a Pepsi when we are thirsty, or long for an iPod when we need music. Memorable brands become part of the fabric in which we make choices as consumers.

That's what business needs from a talent brand when people look for work. When we carefully designate the segments of workers we want our marketing efforts to reach, we recognize that one marketing approach will *not* appeal to all segments the same way nor do all segments need to be equally reached. To brand for talent is to carefully tailor the message to each segment. But that can only happen if the talent brand is carefully crafted to make the journey into the hearts and minds of consumers. How a talent brand makes this journey is what talent brand marketing is all about.

A marketing strategy—for a car, a toothpaste, or a business as a place to work—creates demand to potential buyers. An advertisement—for a car, a home newly listed on the market, or a business as a place to work—tailors specific messages to motivate specific potential buyers to move forward through the buying process. In between the marketing and the selling is a critical step for the buyer to visualize the experience of using the product or service.

The essence of a brand for talent strategy is to lure the right people to do the right work at the right time. When Target declares "See yourself here," it quickly describes what that can mean to administrative support ("Use your organizational and problem-solving skills to help keep our corporate offices running smoothly") and finance/accounting ("We're looking for people who know how to improve the bottom line through financial analysis and planning."[1] The messages are designed to build interest in the business as a place to work. That is what creating demand—and achieving brand recognition—are about. The best messages help potential workers visualize how the business can meet their aspirations, align with their personal values, support their ambitions, reward their efforts, and lighten the burden of going to work every day.

One way to visualize a talent brand is to picture the hurdles that a runner must jump at a track meet. Each hurdle is a barrier, or milestone, a talent brand must successfully surpass. If the talent brand skips or misses a hurdle, it can undermine its overall impact. A global company was concerned that, while being recognized as a brand for talent in North America, they were unknown in other parts of the world where they need to expand. We couldn't approach the challenge for recognition as a global challenge. It had to be addressed one location at a time. A technique to create brand recognition may be appropriate for India, but it might make no sense at all in China, for example. We developed an overall approach to brand recognition—to achieve globally with local reference—as well as a distinct approach to each major market for talent across the world. On the ground, brand recognition happens one consumer at a time, no matter how big the brand.

. . . Mark

Talent Brand Hurdles

To brand for talent, a business must do more than simply develop and distribute tailored messages. It must develop a strategy to enable the brand to jump a series of *hurdles* (as shown in Figure 5.1) to motivate a consumer to take action. This is the same journey whether the consumer is purchasing a pair of shoes or a type of work. A brand must jump a hurdle for new or current workers with support of word-of-mouth, third-party endorsement, and company-sponsored advertising. To jump a hurdle requires creative marketing and careful use of media. That's the essence of a talent brand strategy.

Figure 5.1

Hurdle 1: Be Recognized

First, your business must be recognized as a place to work. Until the workers you want to reach *recognize* your talent brand, they will not absorb any specific messages you send. But talent brand recognition is not as simple as "putting the name out there" for people to see. What it takes for a talent brand to be recognized will vary by segment. For *high brand pressure* segments, the talent brand will likely *not be* immediately recognized or, if recognized, may create a potentially negative response among workers. Either reaction will require a different marketing approach than to *low brand pressure* segments where the marketing effort must sustain a degree of recognition. Before planning the specific *advertising*

to reach workers—such as booths at recruitment fairs or banner ads on websites—here are a few do's and don'ts.

Brand Recognition

Do	Don't
Advertise what is unique about your value proposition.	Simply advertise your business as a place to work without promoting a point of view.
Advertise what your business stands for—the difference you make to the people who work for you.	Simply list the jobs available without describing the work environment, opportunity, or value proposition.
Advertise the meaningful work that people can do.	Assume people know who you are as a place to work simply because they may access you as a place to buy.
Advertise the personal and career growth that people can experience.	
Surprise people with something they may not immediately know about your business.	

You will only know what it will take for your talent brand to be recognized if you carefully compare it to the talent brands of the businesses you compete with for workers. If all the brands are the same, it will be difficult to attract attention. If others are saying what you plan to say, you will need to adjust your approach. Knowing how you must differentiate is essential to be recognized.

The Container Store, for example, became famous for recruiting its customers to become workers. Its marketing parallels the opportunity for workers with the experience for customers. The company leverages its reputation as "an absolutely exhilarating and inspiring place to shop" into "an equally exciting place to work." It continues, "When customers walk into any of our stores, they immediately sense the 'air of excitement' that exemplifies the entire company. This excitement is fostered by the spirit of our store employees."[2] The approach effectively jumps the first hurdle by building upon its retail reputation.

To be recognized, a company may also boast a prominent position on best places to work lists. It may also recognize the value of an article in *Fortune* or *Fast Company* or *Forbes*. While fewer customers may be *reading* magazines these days, the appeal of endorsements from credible third parties remains. Otherwise why would thousands of companies compete each year to be listed on one of the "best places to work" lists? In the fight among brands, such a "seal of approval" can provide a key differentiator, just as it has for generations with consumer products. These endorsements as well as stories in the local and trade press can give a talent brand a chance to be recognized in a crowded market.

The "best places to work" lists provide great opportunities to be recognized as a place to work, but they are not enough. A global information company wanted to reach for talent in all parts of the world. In some places it was known as an employer, in others it was not known at all. Many at the company believed that the challenges could be solved by making a splash on "best places to work" lists. The company secured a spot on a list but did not experience a lift in its efforts to secure talent. They learned that, because most lists primarily focus on North America, successful placements would not help their talent challenges in other parts of the world. They also realized that the nature of the competition focuses on a comparison of overall worker experiences, while the decision to work for a company comes from what is relevant to a specific worker. Securing workers is not as easy as showing up on a list. But it can feel good.

. . . Mark

Hurdle 2: Be Believed

| Recognized | ⇨ | Believed | ⇨ | Personalized | ⇨ | Remembered |

To be recognized as a place to work is a hollow achievement if your business isn't believed as a credible destination. Talent brand recognition will only be valuable if workers believe the messaging authentically reflects the organization. The consumer of work will instantly compare a talent brand message to a collection of perceptions—a combination of what may be read, heard, experienced, and remembered. To be believed, the talent brand must strike a consumer as accurate, fair, and true. A savvy consumer will quickly detect any effort to hype a less-than-authentic experience. And while aspiration is a legitimate approach for a talent brand, that aspiration must live within a realm of possibility. The consumer of work will quickly evaluate whether a talent brand promise can actually be delivered.

General Mills recognizes the importance of brand belief. This emerges, according to Ken Charles, from a unifying message: "You join us and make an impact. We highlight others who have joined and advanced and made a difference. We highlight how, in our flat organization, they can make a name for themselves. And, for experienced workers, how they can move to the next stage in their career by joining us."[3] The marketing connects what the organization delivers by promoting what actually occurs.

At the core of a believable talent brand is an organization that knows itself and makes sure to message with credibility. As Dean Melonas of JetBlue observes, "The key to a successful employer brand is to know your company, every aspect of the product or service, and to be real, to give people an honest story. As we say, 'The pump must come from the heart.'"[4] That's why, as Melonas describes, as JetBlue refines its offerings to customers, it makes parallel refinements in its brand for workers.

How an organization delivers its promises will determine the believability of its talent brand. At a retail organization, for example, a potential worker can observe the work environment. A candidate can see what people do, how they are treated, and whether they care. Savvy organizations create parallel customer and worker experiences. Best Buy leverages its reputation as a place to buy into its brand as a place to work by declaring that working there "feels like going faster than the speed of light, like being two jumps ahead of the competition and widening the gap. It's exhilarating, challenging, and rewarding. And, most of all, it's fun." The brand promises "a place where relationship building is core to our customer interactions. The Best Buy brand is synonymous with great selection, knowledgeable staff, and the belief that technology can be fun. No matter where you work at Best Buy you can learn, work, play, and achieve."[5] Someone who wants to test this promise only has to walk into a store. A consumer of work who receives validation of a brand message from first-hand observation will more likely believe that message.

Likewise, a consumer who plugs into the buzz of a place to work is more likely to believe the commentary of an unknown, unsolicited source than a sponsored source. That's why social networking is essential to talent brand marketing. Any company hoping to achieve brand belief must confront what is shared online. While such sources can't be managed, they can be influenced, and certainly must be monitored. Here are a few do's and don'ts as you plan how to create brand belief:

Brand Beliefs

Do	Don't
Monitor what is being said about your business as a place to work in every possible place—from the media, to the water cooler, to social network chat.	React to everything that is said about your organization as a place to work. Dismiss everything that is said.

Do	Don't
Monitor, especially, what centers of influence may be saying, such as recruiters, industry leaders, pundits, and thought leaders.	Participate in irrelevant best places to work listings simply because they may feel good.
Actually deliver a good work experience.	Try to discourage employees from discussing their experience with your organization.
Actually live your brand.	
Participate in *relevant* listings of best places to work programs.	Discourage participation in conferences and thought leader events.
Give employees internal opportunities to express their opinions so they don't have to go outside.	
Establish a blogging policy that supports fact-based truth-telling versus policing and spinning.	
Encourage qualified employees to be conference speakers and write articles, let your talent speak for your talent brand just by participating.	
Include media relations in your marketing efforts.	

Careers Site. One key opportunity to build brand belief is the "careers" site of a corporate website. This can give your talent brand a face and a voice. It is, for today's worker, the most important element of your marketing strategy, along with the word-of-mouth recommendations of current and former workers.

"The key thing that I've noticed is that prospects expect to be reached online," says Carol Mahoney of Yahoo! "They look at your online presence critically and will dismiss you if you don't bother to engage them. Just having a website doesn't work, especially if it is stale. Five years ago, you needed a basic website. Today you need a robust, interactive, experiential website. Candidates want to be able to check out your careers site, to see what it's really like at the company. That's why we have updated our website so that candidates can hop around and easily find rich content and testimonials."[6] People looking for work today arrive at a company career site with specific expectations. Not only do they want to find a current listing of opportunities, they also want to imagine the experience of working for the company.

Jeanie Mabie of IBM agrees the website can't just be about the company. "It must be about the workers, it must personalize their ambitions, to say they can find a place to work that fits," she says. One way IBM does this is through storytelling. "The new global careers page on our website features videos of employees telling stories. In one moving segment, diverse employees from all over the world read sections of a diversity statement that, even though it sounds like it was written today, was actually written in 1953. This is just one more way to reinforce our fundamental values,"[7] Mabie says, and a key way for the global giant to credibly reach potential workers.

Whirlpool Corporation also uses its website to reveal its priorities. According to Kristen Weirick, "We are big believers in storytelling. Instead of just sharing the nature of our partnership with Habitat for Humanity, we will tell you what it was like to swing a hammer at a Habitat for Humanity build. While we recognize that content must be tweaked for a local market we align the core content to make sure it is authentic."[8] Susan Johnson of Pitney Bowes describes the company's career site with "videos featuring employees talking about their jobs, their work/life balance, their lives. A candidate can click on the job and see what it is really like."[9] The "you are there" approach—marrying various media on one screen—can help a candidate evaluate a potential fit.

Aetna's Caroline Emmons says the company's "Find a Career" web page lists open positions for which it is seeking external candidate interest. Open positions are described functionally and needed skills and knowledge are noted. The site enables candidates to quickly tailor their online experience. "As potential employees enter the site, they can choose portals such as "Returning to Work" or "Student and Recent College Graduates," among others," she describes. "They can sort by many categories, including function, location, or pay opportunity. They are encouraged to read the criteria carefully and to apply online for positions that match their skills and interests." For college recruits, Emmons continues, "Aetna has designed a "Student and Recent College Graduates" web page targeted specifically to career opportunities for students at Aetna. Once a student applies for a position the resume is reviewed by our staffing department against the skills and experience we are seeking."[10] Such an online experience can bring a potential work experience home to a candidate.

How you make your site a *destination* for the customer will drive how much traffic you attract. You must refresh the content and retrofit the look and feel of the site because your consumers will move on if they feel they have seen it all before. Whirlpool Corporation's Kristen Weirick observes, "We want to provide an exceptional candidate experience, free from corporate speak, full of actual employee profiles, perspectives of working for the company, advice, role descriptions, opportunities for growth and development, our leadership model, training opportunities, functional ladders. It's important for people to know what to expect."[11] If the site does its work, potential workers will come back to scan for roles for which they may be interested. And they may tell their friends.

We spent a lot of time and effort on the Yahoo! career site. Our objective was for the site to give prospective employees a glimpse into what it is like to work there every day. On the Yahoo! site, the employee experience is featured in a section called Life@Yahoo!. This section includes the history, benefits, company blog, Flickr Photostream (with photos posted by employees on Flickr), Employee Profiles (Usually Featuring "The Big Thinkers," Events, and Fun Facts. My favorite is a video: "A Day in the Life," a behind-the-scenes video showcasing the Big Thinkers at Yahoo!. This video was made by the summer interns just for fun, but it was so good that the company incorporated it into the careers site.
. . . Libby

Careers Site Tour. The careers site can help a potential worker get to know the place that may offer the opportunity for work. Here are some essential elements.

Talent Brand Messages: A potential candidate who reaches your career site—which, hopefully, is easy to accomplish, depending on the organization of the home page —needs to experience the words and images of your talent brand. Your site should creatively position the talent brand promise and imagery to attract the potential candidate to keep looking. It must, in one glance, tell a complete story of what the value proposition can mean. And it must be believable. Glaceau, the maker of Vitamin Water, exclaims, "Consider yourself warned: it's not all fun and games in here, at the crack of dawn, and into the wee hours, we're busting our butts because we believe in this."[12] The candor of the statement creates immediate interest.

Company Basics: The desire to market can't overwhelm the need to explain the basics of what the company does, what it believes, how it compares. But don't take too much time or space offering these details. Express them in a nutshell. That's one reason to show the employee experience through videos featuring employees at work, events, and testimonials. It's also more real.

Types of Work: Imagine the potential frustration of a candidate who gets excited about what a business offers and wants to learn more, but can't find a simple description of what kind of work the business does. This listing of potential opportunities can be as simple as painting a picture of what it can be like to work for the company or as involved as a video day in the life of the worker. But it's not a collection of job descriptions. They are as passé as resumes! The site should also offer a multi-dimensional view of the actual company experience, including the way people work, events the business offers, and unique aspects of the locations where people work. The more this can be told by people who do the work the better. Real workers can help potential candidates "picture" themselves as part of your business and help them assess your culture.

The "Fit." It's not just a matter of showing a potential worker what the experience can be. The site should enable workers to determine how comfortable they may be in the business. Sites are best if interactive; a self-assessment quiz can help a candidate "match" what is personally important to what a business offers as can "meet the boss" videos that relate leadership thoughts and ideas. Accenture, for example, offers an online questionnaire "to help you sort through these opportunities and identify the 'best fit' within the company based on your preferences, experiences, and interests. We realize there are quite a range of opportunities across Accenture for interested people."[13] By engaging people in the assessment, they acknowledge the firm may not be for everyone. And no company is.

The Career: The site should show the potential candidate how a career at your business can evolve, including the support that will be available, opportunities that may be open, locations, and types of work that may be offered. The more you help the candidates "picture" themselves inside your business, the better chance you have of landing a candidate who "passes" the self-assessment. Once you whet the potential candidate's appetite, carry the momentum to the listing of your potential openings. Reach beyond the traditional description of a job to creatively articulate what the work can be, what it can lead to, and how people work. The listing should not simply be a checklist of requirements and details. It needs wording consistent with every message the potential candidate may see that reflects the brand.

The Process: Nothing can be worse than a career site that stops a potential candidate's momentum with confusing steps to begin an application process or a discussion about career possibilities. The steps you suggest, as well as how you work those steps, will indicate the ease or difficulty of actually working in the business. If the instructions are clear, and the process is easy to follow, you are in good shape. But if the instructions are less than clear and the steps a candidate follows less than user-friendly, you may undermine your employer brand before you get very far with a potential candidate.

The Expectations: A candidate must believe in the integrity of the application process. This requires feedback. An experience that tosses a candidate into a big, black hole may lead a candidate to move to the next opportunity. That's why your career site must accurately describe what the potential candidate can expect. And you must deliver. This includes what happens when a candidate fills out an expression of interest form or submits a resume online, when decisions will be made and, most importantly, how and when a candidate will be notified of the status of a decision. Google, on its website, describes the candidate experience, from the telephone interview ("to assess your technical skills and proficiency to the level of determining whether you should be brought in for in-person interviews") to the onsite interview ("Remember, it's not a question of getting the answer right or wrong, but the process you use to solve it") to the hiring decision by committee ("Everyone's opinion counts, ensuring our hiring process is fair while maintaining high standards as we grow") to the commitment to follow up ("It can take up to two weeks for us to make a definitive decision as to whether we'd like to have you join the team").[14] Your fair dealings with candidates can create positive buzz about your business as a place to work. All it takes is displaying some good manners.

A Worker's Life: Beyond the fundamental facts, the careers site can help a potential worker visualize potential life with the company. JetBlue uses its site, as do many employers, to help potential workers visualize the experience. "To reach a younger worker," according to Dean Melonas, "we are doing more online, such as developing video vignettes for the site to show what an average day in life at JetBlue looks like. We want more informed applicants. We want them to know what they are looking for and that they can find it here."[15] While this may likely include a listing of benefit programs, it must reach beyond to also focus on what the company values, its commitment to social responsibility, environmental issues, and diversity, and its practical approach to such issues as work/life balance.

As we look ahead, we see career sites that will house the sharing of personal work histories, formerly known as resumes. In the new marketplace for talent, the traditional resume will be a relic and the act of applying for a job will be a memory. The best that an organization can hope for—beyond entry-level opportunities—will be that a candidate will express an interest in the company or submit an online interest form to a career site to initiate discussions. You can be ready for this shift by making it easy for a candidate to express interest or to submit background information. Your online submission tool should be as easy to use as an online retailer and as trustworthy as an online bank. The prospect should clearly know what you need, what you expect, and how you will evaluate. And you should clearly explain the screening process you will use to reveal what you will look for and how you will evaluate. Many companies are already taking steps to offer this type of online experience to help create brand belief.

A global financial services company was working to develop a talent brand and they were, simply, getting stuck. They were getting trapped in words, the opportunity to be clever, and letting their creativity get in the way of the message. We went back to the basics. We focused, first, on creating a talent brand statement of up to five words or less. That helped get us out of the word trap, after which we articulated this talent brand for each of the worker segments in the high demand/high brand pressure category the company identified. To lock in the brand, we asked the team to create an advertisement using the brand statement—using up to ten words focusing on points of differentiation. The result was a brand with real meaning and relevance, not just words.

... Mark

Hurdle 3: Be Personalized

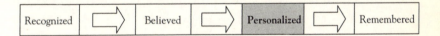

No matter how believable a talent brand may be, it must be relevant to the specific workers you seek to reach. The relevance of your message will determine whether a consumer decides to personalize the talent brand. If the brand speaks directly to the consumer and appeals to what the worker hopes to achieve, the brand message may jump this hurdle. If not, it will be quickly forgotten. The consumer with the short attention span will quickly move to the next brand message.

How do you create brand personalization? Make the brand as personal as possible and give the consumers opportunities to picture themselves as part of the brand. Help candidates imagine the possibilities. For General Mills, making the brand feel personal is a key priority. "On the campus side," according to Ken Charles, "we use web tools; on the experience side, we use other technology to try to reach passive candidates; no matter the tool, we reach out with authenticity. And we quickly make it personal with such events as 'Bring a Friend Night,' where employees can bring friends to our headquarters for a reception and a presentation from someone who recently joined the company. It can be a very soft way to pull a passive candidate into the process."[16] By opening its doors, and making its experience accessible, the company reaches beyond the initial perceptions a consumer may bring to the talent brand.

This means that any marketing plan for a talent brand should include as much face-to-face experience as possible, such as campus recruitment, group interviews, job fairs for entry-level positions, and interactive sessions for technical employees. While recruitment materials and the career website can prepare a candidate, the most important contributor to brand personalization is actual experience. Nothing can personalize a brand more effectively than the personal touch. We are often surprised by the well-branded companies that fall short in this area: the company that, in its marketing materials, proclaims an attentive environment but fails to offer ground transportation to a candidate for a senior position traveling from out of town, or the company that boasts the personal attention it offers but never informs a candidate of the outcome of a job search or interview process. That's no way to personalize a brand. And candidates never forget. Here are a few do's and don'ts:

Brand Personalization

Do	Don't
Manage every touch point a potential worker may experience, make sure to set expectations. Message for each touch point.	View personal contact as outside brand scope. Assume the media dimension of the marketing plan does all the work.

Do	Don't
Create a personal recruitment experience that brings your brand to life.	Assume that candidates don't keep track of how the experience tracks the marketing.
Create an actual on-the-job experience that mirrors what you tell recruits to expect.	Assume that candidates don't share their recruitment experiences.
Separate the efforts to screen a candidate from the efforts to market and sell to a candidate.	

While videos on a career site can add depth to a message, they can also disappear if not carefully created to reinforce a talent brand. A company added every possible new feature to its career site, including a blog, video feature, career assessment, and an opportunity to talk with a live person—all designed to motivate, comfort, and process a candidate. The videos, while well produced, were too slick to be believed, which undermined the potential of that medium to help potential workers picture themselves working for the company. The blogs, while trendy and real, were all about the authors instead of being all about the readers. The assessment feature, while substantive, was a chore to complete and the online application tool was cumbersome. The overall experience created a picture of a company trying to be current, but forgetting to cover its bases along the way.

. . . Mark

A *Talent Concierge*. There is a limit to how even the best website with the best online submission tool can personalize the brand. For a candidate to truly personalize an experience, a business must invest in a face-to-face experience beyond a sophisticated online visit. That's why, at JetBlue, "We make sure the area where we recruit is nice and stress free the minute candidates come through the door," says Dean Melonas. "Every detail is considered for the space to work well, from having all the chairs at the same height, to making sure the window shades are evenly drawn."[17] We remember, years ago, when we reconfigured the candidate "waiting room" at Southwest to be a fun environment filled with on-brand videos and experiences. No matter the outcome of the application, we wanted the applicant to leave absorbed in the company. A business can create a lot of good will by personalizing the follow-up to make sure the candidate savors the parts of the experience that can help close the sale.

As consumers, we savor the service that a concierge provides a hotel. Imagine, for a moment, for your business, how a *recruitment concierge* could contribute to the candidate experience. As Kristen Weirick of Whirlpool Corporation comments, "We focus on the initial candidate touch points. Regardless of how the candidate comes in, we offer the same branded message about who we are as employer. We focus on candidate engagement once we select a candidate for an interview. This is a customized interview experience. We focus on candidate closing, regardless of the outcome, so people walk away feeling positive about who we are. We believe every candidate is a customer, and we want them to remain customers."[18] Picture how a recruitment concierge could carefully plan and script any visit of any candidate to any location. Here are some things a *recruitment concierge* could teach us:

Never leave logistics to chance. Plan each moment of the agenda from arrival to departure. Make the sure the candidate knows (and is comfortable with) all the travel details. If the person is arriving by plane, arrange ground transportation; if by car, provide clear directions and parking instructions; if the person is staying overnight, pre-arrange details at a hotel.

Never let a candidate wonder. Provide a detailed agenda with all the times filled in so the candidate never has to wonder what happens next. If interviews occur in different locations, arrange escorts from one place to the next, so the candidate never has to wander; make sure that interviewers start and end on time.

Never fail to follow up. Make sure to connect with each candidate on next steps, resolutions, and feedback. There's nothing more detrimental to a talent brand than a stray candidate who shares with others—perhaps in social media—the let-down of investing in a place to work, never to hear from the potential employer again. It happens every day.

Make the close an event. Do not—ever—minimize the offer of a job to an electronic message or email. You might as well add the P.S., "We're not all that serious about you joining here, so do what you want." Your candidates will know how quickly you created that message or email and they may assess the value of the offer with the investment of the offering. It it's too easy for you, the business, to make the offer, it can be just that easy for the candidate to move on as well.

Never minimize the details. When making an offer, walk the candidate through the details of the package. If there is an opportunity to confuse a candidate, it will be over the compensation. Many candidates enter such discussions with unrealistic expectations. Some may have inflated views of their own value in the marketplace. The only way to help a candidate think through the pay is to carefully explain your company's approach, detail by detail, with emphasis on how performance is measured and how pay can increase over time. This is the time to be transparent so that a candidate can clearly see how pay is structured, what it takes to advance, and how the approach to pay reflects the importance of people to the business.

Every company has something unique about it, and for Yahoo! it was our yodel. As the company grew, we looked for ways to instill our yodel into our daily life. One of our recruiting leaders had a great idea of how to do this for new hires. He developed an offer package that included a purple box, with the offer letter and several tchotchkes inside. When the candidate opened the box, it yodeled the famous Yahoo! yodel and the inside of the box was filled with pictures of Yahoos! welcoming them onboard. One new hire told us that his wife removed the chip that made the box yodel and installed it on their kitchen cabinet so that every time he opened it, he heard the yodel, and so did the family. That was a great way to get the family involved with the company from day one.

... Libby

Make the offer crystal clear, both for the present and for the future. This is no time to spin. Be as clear and concise as possible. Clearly describe the offer to help the candidate clearly see the financial as well as career dimensions. Tailor the presentation based on what you have learned about the candidate during the recruitment process. If the candidate has shown an interest in a particular location or a specific kind of opportunity, shape the presentation of the offer to put—in priority sequence—emphasis on those things you know will appeal. Carefully show how the value of the offer can grow over time.

Be as personal as possible. Make it difficult for the prospect to say "no." The more one-to-one interaction you offer, the more difficult it will be for the candidate to move on, because of the sense of investment of time. Jump through hoops or do something extra if you can. If the candidate is relocating and needs a special school for her child, help her find just the right place. The little things can make a difference.

Provide documentation for the candidate to share. Depending on the experience level of the candidate, it may be that the candidate has people at home who want to evaluate the offer, too. Be sure the documentation provides details—such as what's behind the non-cash compensation and benefits approach and what's involved with training and development—as well as some of the unique offerings the company can make.

Take no for an answer. No matter how much you want the candidate to say yes, if the candidate says no, remind yourself that, in the end, this candidate could make any decision. The candidates of today look for many different things in work. If, at this time, the candidate decides to try another company, remember that the consumer's attention span can be very short. You can capitalize on its brevity by staying in touch with the candidate long after you receive a negative decision.

> Some candidates regret the decision to join the competition after a month or six weeks. So if we really wanted a candidate, we followed up after six weeks and three months and six months to see how it was going. If it wasn't going as well as expected, or a candidate let on that he or she made the wrong choice, we asked if he or she wanted to reconsider joining Yahoo! Often, we got our person—a little later than we had hoped. If not, we called the person annually to check out his or her engagement status with the other employer. By the way, this works both ways. Rest assured that your competition is using this tactic with your new hires as well.
> … Libby

Never stop marketing. Anyone in retail knows a customer is fickle. While brand loyalty is the Holy Grail, any retailer knows how difficult it is to retain customers when they have so many choices. That's why good retailers never stop selling, even after the customer buys. It's the same with talent. Do not stop the marketing and selling effort when someone agrees to work. That should be the beginning. Continue your marketing and selling efforts through each stage of your relationship with a worker.

Hurdle 4: Be Remembered

If the talent brand succeeds—and effectively motivates the worker to choose the organization as a place to work—the talent brand must be remembered as a key part of that decision. In the same way, if the talent brand succeeds, but the worker does not succeed in securing the work, the brand must still be remembered as a souvenir of a positive experience. Also, when employees leave the organization, a brand should offer a lasting memory. How they remember the talent brand is a fundamental objective for your marketing plan. That's because any brand experience will be shared. And what is shared can influence how other potential and current workers may view the organization.

Sharing the brand is a big part of the General Mills experience, according to Ken Charles. "General Mills has a recruiting culture," he says. "All employees understand that part of their responsibility is to help us recruit. Our long-term employees enjoy the opportunity to bring new people in. Our newer employees get involved, too, because campus candidates want to talk to recent graduates, including alums from their schools at all levels. So our folks go to campus and carry the flag, tell their stories, and establish personal relationships. We have phenomenal leaders who get in front of groups and share their stories. The legitimate, first-person experience works best to sway audiences."[19] The involvement of current workers in the recruitment can also strengthen their sense of engagement. And that can make a difference when you look at how to re-recruit your current workers. That's why some organizations invest in media and alumni networks to celebrate the good experiences. Here are some do's and don'ts:

Brand Memory

Do	Don't
Use every opportunity, every touch point, to reinforce brand messages.	Forget the people who have invested in you from one day of interviews to a lifetime of work.
Carefully follow up with candidates you do not select—or those you defer to a later date.	

Do	Don't
Establish and maintain networks with workers who have invested in the company and choose to leave. Maximize the connections with *all* alumni, including retirees.	Dismiss the importance of re-recruitment as a key talent brand strategy.

Re-Recruiting. Congratulations. You brought the worker in the door. But just as easy as it can be to enter the door it can be just as easy for the worker to walk right back out.

All that discussion—from the first mention of the business and the candidate's potential—focuses on a work experience the worker believes he can find here and not there. So if, when he walks in the door, he doesn't begin to experience what is promised and doesn't see himself in the company, then it may have been for naught. The success of how a company uses its talent brand to create demand, frame the recruitment experience, and close the sale requires the business to use the brand to authentically re-recruit workers.

The search for work never ends. Just because someone works for you today doesn't mean she will continue to work for you tomorrow. You never have the luxury to let up in your brand efforts. Just because someone walks in a door doesn't mean she will stay inside for very long. The notion of loyalty has been replaced by personal priority. As business invents one type of loyalty program after another for the customer, it continues to question how to create brand loyalty among workers.

Re-recruitment begins on day one. The most important day in your efforts to re-recruit is the first day of a new worker's experience. Consider what's going on in the new worker's mind.

The new worker is excited. He or she did, after all, just agree to start a new chapter in life, and most of us are excited when we are about to start something new.

The new worker is filled with hope. That excitement leads to a sense of hope that this will work out well. Even though the worker may be conditioned to anticipate making several changes over a career, there is hope that such frequent change won't be necessary because this company feels like home and delivers the expected opportunity and experience.

The new worker is willing to listen. The ears are the sharpest on day one. The worker can absorb (and retain) key messages on the first day that may be difficult to make stick later on.

The new worker hasn't yet become susceptible to gossip. At every company, gossip travels according to its own pace. It doesn't take long, especially with all the ways for people to connect today, for the gossip to reach the newest worker. A company has only a short window of time to reach the worker with its news.

The new employee is apprehensive. At the same time, the new worker is in a testing mood ready to assess whether the company can really deliver what the employer brand promises. The new worker needs to experience certain *functional* accomplishments from the start—the ability to get things done. Just as important, the new worker needs to begin a sense of *emotional* connection to the people and the business.

On-Boarding. To make the most of the on-boarding experience, balance the focus on the *functional* dimensions of a worker's adjustment along with the *emotional* dimensions of a worker's connection. Think of the first day of work as the delivery of the product. Think of the first day as if it were the delivery of a new car or the opening of a new store. All the hopes come together in a single experience that can define how the company invests in and commits to workers.

The importance of effective on-boarding is supported by Southwest's Jeff Lamb, who remembers, "In 2005, in anticipation of a demographic shift and a competitive marketplace for talent, we increased our emphasis on on-boarding. We reinforced our fundamental focus on putting people first, providing customer service, demonstrating a fun-loving attitude, being a joy to work with, into a 'secrets of our success' theme in 2006 and, in 2007, to 'Operation Kick Tail' that focuses on our core values. As we tell our new Southwest employees, 'Welcome onboard the flight of your life; it's not just a career, it's a cause.' We offer easy access to our online on-boarding site, organized around three values, connect them through the 'love at first bite luncheon' so we can get new hires, from day one, to feel the love and the freedom."[20] The Southwest on-boarding experience is one more indication of how the company continues to leverage its employee and customer focus. Here are some additional tips:

Make sure everything is ready. Nothing can undermine a new worker's confidence faster than getting to work on the first day to be told the company isn't really ready for the arrival. That can happen if a worker doesn't find the expected computer or other available equipment ready to go. Delays can make a new worker wonder if the employer is really ready for him or her.

Make sure there is a plan. A new worker does not necessarily pack patience into the lunch box for the first day; expectations for a plan for the work will walk right through the door on day one. The brand will only come to life if the personal contact the worker receives in the first day is as consistent and personalized as any part of the recruitment experience.

Make the functional dimensions as efficient as possible. Certainly there will be paperwork to complete, online or offline, to officially be put on the books. There is nothing that can let the air out of a new worker's balloon faster than to walk in, enthusiastic, and spend the first day completing paperwork. Consider ways to take care of the necessary paperwork as efficiently as possible. Think about how an electronic tool can help *before* the worker arrives the first day.

Make the new worker feel as prepared as possible for the choices that need to be made. And there will be choices to be made on or near the first day, such as the initial coverage in the company's benefit programs. It will be an "off brand" experience if the new worker feels there isn't adequate time to prepare to make these choices. Even if it means reaching out to the new worker before day one, helping the worker prepare for the first day can create peace of mind. Consider ways to "clue" the new worker what it will take to quickly move from "newbie" to "familiar" as well as get answers, in advance, to the practical questions from where to park to how to get coffee.

Make sure the new worker has help fitting in. The first day on any job is like the first day of school, whether that is first grade or the first semester of college. One way to help the new worker is to actually give the new worker a "buddy." Take the extra step to make it as easy as possible for a new worker to connect with others.

> Part of the Yahoo! on-boarding process was making sure that a new hire met all of his or her key and interdependent contacts early on. We assigned the worker a boss or co-worker to have lunch with for the first week, and we filled the calendar of the new hire with everyone he or she had to know within the first few weeks of employment. Our on-boarding process was a day or two of formal classroom training, but included three months on the job.
> ... Libby

Beyond Day One. The effort to re-recruit cannot let up once a worker is on board. Throughout a worker's lifecycle with a business, you must engage the *functional* dimensions and doing the job as well as the *emotional* experience of connecting. The hazard many businesses fall into—even those that successfully on-board new workers—is forgetting the brand after on-boarding is over. Instead, think of how to bring the brand to life throughout the first year.

Engagement is a fragile thing. While rooted in the practical awareness of doing work in exchange for compensation, it is strongly influenced by less concrete dimensions. These include "the feeling" a worker may get from colleagues, a perception of "treatment" from a leader, a sense of "reputation" of an organization. Especially when times get tough for a business, engagement is a personal issue, only successfully established and nurtured in person by the people who have the most contact and influence with the worker.

Continue the personal contact. For a new worker, the chance to identify and bond with a specific group of people—those who may have joined at the same time or be engaged in similar work—can jump-start the connections. Build a "check in" on how the new worker is doing into the first-year program. A worker will never have more ideas about what a business can do to improve than during the first year. Engage the new worker in a feedback loop to benefit from what the worker has to say and, perhaps more importantly, give the new worker a chance to release ideas about the business, the job, and the world.

Make performance management real. A worker will never express as much hunger for recognition and progression as during the first year. Feed the ambition, curiosity, and hope with concrete feedback on how the worker is performing, what steps the worker needs to take, what development opportunities the worker should pursue, and how it can all add up to create a career. Performance management should not be a process. It should be a way of life and support your efforts to feed the talent pipeline. It should make it easy for the business to look beyond how someone performs in a current role to capitalize on his or her long-term potential, taking into account what a worker wants to do next and how that may match what talent a business may need.

If you hire top talent, as we did at Yahoo!, performance ratings may work against you when it comes to talent retention. Many in our workforce had excelled academically and never received any grade but "A's." They attended the best engineering schools or Ivy League business schools. A performance rating of "average" felt like a "C" to the best and the brightest. This rating system fails the new generation of workers. Remember the ones who all got trophies on the soccer field? So, while you may be sharing one perspective of the worker's performance, that consumer of jobs ... forever searching for greener grass ... may find himself or herself more willing to listen to the competitor interested in luring a candidate with potential of performance versus retention with an average rating. Get your ratings in sync! Or consider dropping the ratings, as we did at Yahoo!. The ratings put a label on a worker that can be cumbersome or even in conflict with your talent brand. A talent review program with a comparison of current performance with future potential worked best for us in terms of evaluating who we most wanted to retain.

... Libby

Make sure career planning supports the brand. Your approach to career planning can open the door to a worker to truly engage. In your company, how does an eager worker learn about opportunities? Is there a formal process or is insight dependent on the willingness of a committed manager? Can a worker go online to determine a career path to any position the company offers? Give a worker a clear picture and the opportunity for face-to-face contact so that he or she feels there is a chance for expectations to be met.

Off-board with class: The commitment to re-recruit can't conclude simply because someone leaves the business. You may want the person to return. Or you may need that person to tell others of the value of his or her experience. At a minimum you want the person to say positive things about his or her time with the company. Great brands never give up on a customer. While people may choose another product or service, great brands keep track of their buyers and consistently market to those who may, for the moment, go elsewhere. They never exclude a former purchaser from targeted, branded messages. What *is* the experience after someone leaves your company? Are people, simply, lost forever? Do you make an effort to keep in touch? Are they targets of your marketing messages? Or do you ignore them, letting the disappointment over departure stop you from reaching out? Great talent brands treat former workers as "alumni" of the company, capitalizing on the allegiance they once experienced. Without embarrassment or hesitation, the company still considers them to be part of the family. Because, over time, customers return to great brands. And so can workers.

Getting to Work

Want to implement a talent brand? Here's how.

First, assess how each segment you place in the high demand, high brand pressure category may react to each type of talent brand.

Second, create a talent brand statement (based on your work in Chapter Three). Use up to five words or less, and try to include a verb.

Third, articulate the promise this talent brand can express to each of the worker segments in your high demand/high brand pressure category. The brand promise is an expanded expression of the shorter statement above—using, in many cases, no more than twenty-five words—and providing depth for those who may need to more fully understand what the brand means. While this promise may never be publicly seen, it is an essential part of the brand tool kit.

Fourth, assess how you bring this talent brand promise to life through each stage of a worker's experience with your company.

Key Lessons: Chapter Five

We have learned many lessons from the efforts to brand for talent. At the top of the list is how necessary it is for a brand to make a realistic journey from idea to implementation. That can only happen if it is carefully applied to each "touch point" that a consumer may experience. Otherwise, the impact can be lost in the words.

Is your business ready to develop and market the talent brand so it can successfully "jump" the hurdles that any brand must jump? Are you ready to invest in what it will take to make any brand come to life, especially one designed to attract the people your business needs to get its work done?

☐ Any brand, whether for a product, a service, a house of worship, or a place to work, must jump a series of hurdles to motivate a consumer to take action. This is the same journey no matter whether the consumer is purchasing a pair of shoes or a type of work.

☐ The talent brand must be recognized. Until the workers you want to reach recognize your talent brand, they will not absorb any of the specific messages you send.

☐ The talent brand must be believed. Talent brand recognition will only be valuable if it leads to a belief, among workers, that the message authentically reflects the organization.

☐ The talent brand must be personalized. A talent brand that is meaningful to a general population is nice to accomplish but fundamentally worthless to the effort to secure workers.

☐ The talent brand must be remembered. If the talent brand succeeds and effectively motivates the worker to choose the organization as a place to work, the talent brand must be remembered as a key part of that decision experience.

☐ Create the campaign around the type of brand to market: aspiration, value, timing, beliefs, experience, action.

Part Three

GET PREPARED

6

ESSENTIAL SIX: SUSTAIN

So many times when we speak to groups about talent brand, we are asked, "What is the 'secret sauce' to create and nurture a culture that will support and sustain a strong brand?" We are questioned: "Can we have a talent brand, implement segmented branding campaigns, and build a strong employer brand if we do not have a supporting culture?" And we hear questions such as: "What are the ingredients for a culture that will align with and support the talent brand?" Unlike a dish in a restaurant, there is no recipe to connect a talent brand and a culture that can automatically apply to any organization. A company's culture is a delicate mixture of people, purpose, and promise, a difficult-to-diagnose but impossible-to-overlook combination of how leaders inspire, how people connect, and how opportunities fulfill. It is, on one hand, an outcome of personal experiences and, at the same time, a foundation or framework that is created and nurtured from a centralized source.

Google promotes a unique culture that is designed to make it easy for people to work. As CEO Eric Schmidt says, "Let's face it, programmers want to program, they don't want to do their laundry. So we make it easy for them to do both." The company, describing its culture in the same way as it describes its services to customers, downplays some of the eccentricities, saying, "And it's not because of the whimsical lava lamps and large rubber balls, or the fact that one of the company's chefs used to cook for the Grateful Dead."[1] In any organization, the culture becomes a message. The key question is what do employees actually experience? And what does the talent brand promise?

Culture and Brand

Culture is not the only necessary ingredient to bring a talent brand to life. To effectively support the talent brand requires the alignment of the culture, corporate identity, and the consumer and employer brands. As Aetna's Robert J. Crowder observes, "The connection to culture is pretty clear; what people say about us is rooted in their experience with us; the experience they have with us is based on the behaviors we exhibit; the behavior we exhibit comes from the espoused values. Our company culture and our employer brand are intrinsically connected."[2] At the core of this relationship is the worker experiences, which must support as well as reflect the other influences. The framework in Figure 6.1 illustrates these connections. The worker experience, in the center, is articulated and reflected by the corporate culture and the employer and talent brands. This worker experience also influences, and is nurtured by, the corporate identity and the consumer brand promises.

The identity of a business is influenced by many things. Certainly how the organization describes itself—what it wants to accomplish, why it believes it must exist, what difference it makes, the "big idea" it expresses—will contribute. More

Figure 6.1

Corporate Culture	Employer Brand	Talent Brand

Worker Experience

Corporate Identity		Consumer Brand

than any controlled factors, a corporate identity will be created in the marketplace by people who experience the company as vendors, customers, shareholders, and communities. Those experiences, now so easy to share, have lasting impact on how a company is perceived as a citizen as well as a place to work. Likewise, the consumer brand—as marketed to and experienced by those who purchase the products or services—will influence the worker experience. The priorities of the corporate identity—coupled with the promises of the consumer brand—define the market expectations the worker experience must meet.

There is no doubt that I have worked for three founder-led companies with legendary corporate cultures. Interestingly, academics wrote case studies about these companies during my tenure at each organization. In 1981, Harvard professors John P. Kotter and John M. Stengrevics wrote a case study about Mary Kay Cosmetics, Inc., it's founder, leadership, organization, and culture (but we didn't call it that at the time). In 1995, Stanford professors Charles A. O'Reilly III and Jeffrey Pfeffer wrote a case study about how Southwest had developed a sustainable competitive advantage against other low-cost start-ups and emphasized the role of human resources in the successful implementation of strategy. In 2006, Dr. O'Reilly and some of his colleagues wrote a case study on internal branding at Yahoo!. All of these case studies are marketed to business school professors through Harvard and, every year, hundreds of students learn about these companies. Almost thirty years later, people remember what they learned about these companies and their cultures in business school.

... Libby

At the same time, the corporate culture, and the employer and talent brands, reflect and articulate what the worker experience must be. The relationship between culture and brand is strong. An organization's culture is created over time by thousands of experiences. A talent brand articulates this culture in a form that is "ready for prime time." But the talent brand cannot exist on its own without the authentic support of the culture. No matter how compelling the talent brand may sound, it will produce a synthetic result if is not true to what actually occurs. In the competition for talent, a talent brand won't do a lot of good for a company if it promises one thing and, when people walk through the door, they experience something quite different.

That's why smart companies focus so much effort on sustaining a culture that enables a talent brand to flourish. According to Southwest's Jeff Lamb, "We don't rest on our laurels. We always focus on what can differentiate us. We know that, because a culture grows organically, we need to get out of the way and let the employees nurture and enhance the culture. We are always trying to strengthen or improve what we do to open the door for our people to experience the culture. It amazed me, for example, when our employees will spend their own money to make and buy baked goods and t-shirts for employee events. It's all about the experience."[3] This experience gives a talent brand momentum. Whirlpool Corporation's Kristen Weirick comments, "Your brand has to reflect the culture today. The only way to be known as a great company is to be a great company."[4] Any talent brand will *only* work if it directly connects with, aligns with, and is supported by the work experience. And that requires a strong connection to the culture.

Here's how the culture and talent brand connect and compare:

	Talent Brand	Corporate Culture
What It Means to the Business	Foundation for the marketing of the organization to current and potential workers	Actual experience created by and delivered to workers at the business

	Talent Brand	*Corporate Culture*
Who Creates It	Internal marketers who develop the talent brand message (with, perhaps, external assistance)	The people who work at the business with significant influence from the leaders of the business
How Developed by the Business	Focus on talent strategy, workforce plan, business strategy and, of course, its external brand	Collection of all the actual experiences created by and delivered to workers at the business
What Results for the Business	Potential workers want to ask the question, "How do I apply to work there?" and current workers want to ask, "What do I do to make sure I stay here?"	Current workers can say, "This is what I experience here, and I helped create it"
What Impact on the Worker	"I understand why I must work for this company, the benefits I will experience, the reputation I will carry forward because I was here."	"I am a part of a culture to which I have the opportunity to contribute every day."
How Connected to the Value Proposition	Marketing of the value proposition to attract workers	Evidence that the value proposition actually exists
How Long It May Last	As long as it is useful to the marketing for workers	As long as people who work for the company want it to last

The lesson of this connection is experienced every day by the legendary magnets for talent. Companies become the places people want to work because they build experiences that few can match. The talent brand, no matter how creative and tailored, will only last if it captures real life. Otherwise, it will just be words.

Leadership Influence

It's true that, while leaders do not create corporate cultures, they strongly influence them through their day-to-day behavior. While marketing slogans do not sustain corporate cultures, they paint cultural pictures. While HR programs do not mandate a work experience, they significantly define its content. Different people, representing segments of an organization, react to culture in different ways. A company's culture survives, perhaps thrives, on its own momentum, fed by the aspirations and experiences of people who work at a company. Sustaining an authentic talent brand requires a multi-dimensional work experience that is signaled by leadership.

Near the conclusion of a talent brand development effort—after the tagline is selected, the artwork developed, the detailed guidelines produced—it is essential for a company to review all of the various programs and processes that contribute to its culture through the lens of the talent brand. As we worked this "audit" with a global retail organization, we assessed each process managed by HR, as well as each communication tool developed by Corporate Communications, to make sure that (a) the culture accurately provides an experience that is consistent with the talent brand; (b) the leadership of the company effectively "lives" the cultural elements that the talent brand articulates; (c) the HR processes are culturally aligned to support the talent brand promise; and (d) the employee communication messages and experience are culturally aligned to support the talent brand promise. The results of the audit pointed to specific gaps in actual programs and messages that, if not addressed, could impact the authenticity of the culture. We emerged with a "to do" list for HR and Corporate Communications to complete in support of the new talent brand.

... Mark

But culture is never something that leaders can control. Certainly they can control the speed of their walk to the front door or the sincerity of a smile to a co-worker or the willingness to hold workers accountable for outcomes and behaviors. The culture, however, evolves from the actual experience of workers, day in and day out, as the company goes about its business. All the small moments a worker experiences contribute, from the discussions with a supervisor to the cleanliness of the break room to the refreshments at the holiday party to the sincerity of a leader's message. It's all part of the cultural fabric of working for a company.

As we began to help a retail organization develop its talent brand, we were questioned by the head of HR about the connection between brand and culture. As we explained, the two, while distinct, are directly connected and interdependent. The brand must reflect the culture and the culture must support the brand. So as we went through the development process and articulated the core of the culture in our expression of the talent brand, we also created the specific cultural elements that must thrive for the company to authentically provide what the brand would promise. By looking at brand and culture in this way—one as articulation, one as support—a company must look directly into what it authentically delivers to support the promises the brand makes. As the company began to implement the brand, it actually refrained from publicizing the words of the brand until it felt assured that the cultural elements were in place, from the behavior and messaging of leaders to the details of an applicant's experience to the specifics of learning and development. Realizing that brand is like an adhesive, with every experience "stuck" for a long time, the company made certain that its culture would "stick" in a positive, brand supportive way.

... Mark

Culture is not something a company can merely hype; it's something a company must savor. Culture is not something a company can "order" from a third-party vendor; it's something that workers create for themselves. Culture is not something a leader can "direct"; it's something that is richer for a leader's natural participation. We find ourselves surprised when savvy business leaders believe they can control the culture or "change" a culture overnight. Culture involves behaviors and years of perceptions and understandings in the hearts and minds of all the workers. It can't be formed or adjusted in a flash.

To affect true cultural transformation, the structure and every system and process must reinforce the aspirations for change. Every leader must embrace new attitudes and conduct their activities in new and different ways. All the leaders can change in a culture is what messages, behaviors, and experiences they inject. No leader can simply click his (or her) heels and hope for a new culture to emerge. No single program from human resources—or the packaging of offerings from communications—can drive the culture. But they will be evaluated by workers as cultural symbols of the organization's willingness to invest in people. The communications employees receive, while not driving the culture, can certainly reinforce the factors important to sustaining the culture.

Thinking back on her many years at Southwest, Libby remembers the early years when the company didn't focus so much on the culture. Academics, the media, and Wall Street began to realize that much of the company's success stemmed from its people-centered way of doing business. That is when the company began to find ways to systemically infuse the Southwest culture into every leader, structure, system, and process.

> When the ranks of Southwest grew to more than 10,000, we realized it was going to take more than just good management and luck to keep our culture alive. Almost twenty years ago, Colleen Barrett, then EVP of Customers, formed a Culture Committee. It started with about one hundred hand-picked employees representing different areas of the company. Members of the committee are now nominated by their predecessors and serve three-year terms. In addition to attending quarterly meetings, committee members are required to participate in "culture events" throughout the SWA system. Culture committee members become alumni and most remain very active in culture programs. This committee sets its own agenda each year based on the most pressing cultural issues and creates initiatives to drive or enhance the culture throughout the organization.
>
> ... Libby

Years later, Southwest continues to nurture the culture that supports its talent brand. As Jeff Lamb observes, "Our culture is a differentiator. Our turnover is less than 5 percent. We find that the majority of turnover occurs during the first year of employment. But if new hires become indoctrinated in the culture, and feel a good fit, it is difficult for them to leave. The culture sticks.

As we focus on how to reduce those first-year losses, we believe the best way is to make sure every new employee gets indoctrinated faster and deeper. We want to prevent losing people due to things we can control. Our culture is sticky enough if we give people the chance to experience it."[5] As Southwest experiences, the key to the culture is what workers encounter every day.

The talent brand can help. It can become *the lens through which each dimension of the worker experience is viewed*. Just as a retail customer's experience is carefully compared to the promises of a customer brand, a worker's experience should be carefully measured against the talent brand. The talent brand can set the standard for what each dimension of the worker experience must contribute.

This begins with leadership. A leader is critical to how an organization develops its culture and sustains its talent brand. A leader has the freedom to express what is important, what is valued, and what is rewarded, as well as what is extraneous, what can be ignored, and what will be dealt with. A leader influences whether a culture is supportive by how he or she handles issues with direct reports, as well as whether a culture innovates by how he or she rewards ideas. A leader influences how personal a culture may be by how much interest he or she seems to take in the well-being of workers. While a leader may not be able to control a culture, he or she can send direct signals about what matters. And, depending on the leader's credibility, workers will decide whether they agree.

We find, however, that leaders don't consistently realize the scrutiny with which their actions will be viewed as cultural icons. Some are surprised that workers wonder whether the CEO is an authentic leader who lives the values that the talent brand articulates. Some do not realize that a CEO's impact can be lost in the morass of corporate-ese and organizational cynicism. When workers look for ways to evaluate the authenticity of a talent brand, they usually start at the top.

This is, certainly, central to the efforts at General Mills with its talent brand: "Our Brand. Your Legacy." While the first part focuses on the contributions the company is committed make ("We nourish lives, give sustenance to the world, it is a sacred charge"), according to Ken Charles, "The second half focuses on legacy, responsibility, and accountability over your career. We focus on developing great leaders as people move through their roles."[6] It's not simply about a leader "talking up" a brand or reinforcing its importance as a business strategy to business leaders. It is about whether the leader's own behavior will undermine or support the essence of the brand and the values it articulates.

> While engaging a leader in a brand is essential, that engagement must be around the content, not simply around the words. To launch a new talent brand for a global energy company, we engaged the CEO to interpret what the talent brand can mean to each part of the company, to each employee. Instead of simply using the leader as a spokesman for the brand, we selected the format of streaming video to candidly reveal what the brand meant to this CEO over a period of weeks. For some eight weeks, each Monday morning, each employee would view a two- to three-minute excerpt of a video interview with the CEO during which he described a dimension of the talent brand. In these spontaneous, candid moments, he would bring the talent brand to life by relating it to a particular piece of work, or cite a specific example of its result and personalize it by bringing it to the perspective of each employee. The talent brand gave him a solid platform from which to demonstrate his leadership, while his leadership gave the talent brand a substantive opportunity to be addressed as a business issue.
> ... Mark

Each day, well-meaning leaders choose how to think, what to say, and how to act and, even though they may not realize whether or not to bring the talent brand to life. Depending on what others see in a leader's behavior, current workers may disengage, potential workers may look elsewhere, and the talent brand may be damaged. Our task isn't simply to craft a talent brand; it must reach to how we help craft actions and coach behavior to influence the choices that leaders make. It is too simple to declare that a leader must be a poster child for a talent brand. A leader must demonstrate, in every moment, every action, living proof that the promise is real.

Workers will look to the leader, more than to any other employee, for the evidence that the talent brand is more than words; it is, simply, how people live in this organization. And that doesn't happen by accident. When people look at leaders, they must see qualities and behaviors the talent brand represents, from authenticity to transparency to fairness. And they must be able to see beyond the decisions a leader a makes to how a leader thinks and what a leader feels, from vision to caring to social responsibility.

As a new start-up, Yahoo! leaders were not in the habit of holding staff meetings, department all hands, team meetings, or even one-on-ones. The first employee survey conducted indicated that employees didn't get enough direction from their leaders. While it wasn't rocket science, just by introducing a framework of team meetings, staff meetings, and one-on-ones, we improved our engagement scores and our leadership-employee culture.
. . . Libby

Leadership Messaging

Before workers can follow, leaders must clearly articulate value propositions to help workers answer the fundamental question, "What's in it for me to work here?" The talent brand can provide a platform for this communication. Workers need to hear, from the highest-ranking source, how the company commits to invest in and support workers. As Dean Melonas of JetBlue observes, "We play close attention to our five values: safety, caring, integrity, fun, and passion. Our leadership takes an additional step by articulating principles of leadership, which are to treat your people right, do the right thing, encourage initiative and innovation, communicate with your team, and inspire greatness in others, which guides how leaders are developed and measured."[7] For maximum impact, leaders should embed a variation of the value proposition in each message they send, from the formal communications created from a centralized source to the informal conversations that occur with workers.

The importance of leadership messaging extends beyond the C-Suite to any role in an organization to which people look for guidance. The leader of a business or the manager of a plant or a work site or the first-level supervisor in a call center are as essential to the cultural foundation of the talent brand as the top leader at corporate. With this responsibility comes a necessity for leaders at all levels to express the value they believe the talent brand contributes to the organization. To be effective, the talent brand can't be perceived as "an HR thing" or "a communications thing." It must be recognized as a business strategy to address the business issue of supplying key talent. As leaders discuss the brand, the supporting behaviors and competencies, the supporting messages and packaging, they cannot "check a box" that appears from a corporate source. They must believe in what the talent brand can contribute.

As leaders clarify the scope and depth of a value proposition, they also have the opportunity to treat colleagues in a manner consistent with the talent brand attributes and personality. This can include how a leader openly expresses thanks to workers for what they contribute. If the talent brand describes a way people work together—and if leadership confirms this expectation—the workers will recognize that the brand is more than a way to tell a story. This reaches to how a leader expresses, in the messaging, what is expected from direct reports.

A talent brand is strengthened when an organization specifies the behaviors needed and the competencies to be measured. But these tasks will only be helpful if, in face-to-face discussions, leaders hold their direct reports accountable for behaviors that exemplify the brand. In an organization, workers learn what is expected and accepted by watching the people ahead of them. What they see, day to day, will significantly impact their perceptions of cultural support for the brand.

Leadership Behaviors

As our mothers once said, "Actions speak louder then words." For a talent brand to succeed, leadership must effectively "live" the cultural and behavioral elements that the brand articulates. Each talent brand—in its statement of promise—directly or indirectly describes the behavior expected of leaders. Workers will hold leaders accountable for "living" the brand as they assume—fairly or unfairly—that leaders can remain above the regular day-to-day intrusions on exemplary behavior. With leadership, success or failure boils down to disappointment. It's impossible for any of us to believe in leaders who disappoint.

As you plan how to bring a talent brand to life, get to know what may disappoint people if they don't see, hear, and experience what the talent brand leads them to expect. Leaders must set an example for others to follow. They must understand the depth and dimension of the talent brand. They must clearly see its value beyond the packaging it promotes to describe the way they want workers to collaborate, support, and contribute. They must see the brand as a set of guidelines for how they should act with others, realizing how their behavior will be held under a corporate microscope.

Leaders come with their own unique personalities. Some may be quiet, less effective as on-stage personalities but better one-on-one. Some may be charismatic but need help in executing. At Aflac, according to Amy Giglio, "We started the Aflac Leadership Academy to groom future leaders at the management level and above for Aflac. One of the results from the Leadership Academy is that everyone uses the same roadmap. This gets all the leaders on the same page, so that the type of talent we hire is consistent. We use behavioral interviewing and have identified over sixty competencies for various career opportunities. These competencies range from listening, action-oriented, and customer service mindsets to integrity and trust. For each job placement, we interview around those core values to ensure that we accurately match a candidate with the career opportunity."[8] As you develop the talent brand, make sure that you don't expect the leader to play a role that doesn't work. A miscast leader is rarely effective.

Every brand carries a set of expectations of how people should act. Every talent brand—no matter how simple or complex—rests on a set of principles of how people should treat each other. These are brand behaviors. When it comes to leadership, these behaviors can make or break the success of the effort simply because of the intensity of the spotlight. There are actions that workers must see in a leader to believe the talent brand is real. At the heart of anyone's disappointment in leader behavior, whether that leader be in politics or business, usually comes down to a disappointment in how the leader treats an individual or a body of people. If the talent brand serves as a set of guideposts of acceptable behavior, then departing that zone of propriety can signal a leadership challenge.

But there are times when the realities of the culture get in the way of what the culture needs to achieve or how the culture needs to change. It is possible that what may be a cultural strength, in one way, can be a severe weakness in another. Central to finding this out is to identify, with leaders, what cultural attributes most frequently guide their decision making and what kind of decision making they guide. If the result paints a picture of a culture at odds with what the business needs to achieve, the business needs to take steps to adjust.

At Yahoo!, after Jerry Yang took over the helm as CEO, we studied what was working and not working in our culture. Previous cultural strengths were now working against us so we needed to change some of our behaviors to change the culture. We identified behaviors needed for moving forward. From there, we worked with a group of our leaders using the Lominger card system and identified what competencies the leaders most needed to lead these changes and we began to hire, train, and promote for these.

... Libby

Leadership Competencies

For every expectation of brand behavior, an organization should consider developing a formal statement of competencies to support the behaviors. While in many organizations competencies are associated with the functional skills and experience someone may bring to work, they are equally important to define leader behavior.

Key to managing the behavior behind the talent brand is a realization that all of us—no matter what work we do or companies we support—are influenced by a structure in which we work. Kristen Weirick of Whirlpool Corporation reflects, "We have a definitive leadership model of twelve behaviors expected of leaders. Within this we look for four key indicators of top talent and three derailers that undermine any leader. Every candidate is assessed against these."[9] To standardize how leaders should support a talent brand requires an organization to document the expected behavior. The result is a set of competencies.

These can be a useful, essential tool to structure the attributes that leaders need to bring to their work. They can "give teeth" to the behavior an organization expects of its leaders and, when added together, can tell a story of what an organization will value and reward. If a fundamental of a talent brand is trust, and a leader consistently demonstrates an unwillingness to trust, the documentation of competencies can help the company address the issue. Likewise, if a fundamental is communication, and a leader consistently demonstrates a strong ability to connect, the competencies can provide an effective framework to recognize and reward.

At the heart of keeping the behavior alive is defining how people in the organization should work together. We learn, with each encounter we have with new consumers of work, how much they are influenced by the collaboration they experience. These consumers, many of whom are products of team-based academic environments, look to leaders to signal how people should work together as well as how the organization respects diversity of thought and idea. A leader must demonstrate a willingness to listen, to share, to reward if he or she expects to be believed. A leader must prompt big thoughts, enhance smaller thoughts, and personalize all thoughts, especially those originated by other people.

As with many business processes, the details behind leadership competencies will determine whether they are effective. As Richard J. Crowder of Aetna relates, "We have instituted a dual rating process for senior executives and leadership that ties compensation decisions not only to the achievement of business goals, but to 'how' you achieved those goals. The 'how' is based on the Aetna Way values of integrity, employee engagement, excellence and accountability, quality service and value. Those values are expressed in behaviors that can be observed," Crowder says, "such as developing and sharing talent across the organization to support the value of employee engagement."[10] While a set of competencies, and the processes to support them, cannot ensure a leader's effectiveness, they can document the behavior needed to sustain the culture and the talent brand.

As a global energy company reached for specific ways to bring its talent brand to life, it reached directly to the people most responsible for setting the tone throughout the organization—the leaders. It committed to make its leadership competencies the first outcomes of the new talent brand. To develop the competencies, we interviewed each of the senior leaders to learn what the new brand meant to them, their part of the organization, what it demanded of leadership, and how it should impact the search for and development of leadership talent. From these interviews we developed a series of competencies that we worked through with the CEO and other senior leaders before they were implemented. Ultimately, they will be the framework for how leaders are selected for the organization, developed for future roles, and measured in current roles. And they add substance and "teeth" to the commitment of the business to the talent brand.

... Mark

Leadership Actions

As much as leader behavior can set a tone for the talent brand and a set of competencies can help an organization monitor whether that behavior consistently occurs, one moment of "off-brand" behavior from a leader can undermine the talent brand in a flash. Unfortunately, leaders are people, and people of all walks have the capacity to walk small and to act small. News stories are filled with accounts of leaders, so capable of doing so much, yet caught for trying to get away with so little.

Somehow, when internal political priorities take over, personal vendettas influence, egos grow beyond seemingly natural boundaries, or there are simply too many mirrors in an office, it becomes too easy for the leader to bypass the brand (and, in some cases, common sense). The talent brand, supported by competencies, can reinforce positive behavior. Paul McKinnon, commenting on Citigroup's employer brand, observes, "We point candidates to our geographic footprint and senior leadership team. We tell people that 'If you are good, you can make it here, regardless of your background.' And, best of all, we can point to the evidence in our senior management team, which is a great reflection of our global tradition and footprint. My sense is that there is a tight connection between what we say and who we are."[11] Smart organizations recognize that leaders must consistently demonstrate what the talent brand demands. Jeanne Mabie from IBM observes: "This world is getting smaller and flatter, increasingly global, and we are going to learn more about what it takes for leaders to support our brand."[12]

Nothing can undermine a talent brand promise faster than a leader who contradicts what the talent brand is all about. Today, with all the available ways to record behavior, from pocket video cameras to smart phones, and all the easy ways to broadcast the results, it is impossible for a leader to prevent negative actions from becoming public displays. This is especially true when people compare a leader to the promises a talent brand makes. If that comparison is unfavorable, credibility can disappear in a moment, no matter what other good a leader may do. People watch and listen before they feel—and before they act. The consumer of work searches for opportunities to broadcast when a leader topples from the pedestal.

Like many things, small actions can be defined by the observer, the beholder, the reactor. When developing a talent brand, it can be very helpful is to consider what actions by a leader can get in the way of the talent brand message. Knowing what "small action" should be avoided and how it could damage will be helpful in managing the leader to steer clear. This can also provide some preparation for how to handle a situation that may threaten talent brand credibility.

Small actions can have big impact. The speed of the grapevine is a reality any talent brand must contend with. On the outside, it is the speed with which disappointed customers share their stories; on the inside, it is the pace at which workers share what they observe, what disappoints and what speculates. So how quickly, in this time filled with gadgets, can bad news travel? Is a "nano-second" not nearly specific enough? In addition to all the social network broadcast tools immediately available, certain industries have their own gossip blogs, which at best are a kind of instant yellow journalism. One misstep on Wall Street, Capitol Hill, Madison Avenue, the Silicon Valley, or Hollywood can become fodder for these bloggers. And what they write will become part of a corporate reputation as a place to work.

For some leaders, the downfalls occur from the totally unexpected, from situations and actions that few ever imagined could have been so misunderstood. But to understand how a worker may separate the significant from the insignificant will give you keen insight into what workers expect. The times when leaders try to downplay an action by labeling a potentially significant act as something that workers *should* consider insignificant can signal a significant credibility challenge. Too many organizations believe that, if they try hard enough, certain moments in organizational evolution can simply disappear. Or they can "spin" their way out.

Others insist that, despite all logic to the contrary, a good CEO can explain his (or her) way out of anything. But workers remember what disappoints. To protect the talent brand requires protecting a leader against intrusion and small thinking and action. Too many people tell leaders what they believe the leader wants to hear. To sustain a talent brand, a leader must behave based on truth.

As we worked with a global services company to assess the impact of leadership support of the talent brand, we asked a few fundamental questions: Do leaders clearly articulate the value proposition to workers? Do they set an example for others to follow? Do they share expectations for talent brand behavior from direct reports? Do they appear to treat people in a manner consistent with the talent brand? Do they appear to value what the talent brand can contribute to the organization? And do they let their personal actions undermine the talent brand? From the answers to these questions we could assess what gaps we needed to fill to authentically position leaders as examples of the talent brand. And through the process we successfully engaged the leaders in the business results this brand could create.

. . . Mark

Dave Ulrich and Norm Smallwood, thought leaders in leadership, describe the concept of a leadership brand as focused less on individual leaders and more on building consistent capabilities among all leaders in an enterprise. How the leadership brand is a shared identity among the leaders can differentiate an organization from its competitors for talent. As Ulrich remarks, "Firms with branded leadership are in a win-win situation. They win with customers because customers have confidence that the leaders will respond to their needs in a consistent and appropriate way. And employees know what to expect and the engagement-draining dissonance is eliminated. Employees see in their leaders what customers expect." As a result, Smallwood suggests, "Companies with strong leadership brands are generally not as strongly affected by changes in management as companies with weaker leadership brands."[13] If leadership is central to the connection between culture and the talent brand, any effort to document the needed behavior is a step forward. In a competitive market for talent, someone is always watching.

Yahoo! produced an innovative toolkit for leaders as part of an overall initiative to drive cultural change and adopt new behaviors. It is called "Have you (. . .) lately?" The first little booklet in the boxed set contains a mirror and asks leaders to reflect where they are before they move forward. A little tool to do that is called the "Yahoo! Mojo Meter." The blanks to fill in include: Checked In? Shown Your Appreciation? Energized? Developed a Yahoo!'s Career? Strengthened a Team? Welcomed New Yahoos!? According to David Windley, CHRO; "The toolkit

is part of an overall campaign; 'Think Purple,' to inspire Yahoos!
to live their lives with an explanation point!"
    ... Libby

Worker Experience

If a leader's words can be precise and can be controlled, a
worker's experience is vague and can only be influenced. That
experience is the product of a range of moments, a collection
of touch points, a myriad of messages. While no organization
can control all the input a worker may receive, any organization must try to send as many positive signals as possible. At
each discussion of the work, each mention of the expectations,
each referral to the experience, the talent brand should be
top of mind for anyone hoping to secure worker retention and
engagement. And for new workers entering the organization, the
experience you deliver will determine the credibility of the talent
brand in the marketplace.

While media and communications are important, they can't
do everything. People have to invest in the talent brand and
use it as a foundation for how they reach out to others. As we
look ahead and see a free talent marketplace, we see how the
business that empowers the talent brand will create communities
to nurture the talent brand. A company that thrives in the
new marketplace for talent will create a talent brand that is so
relevant and compelling that it keeps itself alive; it sustains its
own momentum.

And when it does, the experience is akin to magic—
something special that few can describe yet many want to experience happens when the workers who live and work within the
talent brand move beyond simply participating in the culture to
advocating for its longevity; when they become the sponsors of
the experience and the advocates for the talent brand.

Face-to-Face Interactions

In the end, nothing will bring a talent brand to life faster than a worker participating in conversations that echo the meaning of the brand. Such conversations are rarely lengthy or detailed or content rich. Usually it's a glance, a gesture, an expression to ease a challenging moment, provide a notion of support, motivate a colleague to "stick with it" until completion. The talent brand is an articulation of who you are and what your business stands for, and so it must be a part of every message you deliver. It is the beginning and the end of each presentation, a touchstone and a reminder.

And while there is no way to control a conversation, you can provide on-site managers examples of how to interject brand messages into everyday conversations; you can give on-site managers real examples of handling situations in a brand manner, from dealing with a challenging worker to providing candid feedback to answering a routine question; and you can help on-site managers detect the difference between "delivering the brand" in a conversation and simply delivering information or completing a transaction.

Our work with leaders may set the tone, but it's the efforts of managers and supervisors on the front line that determine the difference between a talent brand trapped in its words and a talent brand that truly comes to life. As we worked with a nationwide retail chain, we strongly suggested a new approach—in order to gain this intensity of manager engagement that would make managers "the owners" of the brand implementations at their sites and so the brand would not get trapped in the "they sent it from corporate headquarters" syndrome. Each manager partnered with a local "brand champion" to create local events and opportunities for workers to engage in what the brand was all about. In addition, managers participated in briefing sessions to review the impact of their behavior on ultimate brand impact. These focused on how managers could deliver messages in a consistent, on-brand tone; how workers could participate in brand events; and how the organization could locally celebrate milestones and achievements to recognize the brand.

... Mark

Worker Events

While conversations ground the culture in a realistic exchange between people, a great deal of organizational influence can emerge from the celebration or party or event that brings a talent brand to life in its full cultural splendor. An organization can effectively focus on what the talent brand is all about by selecting key events for the business to participate in or sponsor—within the company and outside the company—to offer living ways to demonstrate to workers that the talent brand lives for real people.

One key opportunity for an event is when a new worker joins the organization. This gives you the opportunity, as you welcome new people into the talent brand, to help workers already on the inside to re-familiarize and recommit. That door that opens to the outside world—as you welcome new people—can make your talent brand experience so welcoming that new people can join, will want to join, and will soon feel connected because they join. And your current workers, too.

Such events are, as well, an opportunity for the organization to celebrate the "big idea" it may stand for. For some, this is a charity the organization supports; for others, it may be an employee cause; and for others, an annual employee tradition. No matter the nature of the event, the degree to which it becomes a "ritual" offers the opportunity to reinforce key messages about the talent brand. Any talent brand that stands for "a big idea" has a better chance of lasting over time if it focuses on the result of the experience, not only on the specifics of the experience.

And while not all organizations have fun as part of their cultures, those who do are attractive and manage high retention rates.

Worker Recognition

At the crossroads of conversations and events are the individual and collective opportunities to recognize what workers contribute. When we look at all the things an organization can do to make a culture feel real, few can be as lasting as the effort to acknowledge and value the contributions from workers. We all want to believe that what we do matters, that we make a difference, that someone notices. Advancing the talent brand in an organization can be as simple, and as permanent, at sharing the spotlight with as many people as possible. While recognition opportunities do not have to be public, achievements can give you the opportunity to celebrate. And celebrations can make a brand feel very alive and fun.

Cultural Influences

If leadership sets the tone for the cultural alignment to the talent brand, human resources drives the day-to-day reality. To be the "lens" through which the organization looks at each dimension of the worker experience requires HR to define each touch point in a worker's day-to-day life.

Because so much of the worker's experience is influenced by HR programs, it is essential for those programs and services to contribute to an on-brand perception. If a talent brand is a promise to a potential worker that, hopefully, will influence the choice of where to work, then HR has a great deal of influence over the actual experience that a worker discovers when he or she walks through the door to work.

Peet's Coffee's branded leadership program, "Peet's Leadership Blend," is a guide for leaders designed to be at the center of all people practices. The program has tools for leaders to build their own skills and grow their careers as they grow the careers of their team and lead company growth. The program focuses on Business: Strategic Direction and Operational Performance and People: Healthy Relationships and Continuous Development. Competencies are developed for individual contributors, managers, directors, and executives in each category. According to Kristi McFarland, senior director of learning and development and communications, "This work represents a significant step forward for Peet's and begins to establish a common language and framework for how we hire, develop, reward, and advance our people. Commitment from the senior team in launching the program resulted in a high level of engagement from all."

. . . Libby

Human Resources

As long a list as this may produce, one of the first tasks at hand is to study the HR offerings to identify the programs and services with cultural interdependencies that may need to be managed. For example, a key cultural component in a talent brand may be the opportunity to develop a career. This is certainly of high importance to many consumers of work as they build their personal resumes and brands.

Many companies respond with well-developed programs, often with a foundation in technology, to enable workers to develop plans for careers, including the courses to take, tasks to complete, and people to connect with. It's a very hot area with most talent brands.

With each interdependency, the challenge is to fairly diagnose the impact on the talent brand and take whatever steps are needed to ensure that it supports but does not compete. When developing a talent brand, take the step to identify all the processes—mostly administered by human resources—that must provide the worker with a consistent experience on the inside. From goal setting to performance evaluation to salary administration, the challenge for any company is to view the process through the lens of the talent brand and make necessary adjustments in the worker's experience. Within its standard scope of responsibility, HR can significantly impact a culture, from the approach it takes to recruitment and on-boarding to its approach to performance management to benefits and pay, as well as other less-visible efforts. Consider how HR can positively (or negatively) impact the sense of alignment between the talent brand and the culture.

HR Tools and Resources

For many workers, the opportunity to "get things done" becomes a critical way to evaluate the degree to which an organization invests in its people. When we talk with employees and we hear such things as, "I can't get the equipment I need to do my job" or "The Help Desk isn't very helpful" or "Why can't there be customer service people within easy reach?" or "I can't figure out how to get approval to move forward on my project," we observe how satisfaction can influence a worker to believe in what the organization is saying.

The tools and resources have to work. There is no way to achieve brand support if, on one hand, you promise one type of experience, but the worker experiences something very different. This includes the website during enrollment, the claims procedures when using health benefits, and the other online tools providing service to workers. Even the tools to consult when the tools do not work must solve a problem in a way consistent with the brand. Otherwise, they can hollow a brand promise.

At the same time, the interactions that workers have with both the company's human resources staff and the vendors working on behalf of the company impact how workers react. If each voice a worker hears fails to echo a similar tone and message, the brand has as little chance to thrive as if, with each interaction, the brand promise fades farther from view.

Worker Communications

For years, the internal communication function of every organization has struggled with the role it is intended to play. We observed, and participated, as the profession made its journey from the "happy talk" publications of the 1970s to the "corporate journalist" role of the 1980s to the "business spokesperson" role of the 1990s to the "engagement promoters" of this decade. Now, as we imagine the potential of the talent brand and the power of social media, we believe another incarnation is in store.

The internal communicator, by definition, is usually found editing a message for worker consumption, whether it is a release originally intended for the financial community or a leadership message initially targeted to an external audience or a human resources message primarily directed to specific users of company benefits. Its purpose has generally been regarded as to inform without any other real metric of success or accomplishment.

The talent brand, however, brings new focus and opportunity to the internal communicator. Long gone are the days when someone in such a role could claim success simply by transmitting information with clarity. Today, the internal communicator must be closely involved in the marketing of the talent brand—and in nurturing its supporting corporate culture—so the company can make its numbers in new and retained workers. The internal communicator should be setting goals directly related to recruitment and retention in order to shape approaches by focusing on needed outcomes.

Communication—both to and from the worker—is essential to the success of any effort to re-recruit workers. And it's mandatory to any desire to bring a talent brand to life, period.

As employees search for consistency in leadership action and human resource practices, they will also quickly detect whether the official messages coming from the organization support or undermine the talent brand point of view. This evaluation will reach beyond the actual words included in the communications to the overall opportunity for interaction the company promotes, whether messages are relegated to one-direction announcements or whether a commitment to open exchange is easily accessed and experienced.

It's all about telling stories to keep a brand fresh. Yahoo!'s Carol Mahoney recalls a challenging time: "We needed to see if our brand was working. Market research showed it was doing what we needed, but we needed to touch it up. So we revised our marketing campaign for recruitment, 'How Big Can You Think?' into what we called 'Think Big, Think Purple.' This resonated in focus groups we conducted. People didn't always know that purple was the Yahoo! color and or what it stood for, but they 'got' the message."

Mahoney reports a strong response. "In addition to the purchased media, online and offline, we created buzz by sending our hiring messages via scooters and hiring airplanes to pull signs over highway traffic (which happened to fly over the Stanford graduation ceremony)," she recalls. "The activity excited our employees, created buzz, and, most importantly, strengthened our reach. Our candidate pipeline jumped an impressive 30 percent within weeks."[14]

You need your communications to create two types of reactions. On one hand, the functional, you need the worker to say, "I know what we do, what I need to do, and why I am here." At the same time, emotionally, you need the worker to say, "I know the difference my work makes to the business and the difference working here makes to my life." That can only happen when the communications reach beyond the obvious approaches.

Getting to Work

No matter how effective the implementation of a talent brand may be, it must be carefully supported in order to sustain. That effort begins with leadership and is supported by human resources and worker communications. If the support isn't there, the implementation will be for naught.

Key Lessons: Chapter Six

Is your business ready to create an infrastructure to support a talent brand? Or, at the minimum, to use the talent brand as the lens through which to view the culture and the various programs and processes that directly influence how it is perceived?

☐ The relationship between culture and brand is strong. An organization's culture is created over time by thousands of experiences. A talent brand is an articulation of that culture in a form that is "ready for prime time." But the talent brand cannot exist on its own without the authentic support of the organization's culture.

☐ Culture and brand connect the actions of words of leadership; the face-to-face interactions employees experience at each touch point; the products and services delivered by HR; and the messages and content of employee communications media.

☐ The key to the culture is what workers experience. And to ensure the consistency of this experience, the talent brand should be *the lens through which each dimension of the worker experience is viewed.*

☐ A leader is very important to developing a culture and sustaining a talent brand. A leader has the freedom to express what is important, what is valued, and what is rewarded, as well as what is extraneous, what can be ignored, and what will be dealt with.

7

ESSENTIAL SEVEN: SURVIVE

In the world of marketing, the language of brand developed during a time controlled by Madison Avenue. Brands evolved from advertising, when Madison Avenue realized that the "big idea" and the emotional connection were ways to engender customer loyalty over just a purchase. Brands attached meaning to the advertising through the big idea. They were carefully marketed through campaigns targeted to a small number of predictable channels that easily reached the easy-to-identify consumers. Only when consumers talked with each other about their actual experiences with products or services did a consumer brand risk criticism. But those conversations were usually limited to words exchanged over the fence or at the end of the driveway or on the ski lift. Brand dissatisfaction had little opportunity to mushroom.

In the predictable world of talent, as well, the language of employer brand relished in controlled settings. A company could easily articulate its value proposition, advertise its job openings, and brag about its work environment without public scrutiny. Sure, disgruntled applicants would willingly share their experiences, but their conversations were limited to exchanges over the telephone or around the water cooler. Disgruntled employees complained in the break room. Some resigned without complaining. A few sued. Just as with consumers, dissatisfaction with employer brands was contained and of little concern.

Social Media

When the Internet became accessible to millions, workers began to use the medium to share their observations. In the early chat rooms of Yahoo! and other Internet providers, employees of specific organizations would eagerly post their experiences, criticisms, and recommendations. But the reach of the experience remained limited. Even when vault.com began providing a platform where employees and candidates could openly express their complaints and share their opinions about employers, the audience was a small, curious niche rather than a broader group. The old marketplace only found those people who were actively looking for jobs. The new marketplace, thanks to technology, can find people who may not be actively looking. People can now see anything on the inside. They can find the secrets. They can hear the reports. Many job seekers, and many satisfied employees, have a profile and are on it every day,

To say this relatively quiet world has ended is an understatement. Today any talent brand must be able to survive in a social media world in order to have any chance to achieve all that we have described. The nature of the change is simple—immediate access to limitless networks for people to instantly share any idea with millions of people. And while the novelty of the whole thing may be interesting to some, the potential damage to a talent brand is frightening to many. Thanks to the advent of the easy-to-access tools to globally communicate any easy-to-imagine thought, the credibility of a talent brand is potentially in the hands of complete strangers. "The emergence of social networks and blogs demands transparency," observes Yahoo!'s Carol Mahoney. "We have to be part of these discussions. We have to be written about and discussed by the bloggers. Our Talent Acquisition group and key influencers in the company must be part of the experience. On our Yahoo! corporate blog, we link to everything that we think they might want to know."[1]

Thanks to social media, employee communications has moved beyond informing people, to securing and engaging people. It reaches those on the outside interested in coming in and those on the inside the company wants to keep in. Its focus on engaging the consumer of work is a different way to look at the function. The change requires more than simply knowing the tools and how to message the content. It's a matter of knowing how to make the employer brand live in the market for talent so that the business can become the magnet for the talent that it will need, from inside and out. As Mahoney says, "There is wariness about whether or not employers are really who they say they are. So prospects will hunt around and make judgments based on what they can find out themselves about what the company is really like. They want to see, experience, hear from their friends, and validate what they see. You can't just have a careers website; you have to have lots of layers for them to sieve through so they can see for themselves."[2]

It's a new world. Combined with the changes to the talent marketplace and the priorities of the new consumer of work, the new approach to (current and prospective) employee communications must move beyond the single channel approach of the past to create online communities wherein people can address specific issues, connect in specific, relevant ways, and help each other through day-to-day challenges. With social media, the power of information and influence has shifted to people, and rather than be afraid of it, business must embrace it, or else we will put the fate of the talent brand at risk. Yet, no matter its popularity, some take small steps. As Whirlpool Corporation's Kristen Weirick observes, "We are cautious about how to use technology to build relationships. We believe real relationships are built through people so, as we evolve in the space, we must determine the best ways to use enabling technology to maintain relationships."[3]

As we worked with a global information company on their approach to social media and recruitment, we asked a fundamental question, "Are you ready for transparency?" We explained that, in a social media marketplace, the window is open for anyone to observe and comment about anything the company may say or do or anything anyone may experience about the company. There is no control as the traditional media world provides, no opportunity to edit and no chance to limit. But there is an ultimate opportunity to engage, to create connections with prospective workers that traditional media could never achieve. Before starting, we simply asked, "Are you ready for a 360-degree view of who you are, because that is what social media provides."

... Mark

So what do we mean by social media? After the first wave of the web, technology and design combined as an enabler of a more open, creative, and collaborative experience on the web, coined Web 2.0 by pundits. Developers jumped on this trend creating social networking sites, wiki's, web logs (blogs), and other hosted services fostering not only online connections but collaboration. Any open exchange between people—online through the web—that is not monitored, edited, or populated with pre-prepared content could be considered social media. Another way to think about it is that the content is generated by the user and shared with the online world.

While in the early days the concept was confined to those initial Yahoo! and AOL chat rooms, through the first decade of the 2000s, the scope of social media expanded to connect a world of people hungry for response and feedback. Unlike any other social media trend—except, perhaps, the popularization of the television in the 1950s—the advent of social media has completely altered the landscape in which people around the world communicate and collaborate. It has, in the end, created a new set of behaviors that define how people connect. And any talent brand could be easily swallowed in its wake. Let's look, specifically, at how to survive five key challenges that social media has brought to the talent brand.

Yahoo! had a team of sourcers who did nothing but mine the Internet for possible current and future candidates. We built relationships with the candidates and collected their referrals, much like headhunters, at all levels. It isn't unusual for sourcers to have thousands of connections on social network sites like LinkedIn and Facebook. Ours sourcers and recruiters did everything from email contacts to look for candidates to posting openings on their profiles.

… Libby

Survival Tip 1: Communication and Collaboration

One of the hallmarks of social media is collaboration. The idea is how people work together. As explored in the book *Wikinomics*, in just the last few years, traditional collaboration—in a meeting room, a conference call, even a convention center—has been superseded by massive online communities and collaborations. Enlightened organizations are taking advantage of this new source of communal capacity and brilliance to catapult innovation and new growth opportunities.[4]

"The new world of social media is very exciting," according to Amy Giglio of Aflac. "It has revolutionized the way we recruit, by assisting us to build the pipeline, making referrals easier to obtain, and relationship building a bit easier. Social media also help break down barriers when identifying a candidate—and work faster than the telephone. We also use LinkedIn and Facebook to identify targets for passive recruiting as we build relationships with highly sought after candidates. It also helps us protect our brand and increase our credibility internally, when our employees see us proactively and strategically recruiting from various pools of talent."[5] Steve Canale of GE remarks, "We have experimented using Facebook and other social networks for building our brand awareness with the entry-level market. Many of our new hires who are members of GE's leadership development programs create their own private social networks using Facebook to stay connected. Through student and new-hire surveys, we've come to learn that 50 percent of students would actually prefer it if employers did not actively market to them on Facebook. Many students prefer it to remain a neutral space. So we keep that in mind."[6]

Now, you may say, "We have always had instant communication through technology, since Mr. Bell called for Mr. Watson over the first telephone." But that was one man talking with one man. Social media, starting with that first online chat room, enables any number of people to instantly communicate with any number of people. It's a global gathering where anyone can chat with anyone. It's like giving the world-famous speaker's corner at Hyde Park a global megaphone for all to hear. Such a platform can be credited with making the greenhouse effect a social issue for the masses or giving rise to an unexpected U.S. presidential candidate or creating an entirely new vocabulary of non-words, acronyms, and abbreviations. Such a platform can also provide a voice to any worker with anything to say about any business. And say they do, for all of us to hear.

For a talent brand, the challenge imposed by instant collective communication and collaboration is clear. Any negative experience that anyone has with a company during the hiring process or once at work can be instantly shared with millions of people around the world. Nothing from the boss to the food in the cafeteria is immune. To go on any number of social network sites today is to find a smorgasbord of comments about any number of organizations. Have a scheduled interview? Simply go on a social network site, enter the name of the company, and you will read the up-to-the-minute good, bad, and ugly about each step of the experience. From "how you will be treated" during an interview to "what really happens inside the company," the social network sites become like standing around a global water cooler with immediate commentary from any number of unidentified experts.

> One of the most highly sought after jobs in the airline industry is the Southwest Airlines Pilot. Our interview process was a legendary experience. We used a behavioral based interview and some of the questions were unusual for pilots. Some enterprising pilot decided to poll pilots after their interviews and developed a subscription based website for his peers on 'how to pass the SWA interview. . . . Libby

Survival Tip 2: Global Community

Now you may say, "What's wrong with this?" A global sense of connection can be a good thing. And, for many, the opportunities for global links represent the best of what the new world of technology can offer. Social media, since its inception, has offered a place and a space for people from all lands and walks of life to connect with each other, with a nominal admission charge, if any, no set hours of when open and closed, and no need for such prickly details as an actual name—a user name will do. With the click of a mouse, any user can become any persona, complete with an avatar, pose as any worker or leader, and become an authoritative source on any topic. There are not many checks and balances in the new world of social media. Sites offer recruiters the opportunity to connect with potential hires. Companies are creating groups on Facebook to connect.

For a talent brand, the immediate challenge can be one of credibility; the lasting one can be of disconnection. For how can a company respond to criticism if its critics are the faceless behind the screens and keyboards? If, rather than voice their issues directly, they wait until a time and a space when no one can see, but everyone will hear. Simply go to any social network site and you can instantly become a member of any group you establish. But you'll never really know who the members are.

Once an organization confronts and acknowledges the power of social media, it needs to consider the steps to take. Before embarking on a social media strategy for recruitment, we asked a global retail organization to ask itself, "Are the workers in this talent segment inclined to use social media tools? Are the workers familiar with the various tools of social media? Are the workers comfortable using social media? And how do they prefer to use social media?" Rather than guess what the strategy should be, the organization built its strategy around the habits of the people it sought to reach. So they learned that people in their talent space favor Facebook as a social media connection. So it was a natural step for the organization to set up a Facebook page. It learned that, for higher-level positions, potential candidates used LinkedIn as a social network tool. And it learned that, for entertainment, YouTube was the preferred destination. No surprise, it began to actively search LinkedIn profiles and posted videos on YouTube. Like any smart user of media, the organization responded to users. And the users have flocked to the new sites.

. . . Mark

Survival Tip 3: Unchecked Sources

Now you may say, "We've always had a world of unvetted sources, from the mailman who delivered the gossip (and the mail) to the butcher who sliced the rumor (along with the corned beef)." But those opinions were confined to would-be boundaries that effectively protected many ears from many opinions. Now, in a new uncontrolled world, anyone can speak, claim and assert. Consider the power of a tool like Wikipedia to bring instant knowledge to millions. The challenge is, however, that anyone from any source can add or edit that content. Social media removes the role of editor.

For a talent brand, routine without an editor can be a challenge, because the essence of talent message is an essence of control. It's critical when marketing a talent brand to control many sources and channels, just as the originals from Madison Avenue did. But without an editor, control is impossible, leaving a brand open to any type of interpretation from any type of self-proclaimed authority.

Survival Tip 4: Rumors

Now you may say, "Gossip has always been a part of the corporate fabric, along with potato salad at company picnics and bad eggnog at holiday parties." But, just as with many dimensions of this change, rumors, while not controlled, were certainly confined. Or, if they traveled, they had to travel through conventional channels, one person at a time. But now, instantly, a rumor can be everywhere. One email or—worse—a YouTube clip can start a riot or end a career. And the presence of many sources in social media make it even more difficult to prove innocence once guilt has been electronically shared across the time zones. And once it is out there, it never goes away.

For a talent brand, the risk of rumor is intense. A company's reputation as a place to work can be immediately and lastingly damaged by one false accusation by a disgruntled employee spread over the miles in a flash; a leader's reputation for fairness and caring can be undermined by innuendo faster than you can say, "You've got mail."

I was shocked that employees from Yahoo! would leak confidential information to gossip rags and blogs. One of our leadership meetings was "live blogged" while it was happening. To me, this was akin to stealing company material on my integrity scale. I shared this with a thought leaders discussion group. One of my peers gently enlightened me. To these workers, not sharing would be dishonest. They grew up in a world of total transparency and for them, integrity means that they owe the world the honest truth with no filter.

. . . Libby

Survival Tip 5: False Security

Now you may say, "Business has always lived with a false sense of security, always fearing what can happen, but always believing that any issue can be effectively managed by able P.R. work." While the sense of control that business once experienced has been severely weakened by social media, the opportunities of social media create their own sense of control. By having social media at its fingertips too, business can often feel it can "fight back" anything that may be said by anyone in thousands of social media forums. And while that may be logistically possible, it is inconceivable that business would ever let itself get into a "tit for tat" back-and-forth with nameless voices on an electronic device. Yet, many businesses do, despite the inherent risks. The ease of connection makes the decision of where to work, once private, instantly public, as a candidate subjects the decision to public acceptance.

For a talent brand, the potential impact of this false sense of security is strong. If a business decides to use social media channels to "fight back" to "protect its position and turf," the minor skirmishes may be victorious, the arguments may be won, but the ultimate battle may be lost. The damage to the talent brand may be difficult or impossible to immediately repair. Business used to be able to rely somewhat on employee confidentiality. The new generation who grew up with social media believes that transparency is not just a way of life, it is an obligation. Sharing company information to them is not a betrayal, but an act of authenticity.

A global energy company was more than a bit nervous about how to approach the blogosphere. It knew that blogs talked about it; it knew that items about the company appeared on any number of blogs; it monitored what blogs were saying; and it was prepared to respond, to engage in conversation. Before it started, however, we advised them to carefully consider the people they wanted to reach and influence before they instantly jumped into the blogosphere. We asked them, "Do the workers frequent blogs about your industry or organization? And which ones do they frequent? What is the tenor of discussion on those blogs? Are the workers in the segment influenced by what they may hear in the social media about your organization? Are there connections you can foster that can strengthen your reach into this worker segment?" One simple reason for asking these questions is that if a blog discussion evolves into an argument, no company wins. But if a blog offers an opportunity to effectively send a message, a point of view, it can open up healthy conversation and connection.

. . . Mark

How to Develop a Social Media Strategy

It's no surprise that, while many consider social media to be exciting new tools, most communicators and HR types still consider these to be a threat rather than a tool. Our message here is that you can embrace the platform and use it to your advantage instead of fighting it. We have, however, yet to see the true impact on business. It's as if we have completely opened Pandora's box to a new, uncontrolled communications world where anything goes. So how, amidst the chaos and noise, can a talent brand survive in a social media world? And how can the social media world actually support and reinforce the talent brand? Your best talent is already networked on the web. Their skills are in demand by multiple employers. Networks are not only great referral systems but they are also great references, as members can verify that they can perform those skills. And talent trusts networks more than recruiters or, perhaps, even organizations. Business must look at the Web 2.0 as a critical strategy instead of as a threat.

1. Acknowledge That Social Media Is Not Going Away

This is not a passing fancy. Once the power of information has shifted to the consumer of work, there is no going back. The opportunity for immediate connection has become a part of daily life, there is no returning to formal, one-direction channels. When people experience the richness of a global community and the ability to collaborate in an open environment, there is no returning to limited boundaries. Social media is not a new set of gimmicks; it is a redefinition of the communication experience between a company and all of its stakeholders, including current and prospective workers. It also provides new platforms upon which work can be done in the company and with various partners and providers.

2. Acknowledge What Social Media Is and Is Not

This is not a collection of new tools. Social media is an experience of connection, collaboration, communication, and community that is enabled by Web 2.0 technology that opens up the channels between people. The social media interaction, in turn, creates a new set of expectations among consumers, not only for just-in-time information but for openness leading to a range of opportunities to be heard.

Social media can provide a platform for an organization to tell an authentic, not artificial, story. IBM's Diane Gherson relates a situation in India in which business issues caused a temporary delay in the hiring of a large number of workers. Immediately, without perhaps understanding the details, the workers logged on to a social network site, Orkut, and expressed their frustrations with the company. "We could immediately see what concerned them and, rather than shy away from their comments or fear their comments, we actually embraced their comments and welcomed the opportunity to learn about their issues. Before we talked with these employees about the issues, we had a much better idea of what we needed to focus on. We were dealing with a number of young people, many in their first jobs, many working for a big global company for the first time, and the delay was frightening. Because we knew that, we knew how to act, and our local representative invited the parents of these workers to tea for a calm discussion about the issues and the anticipated resolution. The insight we gained from a social network enabled us to take a different route to diffuse a difficult situation."[7]

3. Get to Know Social Media

Social media is the integration of technology, social interaction, and forms of communication that enable immediate exchange between large numbers of people in community settings. So, although the walkie-talkie permits an immediate exchange, it is usually between two people. The virtual community, however, places perfect strangers in a common, virtual environment and encourages them to share. Here is a quick review of the most popular elements of social media. Blogs, online forums, and virtual communities have replaced the chat room, and people now "post comments" versus chat. The only place people really chat are via IM or in some virtual gaming sites. More than twelve million American adults maintain a blog. Fifty-seven million read them.[8]

The Website. Yes, that trusty site on the intranet or the Internet can be a social media experience, especially if the site is open to commentary and interaction. A company website can build a great deal of credibility with workers when "they no longer have to go outside the company to talk with others about the company." By incorporating social media devices, such as blogs and online communities, organizations can foster conversations rather than merely react to them. But, in the talent space, organizations should continue to refine their career sites to be destinations (as we explored in Chapter Five). The most significant change is the introduction of the personal website, developed by an individual worker for positioning in the new talent marketplace. With a personal site, a worker can convert a static resume into a living description of skills, experience, and aspirations. Once you place your resume on your profile, it is there forever. You update it when you change jobs. Theoretically, you never have to look for a job again. It looks for you. And the worker can easily direct would-be employers to the site for instant evaluation.

Facebook. The story of social media can't be told without a salute to this most inventive of tools. The brilliance of Facebook is found in its simplicity. It is, at its root, simply a way for people to connect. What it accomplishes, in its simplicity, is giving a generation a sense of confidence in what change the tool and the experience could create. It gave a generation a new way to express themselves, discover other people, and make connections across traditional boundaries. And, in a step of business brilliance, it took what it accomplished with its initial audience and carefully expanded to other generations as well as the workplace. As Google has with search and Kleenex has with paper products, Facebook has been the standard for how people connect online. It was the first and it remains the most trusted social networking experience.

The Blogosphere. The term "blog" emerged from a contraction of the term "web log." The blog enables any user in any part of the world to easily (thanks to readily available and simple-to-use software) create content and to announce an opinion to the world. Think of the blog as the ultimate in self-publishing: you simply go online, subscribe to a service, set up the blog, declare it "in business," and begin to express any point of view. Blogs run the gamut from news to politics to hobbies or personal diaries, and a vital part of the experience is the readers who post comments in an interactive format. Blogs are socially networked and interconnected through links to websites and other blogs posted by the bloggers. They have become a source of current opinions of hockey moms and NASCAR dads by media and marketers. Services like MyBlogLog, blogspot, and Sitereader allow bloggers to see who is reading and allow readers to set up their own online profiles to be shared on the blogs they frequent. Many bloggers earn revenue from search engine marketing and advertising appropriate to their content topics. In the talent space, the blog has become a standard way for recruiters and candidates to connect and for experts to offer observations, workers to express opinions, and organizations to discuss opportunities. Now, with major search engines each offering services to daily monitor the blogosphere by topic, any online user can easily monitor what is being said on the millions of blogs updated each day.

Blog Governance. It's no surprise that, in the business of building buzz, any number of businesses are taking matters into their own hands. The essential informality of the blog gives a business a chance to speak directly to would-be workers without the formality of traditional advertisements or press releases. In a blog, authors can (and most usually do) say absolutely anything about absolutely anything. Some are short, some are much too long; some are personal, some are much too intimate; some are objective, some are much too subjective; some are real, some are far too imaginative to be authentic. At least, however, they are there and, in the world of blogs, just being available is part of the point. The key to the blog is to say something compelling that users then circulate within their networks. So in the desire to build brand recognition, direct and clear stories of the value of working at a business—with concrete evidence to support the assertions—can build a "grass roots" reputation of a talent brand as an authentic articulation of what a company is all about.

Social Network Sites. When it began, the social phenomenon Facebook was considered a unique tool for the young, web-adept college student audience, an easy way for kids to connect with other kids. MySpace provided a similar online community initially aimed at teens and tweens. From these virtual communities or social utilities at first considered a novelty came a new standard in what it can mean to participate in an online community. Both networks eventually expanded their reach beyond the youth to encompass working adults around the world, an audience also targeted by such sites as LinkedIn, which specifically focuses on working professionals. The premise is simple. A user posts a profile and begins to add friends and acquaintances to build a network of contacts. The various networks converge to form the overall community and, thanks to easy-to-use technology, users can easily search through the greater community for additional users of similar interests to add to their personal networks. The user can easily reach anywhere in the community for anyone who may share a thought, a skill, or an experience. An online developer network has emerged in which developers can add their own applications and tools targeted to interested users. And in the talent space, it gives those looking for workers in the new talent marketplace an easy way to identify and contact workers who may offer just what the organization needs. Southwest, for example, actively uses social networking. "We have a Southwest fan page on Facebook," according to Jeff Lamb, "as well as a blog on our website to which employees from various disciplines within the company can contribute, unfiltered."[9] According to Jeanne Mabie of IBM, "We use a number of social network approaches, LinkedIn as a business network, and Facebook as a way to reach across the generations. We want to be out there and offer something. Our new university page on Facebook —called start@ibm—offers all kinds of groups the chance to learn more about us. We have, as well, offered widgets for our employees to put on their personal Facebook pages. We will offer the tools to our people, to engage them in the effort to secure talent, so it all feels less formal and more real."[10]

Ken Charles of General Mills tells a similar story. "We use Facebook pages and, while it is a good place to tell our brand story and to find people, it is not necessarily a good place to reach out to recruit. To the people on Facebook, that feels like stalking. So rather than blast a message to all of our competitor's interns to recruit them online, we might just take the names and connect with them on campus. Or we may use text messages to reach out to candidates. We really have to understand the landscape."[11]

In 2008 Amazon challenged employees around the world to capture their Amazon story on film in a program entitled "Tell Us Your Story." Amazonians responded, submitting videos that shared their unique perspectives on working for Amazon. Based on thousands of employee votes, winners were chosen and recognized at company-wide meetings. On YouTube, you can see videos from the teams that pack and ship Amazon products, software developers creating a cutting-edge cloud computing platform, and a personal profile from a former superhero finally finding his place in the corporate world.

... Libby

YouTube (Now Part of Google). The world of the video—once delegated to mass presentations at worker meetings—is given a rebirth in brand strategy with the advent of user-generated video sites, such as YouTube. Few social phenomena are as striking as this unique experience, which, since its introduction, has been widely copied by "copy cats" all over the talent landscape. It enables users, as you likely have experienced, to post any type of video production for the world to see. An organization interested in advancing its talent brand can populate these sites as well, offering its own video clips, designed, naturally, to promote the organization and to reinforce the key values of the talent brand.

General Mills is among the organizations that use YouTube to promote a brand as a place to work. Observes Ken Charles, "We post organic videos developed by our consumers to promote our company as a place to work, and we have built our own page on YouTube. That helps connect our recruitment efforts. They search for us on the web, find our careers site, and find our site on YouTube. These informal channels are as important than the formal ones."[12] And such an approach can help an organization effectively segment its offerings to appeal to specific splinters of the worldwide audience, offering yet another way to reach targeted workers. The result? An organization can creatively draw people into an experience that may be appealing. And, because it's all sponsored by a third party, the appearance of clips on a YouTube type of site carries with it an informal endorsement of objectivity, even though it may be submitted with a subjective point of view.

> The design of a YouTube page for a company is an excellent opportunity to set a tone, establish a personality, and personalize a talent brand. As we worked with a global energy company on their YouTube page, we reached well beyond what may have once been included in a traditional web page to create a transparent view into what differentiates the company from its competitors for talent. Through the use of video, commentary, discussion boards, questions and answers, and employee testimonials, we helped a potential worker "picture" what life and work at the company would offer. And we sent clear messages of what type of worker would succeed at the company.
> ... Mark

Online Job Boards. For many consumers of work, the newspaper classifieds are relics from the days of "Ozzie and Harriett." Today a certain segment the workforce—especially those looking for entry-level and high-volume positions—regularly go online to seek the latest opportunities. Sites such as TheLadders.com and Risesmart.com are focused on jobseekers at about the $100k salary range. How you position your company, opportunity, and specific work on these sites is essential to your marketing of your talent brand. The bland explanation will be forgotten, the exaggerated claims will be ignored, leaving only the crisp and clear articulation of your value proposition to be remembered and acted on. You have only a few words to motivate a customer to visualize what your job and company can mean. So use them wisely to point back to your career site. Jeanne Mabie of IBM observes: "We use search engine marketing and optimization to broaden our reach, as we buy specific keywords at different times on specific search engines depending on what talent we need. We carefully select the keywords, how to search for them, and what other tools to leverage, so our opportunities show up as people search online for work."[13]

4. Assess the Impact on the Talent Brand

So what does all this mean to the talent brand you have carefully developed for your business? The handwriting is on the screen: You must develop a strategy for how you use social network opportunities to sustain your talent brand. Otherwise the fate of your talent brand may be in the hands of millions of online users you never see. Create a safety zone around your employer brand that isn't subject to the ups and downs of the business. Your approach to incorporating social media into your talent brand marketing strategy can be simply expressed as the equation shown in Figure 7.1.

Figure 7.1

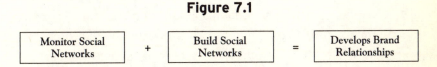

Just as the talent brand must jump the four hurdles described in Chapter Five, it must address the realities of social networks to create an ultimate result: to develop brand relationships. This means, simply, building the loyalty of brand users who experience the organization—and can exchange opinions with the organization—resulting in a sense of relationship with the brand and the organization. Each element of the equation is a fundamental step to follow.

Hundreds of businesses or their customers have created fan sites on Facebook so that the community can share products, services, institutions, and entertainment. A user who spots a topic of interest, whether on a friend's profile or in a News Feed story, can click on the link to that particular page and click the "Become a Fan." LinkedIn allows users to endorse people with whom they have worked or conducted business.

5. Monitor Existing Social Networks

Any organization hoping to attract workers today must constantly monitor what is being said about them in the social media. This can be easy to do: simply go to a favorite search engine and search for websites that have been created with your stakeholders in mind; go to the range of commercial websites in the talent space and look inside for posted comments on your organization; and go to a favorite search engine and search for blogs with content regarding your organization. Or you can hire monitoring agencies to do this for you. Check out general question-and-answer platforms such as Yahoo! Answers for questions asked about your organization or industry. For business gossip, simply go to such sites as Gawker, defamer, wonkette, or jossup.

In Hollywood, on Wall Street, and in the Silicon Valley, online equivalents of *The National Enquirer* have emerged with mostly mean-spirited gossip about the industry. While opinions posted in any of these forums may tend to be generally negative and critical, staying close to these opinions will give you direction for where your push of messages needs to focus. But be careful about how you respond to comments if that is your choice. Once you enter the social fray, it will be difficult to interrupt; entering the discussion may fuel other discussion; inconsistency in points of view from the same organization may increase the commentary and potentially confuse the users.

Clarity is key. Before you respond, clearly develop your key messages and stick with them through all responses. Avoid getting caught up in the emotion that many worker comments may bring out. Simply state facts, provide evidence, and clarify points of view. And once you commit to get started, stick with it. Regularly monitor and consistently respond; otherwise readers may assume you are adopting a "pick and choose" approach by only responding to selected messages.

While monitoring the impact of a talent brand is essential throughout the recruitment and retention effort, it is also essential when it comes to social media. Speed of reputation is a clear opportunity or risk in the social media world and, without careful monitoring, the conversation can undermine the organization. A global information company was concerned because, on any number of recruitment blogs, people openly criticized its recruitment efforts. Anonymous voices reported negative stories about the logistics of interviews not working out, of the company failing to provide promised transportation and transfers and, worst of all, of the company never following up after the interview to inform a candidate whether work had been secured. What made the stories worth serious consideration was not simply the negative view, but the fact that the negative view undermined the talent brand promise the organization had publicly declared. So the answer was not to stem the negative stories, but the answer became how to correct the situation that led to the downbeat reports. We simply asked, "Are these reports true?" "Have these situations occurred?" and "What are you doing to correct them?" In a social media world, all the warts show, and instead of addressing the communication vehicle, the organization needs to treat the wart.
. . . Mark

6. Build New Social Networks

If the true potential of social media is connection, any organization interested in advancing a talent brand should sponsor
opportunities for such conversations. By installing a social media
function on a corporate website—an online forum or virtual
community for potential workers—the organization can effectively position itself as open and transparent in potential issues
that may impact a worker's choice of organization. While each
organization will have its own governance issues to resolve,
a few standards have emerged from the best practices in this
space:

- Make any tool easy to access to create an experience of
  open exchange
- Commit to regularly participating in the online discussions, always following the set of key messages you develop
  to articulate and support the talent brand, and
- Maintain a consistent tone of openness to opinion and
  assertion.

Even if the discussion has a potential to turn negative,
participating in the conversation will add credibility to your
commitment to exchange. Users will be quick to notice any
attempt to "back off" certain discussion points, even though, as
the sponsor of the site, you can choose the degree to which you
participate in the conversation. Because this is *your* site, you
can drive what is discussed, how quickly and thoroughly you
comment, and the tone you follow in your entries. Simply by
posting the opportunity to gather, your organization can send a
positive message to the talent marketplace that you are a business
that is comfortable in its approach, confident in its strategy, and
connected to the opinions and needs of its stakeholders. And
such a feature can help you advance the positioning of your career
site as a destination for potential and current workers.

7. Develop Brand Relationships

Social media can significantly support your efforts to build and sustain a sense of community. Imagine, for a moment, the potential power of reaching a network of people who once worked for your organization or want to work for your organization. Or consider a network of people who influence the choices of workers, such as academic instructors and, of course, parents.

The winner in the social media sweepstakes will be the open organization that clearly sends the message, "We care about what people have to say" and who commits to welcome any user into the experience. The result will be a major opportunity to develop relationships across traditional boundaries with people whose support you need to attract and keep the people you need.

8. Consider How to Use Social Networks

You will most likely have little idea how to answer these questions for each of your top priority segments. As Whirlpool Corporation's Kristen Weirick comments, "In developing an employer brand, it's important to understand the external perception of the organization from both demographic and functional perspectives."[14] This is where some fundamental research into worker use of social media can be very helpful. Before investing time and resource today, get close to what your potential workers are using, and why.

Regardless of what you learn, however, realize that social media is not a gimmick, it is a new reality. The doors that once could close to opinion are now forever open. And the organization that fosters the commitment to open exchange will hold distinct advantage over the organization that chooses to wait "until the dust settles." This online dust will never settle. The new generation of workers entering organizations will not give up their social media habits at the door. They will bring expectations for instant connection with them on day one. And they won't stay patient for very long.

As we worked with an energy company on its social media strategy for recruitment, we carefully looked at the talent segments of highest priority. Following the steps discussed in this book, we also reviewed the pressure on the brand and the habits of the users to determine which social media offered the greatest opportunities for gain in reaching targets of talent. We considered what connections the organization could foster through social media that could strengthen its reach into each priority worker segment, how a proactive approach to social media could help the organization gain recognition among targeted workers of their talent brand, and how the organization could differentiate its brand through its use of social media. Just like every other new medium we encounter in this work, the novelty ultimately wears off, and once social media is the norm, only the most creative and strategic uses will prevail.

. . . Mark

9. Develop a Social Media Marketing Plan

Choose one of the top priority worker segments you identified in Chapter Four. Now consider how your use of social media can help your brand jump the hurdles identified in Chapter Five. This can play a key part in your talent brand marketing approach.

Your talent brand can, and will, survive social media if you commit to its inclusion in your marketing plans. Avoiding social media today will only make it more difficult in the future to credibly enter the space. Finding your social media niche today can pay immediate dividends, differentiate you from the competition, and engage your stakeholders in a way that may be most meaningful to them. Plus, it will give you the chance to listen to what others say, which, in itself, can be an important step to developing brand relationships.

Getting to Work

Want to make sure that your talent brand survives the new world of social media? Here's how. First, get close to social media, what it is, how it works, what contributions it can make, what impact it can create (or, perhaps, havoc), and how you must adjust your thinking about what a brand management process must contain.

Second, check what's going with social media and your organization. Do you blog? Do others blog about you? How do potential and current workers exchange observations of you, the value you provide, the leadership? How have you (or do you fear you could be) surprised by social media? How vital is social media to the consumers of work you seek to attract and engage?

Third, develop a strategy to not only confront social media, in a potentially reactive manner, but to use social media to advance your reputation, in a proactive manner. In fact, any brand for talent strategy must include a thriving social media component. It's just the way the world works now.

With these steps in mind you can live the lessons of Chapter Seven.

Key Lessons: Chapter Seven

No matter how careful your plan, segmented your strategy, or creative your talent brand, it could all go up in smoke based on one well-reported, negative experience in social media. No longer can any business control what people say. Today there are so many ways for voices to be heard that a bigger challenge is how to control the volume. So you'd better figure out how to incorporate social media into your plans.

Is your business ready to confront the most significant change in how people communicate since Mr. Bell invented the telephone? Are you ready to open your business up to the freedom (and consequence) of transparent conversation? And are you ready to invest in what it may take to influence and monitor this social phenomenon that can directly influence how people perceive your brand?

☐ Thanks to social media, worker communication has moved beyond informing, even engaging people, to securing and engaging people—those on the outside to come in, those on the inside to stay in—all to drive the talent brand to the consumer of work.

☐ Combined with the changes to the talent marketplace and the priorities of the new consumer of work, the new approach to (current and prospective) worker communications moves beyond the single channel approach of the past to create online communities where people can address specific issues, connect in specific, relevant ways, and help each other through day-to-day challenges.

☐ Any negative experience that anyone has with a company during the hiring process, or once at work, can be instantly shared with millions of people around the world.

☐ For a talent brand, the immediate challenge can be one of credibility; the lasting one can be of disconnection. For how can a company respond to criticism if its critics are the faceless behind the screens and keyboards?

☐ For a talent brand, the risk of rumor is intense. A company's reputation as a place to work can be immediately and lastingly damaged by one false accusation by a disgruntled worker spread over the miles in a flash.

☐ For a talent brand, the potential impact of this false sense of security is strong. If a business decides to use social media channels to "fight back" to "protect its position and turf," it may be victorious in the minor skirmishes, the argument may be won, but the ultimate battle could be lost and the damage to the talent brand might be difficult or impossible to repair immediately.

Part Four

WHAT IT MEANS TO YOU

8

BUILD A TALENT BRAND LEGACY

When we started thinking about employer brand many years ago, we never imagined it would occupy so much of our collective professional lives. But as we worked the possibilities—as the talent marketplace became more complex and as the importance of talent brand emerged—we knew we were hooked.

We also knew, from experience and from instinct, that when a talent brand works it sets a tone for an organization to succeed. Few can discount the smart moves that the leadership of Southwest Airlines have made over the years; yet, at the same time, few can discount the value of its talent brand to pave the way for the airline to continuously hire and develop strong people. Because that is what talent brand is all about—the commitment to do what it takes to get good people in the door to do the work, to keep them as long as you need them and they are relevant to your work priorities, and to end your working relationship on good terms so that, in the future, they may return or, certainly, tell their friends that you are a good place to work.

While more than 60 percent of companies now have an employer brand and another 25 percent report that they are working on one, few employer brands are ready for the new talent marketplace.[1] To be ready; a talent strategy supported by a talent brand and a branded marketing approach for each talent segment will be critical.

So what can a solid talent brand contribute to a business? Let's look at the twelve key contributions and what the lessons of this book can help you achieve.

1. The New Marketplace for Talent Will Have a Clear Understanding of Why Someone Should Work for You

The marketplace for talent is complex, changing, and noisy, filled with new consumers of work who simply want to build a strong resume and a compelling personal brand by making smart moves to work smart places. At the same time, some in this new generation of workers and others in older generations are not looking at building a career but at how they want to work and what they want to do on their own terms. This is the world in which a talent brand can and must thrive, differentiate, and tell a story of your business as a place to work for different segments of workers. If you carefully develop your talent brand and use it as the foundation for how you market your business as a place to work to each critical segment, you can break through the noise to create understanding. But that will only happen if you approach the marketing of your talent brand with the zeal and precision as you market your brand to customers.

2. You Will Become a Magnet for Talent

From the point of view of the new consumer of work, the marketplace for talent needs magnets—places in which consumers of work simply know they need to work—to simplify the clutter. An easy-to-identify magnet simplifies the search. By knowing what a magnet offers, and what kind of worker a magnet demands, a consumer of work can assess whether he or she will thrive in the environment and can package himself or herself to fit the tailor-made guidelines. That saves the ever-busy consumer some steps, shortens the decision-making process, and keeps the consumer in the driver's seat of the hiring process, which is just where this consumer wants to be. And it makes you the place where everyone wants to work.

3. You Will Increase the Number of People Who Want to Work for You

You will, essentially, increase your supply because you generate demand. The marketplace is so crowded that the old way to find people to work for you—by reacting to a need and filling a job after the fact—is simply too slow and takes too much time. Developing a new talent brand can, however, help you manage how you market for talent the same way you manage other aspects of your business—with a strong focus on supply, demand, and results. Aggressively marketing your talent brand—to create buzz for your business as a magnet—can help you reach formerly untapped sources to deliver candidates to each critical segment.

4. You Will Target the Segments of the Talent Marketplace

This marketplace for talent is defined by its segments rather than viewed in the aggregate. This means that, as business markets the talent brand, it must tailor the brand message for each segment, carefully targeting its message according to the net supply and demand and necessity for each type of worker. Segments will change over time and, just as a business carefully uses market research to "get inside" the heads of customers, it must relentlessly focus on what motivates the new consumer of work. According to Jeanne Mabie of IBM, "We use our brand to reach different segments of potential workers, from those out of school to experienced professionals. The mindsets are very different, such as the active seeker of work compared to the passive seeker, who may not be looking but may be open to hearing about an opportunity. We have to segment our population in many ways, from the kind of work they do to their geographies and constituencies, and once we segment, we tailor our messaging to reach hot skills around the globe, using different media, marketing tools, websites, and search engines. We also rely on employee referrals as we focus on building a global talent network that we can tap into."[2]

5. Your Sourcing Strategy Will Look More Like a Consumer Marketing Strategy

Rather than the current focus to ignite interest from job candidates who are actively looking for new opportunities and qualified passive candidates who are not seeking a new job opportunity to fill current needs, your new strategy will consider broad sourcing and whether to buy, build, or borrow talent from anywhere in the world. A targeted branded marketing campaign aimed at each critical talent segment will provide ways to sequence recruiting through multi-channel marketing. With a talent brand and a multi-channel branded talent marketing approach, you will employ new sourcing strategies for each segment. Each marketing campaign will be targeted to the right audience. You will connect your prospects with the big idea of spending at least part of their careers with your firm as the talent brand starts and develops the relationship with people who fit the profile in your various segments.

6. You Will Be Able to Filter Your Candidates to Meet Your Desired Profiles

The noise of the marketplace can, as well, contribute to misunderstanding of what a business expects from its people. Unlike responding to the specifics of a mundane job posting, a potential candidate responding to the messages of a talent brand will have an opportunity to learn what a company may expect. That's why a talent brand—in its clear messages and subtle references—acts as a filter that can help a potential "pre-qualify" if he or she has the attributes and behaviors to succeed at the company. Further, magnets have a built-in filter, which simplifies for them (as the talent acquirer) the process of acquiring the right talent. The specifics of the work will still have to be explained; the talent brand, however, can help the candidate determine whether it can be "a fit" before moving to the details.

7. You Will Streamline Your Talent Acquisition Programs and Processes

Talent acquisition involves the planning, sourcing, assessing, hiring, and on-boarding of talent; as well as programs to support back-office processing, candidate experience, and the segmented approach. With a laser-like focus on each critical segment and a talent brand that attracts the right candidates, the entire process of bringing new talent on board is well understood and reliable. Processes, roles, decision frameworks, and handoffs are in place. Centralized talent acquisition provides an overall strategic program and shared services to the business—or it is distributed with a shared mindset throughout the enterprise—while hiring leaders work with talent acquisition partners to ensure that the overall candidate experience at various touch points is consistent with the talent and employer brands. Technology supports programs and processes in a seamless and functional way.

8. Your Recruiters Will Finally Move Beyond the Order-Filler Role

You move beyond your competition for talent by removing the requirement to find people, one person at a time—to fill specific requisitions with specific skills and experience criteria, to do specifically described work—to a true search for talented people who fit the profile in specific critical segments and who will take your organization where it needs to go. You fill many critical needs from within your internal talent that you have built over the years. Less critical needs are filled by borrowed (outsourced or contracted) people who sign on to do specific work for specific time periods. The conversation about talent in weekly executive team meetings shifts from number of requisitions filled to a holistic look at "the talent we need versus the talent we have," from "how many people we hired" to "how we are doing at developing and growing the talent we have on board." And discussions around auxiliary talent are strategic rather than about cost-cutting alone. Rather than counting the number of diversity candidates hired, you can highlight the high levels of engagement and success rate of the most talented workers, who are diverse in what they bring to the company. As Paul McKinnon from Citigroup observes, "We try to emphasize diversity in its broadest form: If you have talent, you can succeed here, no matter what your background or where you are from."[3]

9. You Will Give Your Internal Communications New Purpose

In a crowded marketplace, the role of the internal communicator has shifted from corporate journalist to marketing strategist. A communicator must actively support the talent strategy of a business by aggressively taking the talent brand to market, using the fundamentals of the brand to frame messages, define content, and direct the approach. No longer is it acceptable for an internal communicator to simply adapt messages once created for external audiences for internal use. Now the communicator must use the skills of the craft to define a relationship between the company and the worker.

10. You Will Give Your Leadership a New Voice

The confusion of the marketplace for talent demands a new clarity from business leaders on what they need, what they expect, and what they will offer. Gone are the days when workers will take a "wait-and-see" approach to advancement and rewards. Today's worker wants it all spelled out, in black and white, well before accepting the opportunity to work. And once they are on board, they expect to see progress much more frequently than those entering the workforce in the past. This places a new burden—or opportunity—on business leaders to clearly articulate what the business offers, expects, and rewards. It also places pressure on leaders to transparently live the values of the talent brand because, in a marketplace filled with social media, any mishaps will be quickly and widely reported.

11. You Can Redefine Your Relationship with Your Workers

In the marketplace for talent, the eager consumer of work looks for opportunities to build skills and enhance a personal brand rather than the next job. This is a different relationship from the one that business once enjoyed with long-term employees. In today's marketplace, a worker will stay only as long as a company and its opportunities remain relevant. As a result, the business must use its talent brand to creatively articulate and reinforce this relevance in terms that will be meaningful to the consumer of work. And the effort never ends; the work to market the talent brand is constant for a business looking for workers. The talent brand allows an ongoing discussion with workers both as a group and one-on-one about the criticality of their roles now.

12. You Can Establish a Talent Brand Legacy at Your Organization

For you, implementing a successful talent brand can create the legacy you build in your business and your profession. You can become a voice for what the business stands for, can potentially mean, and can consistently achieve. You can serve as a "conscience" for the organization and, at times, as a voice of reason. In this unofficial role you can offer:

- A *reality check:* What is happening on the outside? Talent brand is more than a language; it's a way of thinking, grounded in the reality of a customer making a choice. You can bring this realistic, retail perspective to every discussion.
- A *gut check:* What is happening on the inside? The talent brand must live in an organization's fiber, and part of your role as champion is to keenly observe how deeply the talent brand is felt throughout the organization.
- A *creative check:* What the talent brand can become as you continue to foster its development.

Lessons We Have Learned

So, as you prepare for this role, think over some of the key lessons we've discussed in this book and what we've learned along the way. Over the years we have had numerous opportunities to partner with both the best people and the best places. Here's a quick look at what they taught us.

Talent Will Never Look the Same

It's not just about jobs to fill or people to reach. To brand for talent is to appeal to a worker searching for opportunities in a new marketplace. Gone forever are the days when people simply looked for jobs from classified advertising or waited to be contacted by a head hunter or recruiter. Today and increasingly tomorrow, it will be a free-flowing exchange of work and workers, with the talent brand as corporate centerpiece.

HR Will Never Look the Same

After discovering the power of employer brand and establishing a well-known talent brand at Southwest, we knew that we could never practice HR in the same old ways again. We began to see HR as a business that supports a business. The business of HR is to produce the right talent for the organization, as another partner might produce a component or resource the business uses to produce a product. The right talent drives the value expected by customers, shareholders, executives, and the workforce. The right talent creates the customer experience and delivers on the brand promise.

It's Not Just About the Talent Brand

To produce the right talent, you need a brand. That's true. But you need a mission, values, strategy, priorities, programs and processes, a supply chain, and forecasting and accounting to predict and measure results. You need a product group (HR specialists) that creates the programming to support your employer brand, culture, talent, and business initiatives. And you need sales, distribution, and support systems (HR generalists and recruiters) to partner with the business to deliver the programs and products to bring in, build, or borrow talent resources.

Just Wanting a Talent Brand Is Not Enough

Where the organization is in its life cycle and growth affects whether it is ready for a brand that will stick. Organizational readiness is essential. If an organization has not yet evolved to a point at which it can articulate what it stands for and what it promises to customers and workers, or its talent profile and opportunity, it should not try creating a talent brand. Rather, advertise what you offer now and where it may go in the future. Advertising campaigns can come and go, and it should be understood that the advertising is for specific purposes rather than for longer-term meaningful branding. Southwest was more than twenty years old before it was ready for a consumer and employer brand, and those brands have stood the test of time. But over the early years we used many successful advertisements that built the foundation for later branding initiatives.

Your Organization Can Be a Magnet for Talent

Very few employers are as well-known for their talent as they are for their consumer brand, yet every decade or so, a few companies emerge at the top of the list. Most often it takes years to get there; yet sometimes it just takes a great new idea to disrupt the equilibrium. Creating the legend takes an entire organization focused on talent—not just hiring great talent, but keeping the right talent and getting rid of people as appropriate to make room for new ideas and new ways of doing things. Most companies have mastered the art of bringing people in; fewer have learned the art of developing and grooming talent for future needs.

Final Thoughts

Three years ago, when we finished *Brand from the Inside*, we never imagined we would find ourselves in a marketplace so changed that we would explore the issues a second time. Our work with organizations around the world teaches us, time and time again, (1) that a culture is fragile, (2) a brand can be used in many different ways, (3) people want to believe in where they work, and (4) transparency always provides the best organizational vision. You have your best opportunity to create a talent brand legacy by keeping the focus on people—because they matter and because they vote with their feet every day.

Notes

Chapter One

1. Conversation with Ken Charles, General Mills
2. Conversation with Steve Canale, General Electric
3. Conversation with Janice Ellig, Chadick Ellig
4. Conversation with Jeanie Mabie, IBM
5. Conversation with Jim Citrin, Spencer Stuart
6. Conversation with Robert J. Crowder, Aetna
7. Conversation with Kristen Weirick, Whirlpool Corporation
8. Conversation with Steve Canale, General Electric
9. Charlie Boss, Fresh Mind's Talent Blog, August 19, 2008
10. Conversation with Caroline Emmons, Aetna
11. Joshua Jones, Jobing.com, July 31, 2008
12. Conversation with Steve Canale, General Electric
13. Conversation with Richard Spitz, Korn/Ferry International
14. Conversation with Richard Spitz, Korn/Ferry International
15. Conversation with Jim Bagley, Russell Reynolds
16. Conversation with Jim Bagley, Russell Reynolds
17. Conversation with Janice Ellig, Chadick Ellig
18. Conversation with Janice Ellig, Chadick Ellig

19. Conversation with Amy Giglo, Aflac

20. Conversation with Janice Ellig, Chadick Ellig

21. Rise Smart, *USA Today*, June 5, 2008

22. Conversation with Caroline Emmons, Aetna

23. Joshua Jones, Jobing.com, July 31, 2008

24. Conversation with Jim Bagley, Russell Reynolds

25. Conversation with Ken Charles, General Mills

26. Jennie Flynn Dobies, Yahoo!

27. Jennie Flynn Dobies, Yahoo!

28. Conversation with Janice Ellig, Chadick Ellig

29. Conversation with Kristen Weirick, Whirlpool Corporation

30. Conversation with Jeanie Mabie, IBM

Chapter Two

1. Conversation with Jack Murphy, Dresser Industries (1990)

2. Conversation with Bernard Claude, Total Petrochemicals USA

3. Conversation with Janice Ellig, Chadick Ellig

4. Conversation with Jim Citrin, Spencer Stuart

5. Conversation with Jim Citrin, Spencer Stuart

6. Conversation with Diane Gherson, IBM

7. Conversation with Steve Canale, General Electric

8. Conversation with Janice Ellig, Chadick Ellig

9. Conversation with Susan Johnson, Pitney Bowes

10. Conversation with Robert M. Melançon, Melançon & Company

11. Conversation with Dean Melonas, JetBlue

12. Conversation with Dean Melonas, JetBlue

13. Conversation with Carol Mahoney, Yahoo!

14. Conversation with Ken Charles, General Mills

15. *Taking the Pulse: Talent Branding Survey*, Institute for Corporate Productivity, in conjunction with HR.com, October 2008

16. Conversation with Kristen Weirick, Whirlpool Corporation

17. Conversation with Robert J. Crowder, Aetna

18. Conversation with Caroline Emmons, Aetna

19. Conversation with Steve Canale, General Electric

20. Conversation with Jim Citrin, Spencer Stuart

21. Conversation with Paul McKinnon, Citigroup

22. Conversation with Susan Johnson, Pitney Bowes

23. Conversation with Amy Giglo, Aflac

24. Employment Digest Net, September 8, 2008

25. Jennie Flynn Dobies, Yahoo

26. Conversation with Robert M. Melançon, Melançon and Company

27. Conversation with Amy Giglo, Aflac

28. Conversation with Ted Hoff, IBM

Chapter Three

1. Conversation with Jeff Lamb, Southwest Airlines

2. Conversation with Dean Melonas, JetBlue

3. Conversation with Robert M. Melançon, Melançon and Company

4. Tim Brown, *The Employer Brand, A Strategic Tool to Attract, Recruit, and Retain Talent*, Society for Human Resource Management, April–June 2008

5. Tim Brown, *The Employer Brand, A Strategic Tool to Attract, Recruit, and Retain Talent*, Society for Human Resource Management, April–June 2008

6. www.whirlpool.com

7. Conversation with Diane Gherson, IBM

8. Conversation with Richard Spitz, Korn/Ferry International

9. LinkedIn survey response from Tom Janz, March 9, 2007

10. Conversation with Richard Spitz, Korn/Ferry International

11. LinkedIn survey response from Tom Janz, March 9, 2007

12. Conversation with Kristen Weirick, Whirlpool Corporation

13. Conversation with Jim Bagley, Russell Reynolds

14. www.aetna.com

15. Conversation with Richard Spitz, Korn/Ferry International

16. www.generalmills.com

17. LinkedIn survey response from Peter Nguyen, March 12, 2007

18. www.ebay.com

19. Conversation with Richard Spitz, Korn/Ferry International

20. Conversation with Jeanie Mabie, IBM

21. Conversation with Ted Hoff, IBM

22. www.accenture.com

23. www.ebay.com

24. www.jetblueb.com

25. www.containerstore.com

26. www.heinz.com

27. www.google.com

28. LinkedIn survey response from Chris Warrender, March 9, 2007

29. www.google.com

30. Conversation with Kristen Weirick, Whirlpool Corporation

31. LinkedIn survey response from Peter Nguyen, March 12, 2007

32. Conversation with Paul Rogers, Hewlett-Packard

33. www.amazon.com

34. Conversation with Dean Melonas, JetBlue

35. Conversation with Robert J. Crowder, Aetna

36. www.traderjoes.com

Chapter Four

1. www.americanapparel.com

2. Conversation with Ken Charles, General Mills

3. Conversation with Ken Charles, General Mills

4. http://hrhorizons.nacubo.org/x153.xml)

5. Conversation with Kristen Weirick, Whirlpool Corporation

6. Conversation with Diane Gherson, IBM

7. Observations of Libby Sartain as a member of the Peet's Coffee board

8. www.cocacola.com

9. www.apple.com

10. www.intel.com

11. www.ikea.com

12. www.disney.com

13. www.mcdonalds.com

14. www.nokia.com

15. www.microsoft.com

16. www.ibm.com

17. www.starbucks.com

18. www.americanexpress.com

19. www.hp.com

20. www.honda.com

21. www.oracle.com

22. www.kelloggs.com

23. www.harleydavidson.com

24. www.pepsico.com

25. www.loreal.com

Chapter Five

1. www.target.com

2. www.containerstore.com

3. Conversation with Ken Charles, General Mills

4. Conversation with Dean Melonas, JetBlue

5. www.bestbuy.com

6. Conversation with Carol Mahoney, Yahoo!

7. Conversation with Jeanie Mabie, IBM

8. Conversation with Kristen Weirick, Whirlpool Corporation

9. Conversation with Susan Johnson, Pitney Bowes

10. Conversation with Caroline Emmons, Aetna

11. Conversation with Kristen Weirick, Whirlpool Corporation

12. www.glaceau.com

13. www.accenture.com

14. www.google.com

15. Conversation with Dean Melonas, JetBlue

16. Conversation with Ken Charles, General Mills

17. Conversation with Dean Melonas, JetBlue

18. Conversation with Kristen Weirick, Whirlpool Corporation

19. Conversation with Ken Charles, General Mills

20. Conversation with Jeff Lamb, Southwest Airlines

Chapter Six

1. www.google.com

2. Conversation with Robert J. Crowder, Aetna

3. Conversation with Jeff Lamb, Southwest Airlines

4. Conversation with Kristen Weirick, Whirlpool Corporation

5. Conversation with Jeff Lamb, Southwest Airlines

6. Conversation with Ken Charles, General Mills

7. Conversation with Dean Melonas, JetBlue

8. Conversation with Amy Giglio, Aflac

9. Conversation with Kristen Weirick, Whirlpool Corporation

10. Conversation with Robert J. Crowder, Aetna

11. Conversation with Paul McKinnon, Citigroup

12. Conversation with Jeanie Mabie, IBM

13. Conversation with Dave Ulrich and Norm Smallwood

14. Conversation with Carol Mahoney, Yahoo!

Chapter Seven

1. Conversation with Carol Mahoney, Yahoo!

2. Conversation with Carol Mahoney, Yahoo!

3. Conversation with Kristen Weirick, Whirlpool Corporation

4. *Wikinomics: How Mass Collaboration Changes Everything*, by Don Tapscott and Anthony D. Williams

5. Conversation with Amy Giglio, Aflac

6. Conversation with Steve Canale, General Electric

7. Conversation with Diane Gherson, IBM

8. Donald E. Breckenridge, Jr., *The Fordyce Letter*, April 4, 2008

9. Conversation with Jeff Lamb, Southwest Airlines

10. Conversation with Jeanie Mabie, IBM

11. Conversation with Ken Charles, General Mills

12. Conversation with Ken Charles, General Mills

13. Conversation with Jeanie Mabie, IBM

14. Conversation with Kristen Weirick, Whirlpool Corporation

Chapter Eight

1. Tim Brown, *The Employer Brand: A Strategic Tool to Attract, Recruit, and Retain Talent*, Society for Human Resource Management, April–June 2008

2. Conversation with Jeanie Mabie, IBM

3. Conversation with Paul McKinnon, Citigroup

Acknowledgments

The collaborative experience to put ideas into a book involves many people.

We are very grateful to those who helped us shape our ideas, substantiate our point of view, and bring our thinking to life with their examples—from the initial HR experts who helped us frame the discussion to the representatives of some of the world's leading brands who openly shared their thoughts and their work.

A big thanks to Kurt Basler at LyondellBasell, Carolyn Sanders at Total Petrochemicals USA, Leon Potgeiter at American Express and Brooke Brownlow at H-E-B who, through how they work and challenge and think, help open our minds to new ways to look at the potential of a talent brand.

A special acknowledgment to IC4P for contributing research—and to Yahoo! HotJobs for contributing thoughts and research. And to Suzanne and Chris Salvo for the great photograph for the jacket.

An essential recognition goes to the places we work, and have worked, and the companies we work for, and have worked for—for all that we have learned along the way from people who supported and challenged and engaged us.

A note of deep gratitude to a great writer from Generation Y, Jonathan Schumann, who kept us connected to his generation and made many suggestions that strengthened the book.

A special message to thank each other. Almost 20 years ago, we began a journey to help organizations develop corporate reputations as great places to work. Almost five years ago, we began to document what we achieved, learned, hoped and created. Today, we look back on a most rewarding collaboration that brings out the best in each other and brings the best to the places where we work. So, Mark thanks Libby, and Libby thanks Mark.

And thank you for reading our books.

Index

Numbers

2008 financial crash, 46

A

Accenture, 'best fit'
    questionnaire, 154
accountability, of leadership,
    190
actions
    as basis of talent marketing,
        139–140
    leadership, 194–198
    speaking louder than words,
        190
advertising
    brand recognition and,
        145–146
    creating demand by,
        143–144
    Madison Avenue and, 207
    marketing and, 41
    moving online, 61–62
    not getting stuck in
        traditional methods, 100
    preventive branding and,
        131
Aetna
    college recruiting strategy,
        59–60
    consumers of work
        preference for online job
        searches, 28
    culture and brand
        relationship, 178
    expectations and standards
        of new worker and, 17
    Find a Career web page, 152
    leadership rating system, 193
    parental involvement with
        new workers and, 20–21
    reputation as benefit in
        talent marketplace, 59
    welcome message to
        potential workers, 86

welcoming nature of talent
    brand, 101
Aflac
    expectations regarding what
        company can do for
        applicants, 26
    grooming leaders at, 190
    recruitment by, 64
    social networking as means
        of maintaining applicant
        relationships, 63
    uses of social media, 211
Amazon
    talent branding efforts, 100
    Tell Us Your Story
        campaign, 223
American Apparel, 111
American Express, value
        basis of talent marketing,
        135
Apple, marketing approach,
        132
applicants
    recruitment expectations,
        25–26
    social networking as means
        of maintaining relationship
        with, 63
application process, on careers
        site, 155
aspiration, as basis of talent
        marketing, 132–134
attention span, of new
        consumers of work, 22
auditing talent brand
        development, 182–183
authenticity
    brand belief and, 151
    creativity and engagement
        resulting from, 93
    expectations of consumers of
        work regarding, 31–34
    leadership and, 186
    talent brand marketing and,
        86–87

B

Baby Boomers
    Generation Y and, 3
    retirement creating demand
        for new workers, 39
    sensibilities of, 41–42
    workforce exceeding supply
        during Baby Boomer era, 40
background information,
    checking online, 22
Bagley, Jim
    on connectedness of new
        consumer of work, 29
    on importance of brand on
        resumes, 23
    on importance of employer
        brand, 86
Barrett, Colleen, 185
behaviors
    brand behavior, 191
    leadership behavior,
        190–192
beliefs
    as basis of talent marketing,
        137–138
    believability of brand. see
        brand belief
"best buy" lesson, retail
        marketplace, 18
Best Buy, role of brand belief in
        attracting talent, 149
best places to work lists
    brand recognition and, 147
    not substitute for talent
        brand, 99
    recruitment strategies and,
        60
    Southwest Airlines on, 73
best practices, for building
        social networks, 228
beyond day one, 168–171
"big idea"
    Madison Avenue and, 207
    story communicating, 92–94

"big idea" (*Continued*)
  welcoming events
    celebrating, 200
blogs/blogosphere
  global energy company's
    approach to, 216–217
  gossip regarding corporate
    leaders, 195–196
  governance of, 221
  impact of critical blogs on
    corporations, 227
  replacing chat rooms, 219
  social media strategy and,
    220–221
  transparency and, 208
blogspot, 221
Bluechipexpert.com, 123
Boudreau, John, 114–115
BountyJobs.com, 123
brand
  attracting top talent via, 56
  awareness of new worker
    regarding, 15
  categories of, 140–141
  fact-based communication
    replaced by branding, 105
  globalization and, 57–59
  importance on resumes, 23,
    45
  localization of brand
    messages, 127–128
  as means of pre-selling
    candidates, 74
  online access to, 57–58
  segmentation, 84
  social media for building
    brand relationships,
    229–230
  time required to build, 58–59
  types of, 2–3, 79–80
  unified approach to, 113
brand behaviors, 191
brand belief, 148–157
  careers site for building,
    150–157
  do's/dont's, 149–150
  overview of, 148–149
brand for talent. *see* talent
  brand
Brand from the Inside, 2
brand intensity, 122–126
brand loyalty
  in good and bad times, 2
  overview of, 6–8
brand memory, 163–171
  beyond day one, 168–171
  do's/dont's, 164–165
  marketing for talent and, 53
  on-boarding experience and,
    166–168
  overview of, 163–164
  re-recruiting and, 165–166

brand personalization, 157–163
  do's/dont's, 158–159
  overview of, 157–158
  talent concierge for,
    159–163
brand pressure
  high brand pressure/high
    worker demand, 127
  high brand pressure/low
    worker demand, 128–129
  low brand pressure/high
    worker demand, 129–130
  low brand pressure/low
    worker demand, 130
  overview of, 126–127
brand recognition, 145–147
brand segmentation. *see*
  segmentation
buzz, talent brand and, 87

C

call to action, talent brand as,
    98–101
Canale, Steve
  on college recruiting
    strategy, 60
  on competing in the talent
    marketplace, 47
  on demographics and
    expectations of current
    workforce, 21
  on email as recruitment
    vehicle, 14
  on social media, 212
  on worker expectations, 20
candidate expectations section,
    of careers site, 155–156
candidates
  accepting the "no" decision
    of, 162–163
  assessing, 125
  checking back with
    candidates who turned
    down offers, 163
  description of Google
    experience, 155–156
  documentation provided to,
    162
  expectations section of
    careers site, 155
  face-to-face experience of,
    162
  filtering to meet desired
    profiles, 238–239
  following up with, 160–161
  personal approach to, 160
  pre-selling, 74
  quality expectations of, 52
  reaching prospective, 56
career section, of careers site,
    154–155

CareerBuilder job board, 62
careers
  Baby Boomers orientation
    towards stability, 40
  GE reputation for career
    building, 45
  planning to support brand,
    170
  work experience vs. job, 21
careers site
  candidate expectations
    section, 155–156
  career section, 154–155
  company information
    section, 153–154
  as face of talent brand,
    150–153
  Pitney Bowes example,
    151–152
  talent brand section, 153
  work application section,
    155
  work availability section, 154
  worker life
    section, 156–157
  Yahoo! example, 153
CEOs
  actions of, 196
  authenticity of, 186
  difficulty finding/engaging
    workers, 37–38
  role in changing
    organization's talent brand,
    39
Charles, Ken
  on attracting top talent, 56
  on being in the channels the
    new generation
    frequents, 14
  on brand belief, 148
  on brand personalization,
    158
  on development of leaders,
    187
  on recruitment culture, 164
  on social media, 222–223
  on social networking, 29
  on unified branding, 113
  on YouTube, 223–224
chat rooms
  blogs replacing, 219
  Yahoo! and, 208
Citigroup
  actions of leaders, 194
  diversity at, 240
  targeting talent in global
    marketplace, 61
Citrin, Jim
  on company reputation for
    handling talent, 45
  on employer brand, 17, 60
  on executive search, 44

clarity
　of brand message, 87
　of company story, 92–94
　demanded of leadership, 240
　of job offers, 162
　as key in responding to
　　online gossip, 227
classified ads, traditional job
　hunting and, 40
Claude, Bernard, 38
closing process, in recruitment,
　161
Coca-Cola, 131
collaboration
　social media and, 211–213
　Web 2.0 and, 210
college graduates
　attracting talent, 59–60
　recruiting, 152
commitment to talent brand
　lasting nature of, 101–105
　organizations making,
　　99–100
　talent brand as statement of
　　commitment, 110
communication
　fact-based communication
　　replaced by branding, 105
　internal, 240
　by leadership, 188–190
　uncontrolled in era of social
　　media, 217
　by workers, 204–205
companies. see organizations
company information section,
　of careers site, 153–154
competencies, leadership,
　192–194
competition for talent
　among top corporations, 115
　brand pressure and, 126
　checking back on candidates
　　who turned down job
　　offers, 163
　comparison with
　　competitors, 119–121
　danger of ignoring
　　competitors, 129
　global marketplace and,
　　47–48, 50, 61
　reputation as benefit in, 59
　segmentation and, 56–57
conferences, 123
connection-orientation
　how workers connect, 123
　new consumer of work and,
　　28–31
consumer brand, 179
consumers
　brand awareness of, 15
　habits of, 17–18
consumers of work

brand loyalty and, 7
brand-saviness of, 6
changes in worker
　expectations and, 4–5
connection-orientation of,
　28–31
demographics and, 14
description of new consumer,
　13
employees compared with,
　104
engagement of, 47
impatience as quality of, 24
looking for work experience
　not job, 21
self-centeredness of, 18
targeting segments of,
　110–111
Container Store, 146–147
coolness factor
　employer brand and, 17
　Yahoo! and, 115
core work, 117
corporate culture
　adjusting, 191
　brand and, 178–182
　creating high performance
　　culture, 100
　Google's emphasis on, 97,
　　177
　HR programs and, 201–204
　leadership actions/behaviors
　　and, 184–185
　leadership not controlling,
　　183–184
　marketing to attract workers,
　　71–72
　mixture of ingredients in,
　　177
　nurtured by talent brand,
　　91–92
　Southwest Airlines focus on,
　　185–186
　talent brand and, 180–184
　worker engagement and, 41
corporations. see organizations
cost reductions, 2008 financial
　crash and, 46
creative check, for talent
　brand, 242
creativity
　resulting from authenticity,
　　93
　uses of social media and, 230
　Yahoo! careers site organized
　　by creative and technical
　　needs, 119
critical for operations,
　prioritizing by, 116
Crowder, Robert J.
　on culture, 178–182
　on employer brand, 101

on leadership rating system,
　193
on talent marketplace, 59
on worker expectations and
　standards, 17
culture. see corporate culture
customer brand, 2, 79–80
customers, keeping track of
　wants and needs of, 124
cyberspace, 61–64
　advertising for talent moving
　　online, 61–62
　social networking as
　　channels for sharing work
　　experience, 62–64
cybersurfers, 87

D

debt, college expenses and, 25
decision making,
　connection-orientation of
　　new consumer and, 30
defamer, 226
demand. see supply and
　demand
demographics
　consumers of work and, 14
　of current workforce, 20–21
　as perspective on employer
　　brand, 229
　segmentation and, 114
development, filling talent
　pipeline, 83
differentiation. see also
　segmentation
　of brand message, 94–96
　from competition, 120
　culture as basis of, 185
　finding quality talent by, 58
　new marketplace requiring,
　　236
　reaching workers and, 54
　Southwest Airlines focus on,
　　180
　value proposition as basis of,
　　91
digital technology, 3. see also
　technology
Disney, 133
documentation, providing to
　work candidates, 162
Doubletree Hotels, 38
Dresser Industries, 38

E

eBay
　talent brand message, 91
　work environment of, 48–49
economic environment, brand
　loyalty and, 2

Ellig, Janice
   on applicant expectations,
      26
   on brand awareness of new
      worker, 15
   on imbalance created by
      search for talent, 39
   on impact of negative press,
      32
   on short term outlook of
      workers, 23
   on talent marketplace, 47
email, as recruitment vehicle,
      14
Emmons, Caroline
   on Aetna's Find a Career
      web page, 152
   on college recruitment
      strategy, 59–60
   on online job searches, 28
   on parental involvement
      with new workers, 20–21
emotional dimension
   branding and, 207
   communication with
      workers, 205
   re-recruiting and, 168
employees. see also workers
   educating potential, 16–17
   having necessary resources,
      203
   referral programs, 123
   social media changing
      communication patterns of,
      209
   thinking of as consumers,
      104
employer brand
   Aetna example, 101
   attracting entry-level
      workers, 71–72
   coolness factor, 17
   corporate reputation and, 53
   demographic and functional
      perspectives of, 229
   as factor in worker
      engagement, 57
   filling talent pipeline and, 52
   as filter for strategic
      planning, 60
   marketing employer brand
      vs. marketing talent brand,
      111–112
   not enough as basis for
      marketing, 109
   not longer enough in finding
      talent, 40
   organizational understanding
      of, 61
   reasons for developing, 88
   reasons for engaging, 96

rebranding effort of IBM,
      78–79
relevance to new generation
      of workers, 8
SHRM survey regarding,
      77–78
Southwest Airlines example,
      72
as statement of purpose, 97
talent brand compared with,
      75, 79, 84–86
talent brand extending,
      74–76
time required to build, 58–59
types of brands, 2–3, 79–80
value proposition and, 2,
      76–77
employers
   social networking for
      checking out, 118
   worker/candidate wariness
      regarding, 209
employment, portability of, 45
endorsements
   brand recognition and, 147
   on LinkedIn, 226
energy, talent brand and, 87
engagement
   attendance vs., 41
   authenticity and, 93
   of consumers of work, 24–27,
      47
   difficulty of finding/engaging
      workers, 37–39
   employer brand as factor in,
      57
   online, 151
   reasons for, 96–98
   re-recruiting and, 169
   talent brand for securing and
      engaging workers, 9
environment, examples of
      corporate work
      environments, 48–49
events, celebrating workers,
      200–201
excellence, worker viewpoint
      regarding, 25–27
ExecuNet, 63
executive search, 44
expectations
   of applicants during
      recruitment process, 25
   authenticity as, 31–34
   brand carrying set of, 191
   candidate expectations
      section of careers site,
      155–156
   changes in worker
      expectations, 4–5
   Generation Y, 3–4, 20–21
   quality as, 52

what's in it for me, 5, 26
workers, 17, 20–21
work/life balance as, 27,
      127–128
experience. see worker
      experience

F

Facebook
   Aflac uses of, 211
   companies setting up
      Facebook page, 214
   corporate uses of social
      media, 222–223
   GE's uses of, 212
   maintaining and updating
      resume on, 17
   OfficeBook application, 62
   Pitney Bowes uses of, 63
   as standard for online
      connection, 220
face-to-face experience
   personalization and, 158, 162
   worker participation in
      talent brand, 199–200
false security, social media and,
      216–217
Fast Company, 147
Find a Career web page, Aetna,
      152
fitting in, on-boarding
      experience and, 168
follow up, with potential
      candidates, 160–161
Forbes, 147
Fortune, 147
functional dimension
   perspectives of employer
      brand, 229
   segmentation by, 115–116

G

game changing work, 117
Gawker, 226
GE. see General Electric (GE)
General Electric (GE)
   career building reputation of,
      45
   college recruiting strategy at,
      60
   competing in the global
      talent marketplace, 47
   demographics and
      expectations of current
      workforce, 20–21
   email as recruitment vehicle,
      14
   talent acquisition, 20
   uses of social media, 212
General Mills

attracting top talent, 56
being in the channels the
   new generation frequents,
   14
energy in talent brand
   message, 88
importance of brand belief
   at, 148
importance of brand
   personalization at, 158
leadership development,
   186–187
recruitment culture at, 164
social media uses at, 222–223
unified brand approach at,
   113
YouTube uses at, 223–224
Generation X, 20
Generation Y
as brand-conscious shoppers,
   4
demographics of consumers
   of work, 14
expectations, 3–4, 20–21
opportunity-orientation of,
   15
reaching prospective
   candidates, 56
generational change
being in the channels the
   new generation frequents,
   56
expectations of Generation
   Y, 3–4
geographic boundaries. see also
   globalization
no longer a limit on supply of
   talent, 54
traditional hiring territories
   vs. global marketplace, 5
Gherson, Diane
on changes in competition,
   119
on IBM rebranding itself,
   78–79
on recruitment, 46
on social networking,
   218–219
Giglio, Amy
on applicant expectations,
   26
on leadership, 190
on recruitment, 64
on social media, 211
on social networking, 63
Glaceau, 153
glassdoor.com, 62, 125
global community, social media
   and, 213–214
global marketplace. see also
   marketplace

competition for talent and,
   47–48, 61
freedom of competition in,
   50
globalization
adapting global message to
   local challenges, 65
brand and, 57–59
communication and, 208
social media and, 212, 218
values and, 93
Google
candidate experience at,
   155–156
competition for talent, 115
culture at, 177
culture in talent branding
   message, 97
work environment of, 48–49
YouTube now part of, 223
gossip
sources of business gossip,
   226
threats posed by social
   media, 215
gurus, Yahoo!, 81
gut check, for talent brand, 242

H

habits, of new consumers,
   17–18
Harley-Davidson, 138
Heinz, 96
Help Desk, employee resources,
   203
Hewlett Packard, 135
high brand pressure
action as basis of talent
   marketing, 140
aspiration as basis of talent
   marketing, 133
beliefs as basis of talent
   marketing, 137
brand recognition and, 145
experience as basis of talent
   marketing, 138
high worker demand, 127
low worker demand,
   128–129
timing as basis of talent
   marketing, 136
value as basis of talent
   marketing, 135
high worker demand
high brand pressure, 127
low brand pressure, 129–130
high-intensity approach, to
   marketing brand, 122
Hoff, Ted
on adapting global message
   to local challenges, 65

on values jam session, 93
Honda, 135
honesty, brand belief and. see
   authenticity
howsthatjob.com, 125
HR. see human resources (HR)
human resources (HR)
changes in role of, 64–66,
   243
creating high performance
   culture, 100
identifying programs and
   services with cultural
   interdependencies,
   202–203
influence on worker
   experience, 201
tools and resources of,
   203–204
viewing social media as
   threat, 217
hurdle analogy from track. see
   talent brand hurdles

I

IBM
aspiration as basis of talent
   marketing, 133
authenticity at, 33
competition for talent, 119
educating potential
   employees, 16–17
global message adapted to
   local challenges, 65
leadership actions supporting
   brand, 195
rebranding effort of, 78–79
search engine used for
   finding talent, 225
segmented approached to
   finding workers, 237
shift from production to
   consulting, 46–47
social media uses at, 222
social networking feedback,
   listening to, 218–219
storytelling as means of
   engagement, 151
values as basis of talent
   branding, 93
values jam session, 93
IKEA, 133
implementation, of talent
   brand, 143–144
information, social media
   shifting power to people,
   209
input orientation, work vs. jobs
   and, 50
integrity, 215. see also
   authenticity

Intel, 133
interactivity
  career sites and, 154
  online engagement, 151
internal communication
  purpose of, 240
  workers engaging in,
    204–205
Internet, job hunting via, 62
investment work, prioritizing
    work based on value added,
    117
iPods
  connection-orientation of
    new consumer and, 28
  memorable brands, 143

J

Janz, Tom
  on optimal brand messaging
    to attract right talent, 81
  on selectivity in attracting
    top talent, 83
JetBlue
  advertising methods, 100
  communication role of
    leaders, 188–189
  employer brand, 74
  importance of brand belief
    at, 148
  importance of corporate
    reputation, 53
  picture of worker life on
    career site, 156
  recruitment area at, 159
job hunting
  consumers of work
    preferences, 28
  as never ending process, 17,
    22
  online, 7–8, 62
  online job boards, 28, 224
  social media and, 64
job offers
  accepting the "no" decision
    of a candidate, 162–163
  checking back on candidates
    who turned down, 163
  clarity of, 162
  closing process and, 161
jobs
  consumers of work looking
    for work experience not
    job, 21
  evaluating demand by
    segments, 118–119
  focusing on work instead of
    jobs, 49–50, 103
  market for jobs compared
    with market for talent,
    50–51

meeting demand for work vs.
    identifying job candidates,
    81
  online reviews, 125
Jobvite.com, 123
Johnson, Susan
  on Pitney Bowes careers
    website, 151–152
  on social networking, 63
  on talent market, 48
jossup, 226
just-in-time management, of
    worker pipelines, 51

K

Kelleher, Herb
  on ability to find/engage
    workers, 38
  on assessing desired qualities
    in job candidates, 125
  on Southwest Airlines, 73
Kelleher, Rick, 38
Kellogg's, 137
Kleenex, 143
Korn/Ferry International
  challenging careers, 21
  communication/demonstration
    of special values, 92–94
  demand for work vs.
    identifying job candidates,
    81
  importance of authenticity,
    87
Kotter, John P., 179

L

labor markets, freedom in, 46
Lamb, Jeff
  on culture as a differentiator,
    185
  on differentiation, 180
  on employer brand, 72
  on on-boarding, 164
  on uses of social media, 222
Lawless, Marcy, 125
leadership
  accountability for finding
    talent, 38
  actions, 194–198
  behaviors, 190–192
  challenges of 1970s and
    1980s, 44
  competencies, 192–194
  conduct creating a cultural
    symbol, 184–185
  as demonstration, 188
  developing at General Mills,
    186–187
  impact on talent brand,
    196–197

messaging role, 188–190
  new voice for, 240–241
  not able to control culture,
    183–184
  role in sustaining talent
    brand, 182
  sending signals about what
    matters, 186
leadership toolkit, Yahoo!,
    197–198
legacy, talent brand
  building, 235
  establishing, 241–242
life expectations. *see also*
    work/life balance
  worker life section of careers
    site, 156–157
  work/life balance as,
    127–128
LinkedIn
  Aflac uses of, 211
  corporate uses of social
    media, 222
  endorsements on, 226
  resumes on, 17
  as social networking tool, 63,
    214
  working professionals as
    focus of, 222
localization
  adapting global message to
    local challenges, 65
  of brand messages, 127–128
  relevance of values and, 93
logistics, of candidate
    recruitment agenda, 160
L'Oréal, 140
low brand pressure
  action as basis of talent
    marketing, 140
  aspiration as basis of talent
    marketing, 133
  beliefs as basis of talent
    marketing, 137
  brand recognition and, 145
  experience as basis of talent
    marketing, 138
  high worker demand,
    129–130
  low worker demand, 130
  timing as basis of talent
    marketing, 136
  value as basis of talent
    marketing, 135
low worker demand
  high brand pressure,
    128–129
  low brand pressure, 130
low-intensity approach, to
    marketing brand, 122
loyalty, 6. *see also* brand loyalty

M

Mabie, Jeanie
  on avoiding "the plastic
    fantastic", 33
  on educating potential
    employees, 16–17
  on job searches, 225
  on leadership actions
    supporting brand, 195
  on segmented approached to
    finding workers, 237
  on storytelling as means of
    engagement, 151
  on talent brand being based
    on values, 93
  on uses of social media, 222
Madison Avenue, 207
magnet for talent
  becoming, 236, 244
  being known in industry as, 1
  making talent as famous as
    brand, 13
  overview of, 90–92
  segmentation approach and,
    121
  Southwest Airlines as, 71, 73
Mahoney, Carol
  on blogs, 208
  on finding talent for specific
    segments, 54
  on online engagement of
    candidates, 151
  on recruitment marketing
    campaign, 205
  on wariness regarding
    employers, 209
Main Street, changes in, 57
marketing
  action as basis of talent
    marketing, 139–140
  advertising and, 41
  aspiration as basis of talent
    marketing, 132–134
  beliefs as basis of talent
    marketing, 137–138
  brand intensity and,
    122–126
  culture as means of
    attracting workers, 71–72
  demand created by, 143–144
  vs. describing, 104
  experience as basis of talent
    marketing, 138–139
  HR departments and, 65
  never stopping, 163
  overcoming resistance, 121
  preparing for, 131–132
  preventive branding and,
    131
  recruitment campaign, 205
  segmentation and, 110–112

social media plan, 230
  for talent, 53
  testing, 99
  timing as basis of talent
    marketing, 136–137
  value as basis of talent
    marketing, 134–136
marketplace. *see also* global
    marketplace; talent
    marketplace
  company reputation as
    benefit, 59
  competing in, 47–48
  freedom in labor market, 46
  freedom of competition in,
    50
  Main Street no longer focus
    of, 57
  supply and demand in, 7–8,
    55–56
  for talent currently, 236
  for talent in 1970s and
    1980s, 45
  talent marketplace and, 5
  targeting segments of,
    237–238
Mary Kay Cosmetics, Inc., 179
McDonald's
  aspiration as basis of talent
    marketing, 133
  competition for talent, 59
McFarland, Kristi, 201–202
McKinnon, Paul
  on diversity at Citigroup, 240
  on global marketplace, 61
  on leadership actions, 194
media. *see also* social media
  ability to control traditional,
    210
  not sole means for
    marketing, 103
Melançon, Robert M.
  on branding as means of
    pre-selling candidates, 74
  on demand for top quality
    candidates, 52
  on HR, 64
Melançon & Company, 52
Melonas, Dean
  on advertising methods, 100
  on corporate reputation, 53
  on employer brand, 74
  on importance of brand
    belief, 148
  on leadership messaging,
    188–189
  on personalization, 159–160
  on worker life at JetBlue, 156
memorability of brand. *see*
  brand memory
Microsoft

aspiration as basis of talent
    marketing, 133
  competition for talent, 115
mission statement (Southwest
    Airlines), 73
mobility
  of new workforce, 22–24
  portability of employment
    and, 45
"mom-and-pop" stores, 57
monitoring social networks,
    226–227
Monster job board, 62
Murphy, Jack, 38
MyBlogLog, 221
MySpace, 221

N

National Association of
    Colleges and Employers
    (NACE), 60
networks, values of, 217. *see
    also* social networking
Nguyen, Peter
  on "best places to work" lists,
    99
  on not creating talent brand
    prematurely, 89
Nokia, 133

O

off-boarding with class,
    170–171
OfficeBook application,
    Facebook, 62
offshore workers, 46
on-boarding experience,
    166–168
online experience
  collaboration and, 211
  getting scoop on
    companies/work
    opportunities before
    applying, 16
  job hunting, 7–8, 28
  necessity of online
    engagement for
    corporations, 151
  resumes, 125
online job boards
  changing how people look
    for work, 62
  social media strategy and,
    224–225
opportunity
  applicant expectations
    regarding, 26
  loyalty and, 6
  opportunity-orientation of
    Generation Y, 15

opportunity (*Continued*)
  talent freedom creating,
    45–46
  worker expectations and, 20
Oracle, 136–137
O'Reilly, Charles A., 179
organizations
  attracting talent, 1
  authenticity in delivery of
    promises, 86–87
  clarity of company story,
    92–94
  commitment to talent brand,
    99–100
  corporate reputation and the
    web, 16
  difficulty of finding/engaging
    workers, 37–39
  impact of negative press on,
    32
  reputation as benefit in
    talent marketplace, 59
  responding to social media
    attack, 213–214
  shifting from employer brand
    to talent brand, 78
  trends in 1970s and 1980s,
    43
  understanding what
    employer brand is, 61
  websites protecting online
    reputation, 64
output orientation, work vs.
  jobs and, 50
outsourcing
  freedom in labor markets
    and, 46
  portability of employment
    and, 45

P

paperwork, on-boarding
  experience and, 167
parental involvement
  as coaches for younger
    workers, 30
  Generation Y and, 20
  worker expectations
    resulting from, 4
PDAs, 28
Peet's Coffee, 201–202
PepsiCo
  experience as basis of talent
    marketing, 139
  memorable brands, 143
performance management,
  beyond day one, 169–170
personalities, leadership, 190
personalization of approach to
  candidates
  beyond day one, 169

face-to-face experience and,
    158, 162
personalization of brand. *see*
  brand personalization
Pfeffer, Jeffrey, 179
pipeline of workers, 51–55
  employer brand as means of
    filling, 52
  vs. filling jobs, 55
  geography no longer a limit
    on supply, 54
  overview of, 51
  planning to meet demand for
    workers, 52
  re-recruiting current
    employees, 54
  talent brand as means of
    filling, 82–84
Pitney Bowes
  careers website, 151–152
  social networking at, 63
  talent market and, 48
pivot points/pivotal talent,
  identifying in segmented
    approach, 114–115
pivotal work, prioritization as
  basis of segmented
    approach, 117
Plaxo, 17
portability
  of employment, 45
  of new workforce, 22–24
pre-qualifying candidates,
  238–239
press, impact of negative, 32
preventive branding, 131
prioritization, segmentation
  based on, 116–118
privacy, transparency vs., 29
productivity, financial crisis
  and, 46
profiling consumers of work, 19

Q

quality, marketing for talent
  and, 53
quality circles, 41

R

rating system, for leadership,
  193
reality check, for talent brand,
  242
recognition, of worker
  contribution, 201
recruitment
  closing process, 161
  college graduates, 59–60,
    152
  engaging applicants, 25

filling talent pipeline, 83
  at General Mills, 164
  at IBM, 46
  at JetBlue, 159–160
  marketing campaign for, 205
  moving beyond order-filling
    role, 239–240
  re-recruiting and, 54,
    165–166, 168–169
  role of HR department, 64
  search engines as tool in, 63
  social networking and, 211
  technological tools for, 14
recruitment concierge, 160
references, checking online, 22
referrals
  employee referral programs,
    123
  marketing for talent and, 103
  as means of filling talent
    pipeline, 83–84
relationships
  caution regarding using
    technology for building,
    209
  developing brand
    relationships via social
    media, 229
  as means of filling talent
    pipeline, 83–84
  online world redefining, 29
  redefining worker
    relationships, 241
  vs. transactions, 104–105
relevance, personalization and,
  157
reputation, corporate
  attracting entry-level
    workers, 71–72
  as benefit in talent
    marketplace, 59
  differentiating from
    competition, 120
  for handling talent, 45
  impact of negative press on,
    32
  importance of maintaining,
    53
  magnets for talent and, 121
  recruitment strategies and,
    60
  social media and, 227
  websites protecting, 64
ReputationDefender.com, 64
re-recruiting. *see also*
    recruitment
  beyond day one, 168–169
  filling talent pipeline, 83
  as ongoing process from day
    one, 165–166
research, social networking
    and, 229

resumes
  importance of brands on, 23, 45
  importance of moves on, 22–24
  online, 125
  profiles on social network sites as supplement to, 22
  sites for maintaining and updating, 17
  retail marketplace, "best buy" lesson, 18
Risesmart.com, 224
Rogers, Paul, 100
rumors, threats posed by social media, 215
Russell Reynolds, 23

S

salary, work/life balance and, 27
Sartain, Libby, 1
Schmidt, Eric, 177
Schumann, Mark, 1
search engines
  executive recruiters use of, 63
  finding talent, 225
  monitoring social networks, 226–227
security
  Baby Boomers orientation to, 41–42
  social media and false security, 216–217
segmentation
  action as basis of talent marketing, 139–140
  addressing brand segmentation, 84
  aspiration as basis of talent marketing, 132–134
  beliefs as basis of talent marketing, 137–138
  brand intensity and, 122–126
  brand pressure and, 126–130
  brand segmentation, 84
  branding for talent and, 110
  competition for talent and, 56–57
  differentiated approach to worker segments, 19–20, 54
  differentiating from competition, 119–120
  difficulty of finding talent for specific segments, 54
  evaluating demand by segments, 118–119
  experience as basis of talent marketing, 138–139

how to segment talent, 113–116
  identifying segments, 120–121
  as key in talent brand, 80
  marketing and, 110–112
  preparing to market and, 131–132
  prioritization as basis of, 116–118
  of talent marketplace, 237–238
  timing as basis of talent marketing, 136–137
  value as basis of talent marketing, 134–136
  value proposition converted into targeted message, 91
self selection, by workers, 125
self-assessment questionnaires, 154
self-centeredness, of new consumers of work, 18
seminars, 123
service award program, Yahoo!, 139
SHRM (Society of Human Resource Management), 77
Sitereader, 221
Smallwood, Nomr, 197
smart phones, 28
social media, 208–231
  building social networks, 228
  collaboration and, 211–213
  communicating with workers and, 5–6
  connection-orientation of new consumer and, 28–29
  corporate uses of, 222–223
  developing brand relationships, 229–230
  false security and, 216–217
  global community and, 213–214
  impact on talent brand, 225–226
  job hunting and, 64
  marketing plan for, 230
  monitoring social networks, 226–227
  overview of, 208–211
  rumors and, 215
  unchecked sources and, 214–215
  worker preferences and, 20
social media strategy
  acknowledging that it is not going away, 218
  acknowledging what is and is not, 218–219
  blogosphere and, 220–221
  Facebook as tool of, 220

getting familiar with, 219
  online job boards, 224–225
  overview of, 217
  social networking sites, 221–223
  website for, 219–220
  YouTube, 223–224
social networking
  benefits of listening to, 218–219
  building social networks, 228
  as channel for sharing work experience, 62–64
  checking out potential employers via, 118
  employee referral programs and, 123
  extent of, 29–30
  job hunting via, 28–29
  LinkedIn as tool for, 214
  monitoring social networks, 226–227
  profiles on social network sites as supplement to resume, 22
  sites, 221–223
  talent brand marketing and, 149
  technology of information exchange and, 5
  transparency and, 208
  workers participation in, 125
social responsibility, authenticity at Whirlpool, 32
Society of Human Resource Management (SHRM), 77
sourcing strategy, 238
Southwest Airlines
  assessing job candidates, 125
  attracting entry-level workers, 71–72
  case study, 179
  difficulty finding/engaging workers, 38
  employer brand at, 2, 72
  focus on corporate culture, 185–186
  focus on differentiation, 180
  focus on employee experience, 45
  leadership of, 235
  meeting year 2000 labor shortage, 89–90
  on-boarding experience, 164
  online tips on how to pass pilot interview process, 213
  social media uses at, 222
  waiting room at, 160
specialization, executive search in age of, 44

Spitz, Richard
  on authenticity, 87
  on communica-
    tion/demonstration of
    special values, 93
  on meeting demand for work
    vs. identifying job
    candidates, 81
  on mobility of new
    workforce, 22
  on need for challenge in
    careers, 21–22
  on rehiring process, 83
stability, Baby Boomers
  orientation towards, 40
standards, worker, 17
Starbucks
  competition for talent, 59
  value as basis of talent
    marketing, 135
statement of commitment, 110
statement of purpose, employer
  brand as, 97
statement of value, 76. see also
  value proposition
Stengrevics, John M., 179
stories/storytelling
  Amazon's Tell Us Your Story
    campaign, 223
  brand belief and, 151
  clarity of company story,
    92–94
  talent brand as, 76, 89
  worker communication and,
    205
supply and demand
  evaluating demand by
    segments, 118–119
  following 9/11, 46
  increasing supply of workers,
    237
  maintaining worker pipeline,
    51–55
  marketing to create demand,
    143–144
  marketplace regulating,
    55–56
  in new marketplace, 7–8
  trends in 1970s and 1980s,
    43–44
supply chain management,
  80–81
surfers, Yahoo!, 87
survival tips, for social media
  world
  communication and
    collaboration, 211–213
  false security and, 216–217
  global community, 213–214
  rumors and, 215
  unchecked sources, 214–215

T

talent
  acquisition programs, 20, 239
  attracting, 56
  changes in marketplace and,
    242
  competing for, 47–48
  identifying pivotal, 114–115
  increase in competition for,
    56
  market for jobs compared
    with market for talent,
    50–51
  marketplace for, 236
  marketplace of 1970's and
    1980s, 45
talent, changes in
  brand loyalty, 6–8
  consumers of work, 4–5
  generational change and,
    3–4
  overview of, 3
  social media and, 5–6
  talent marketplace and, 5
talent brand
  applying, 88–90
  brand loyalty and, 7
  brand pressure and. see brand
    pressure
  branding for talent, 76–80
  career site as face of,
    150–153
  CEO's role in changing, 39
  commitment to, 101–105
  contributions of, 236–242
  corporate culture and,
    180–181, 183–184
  creating, 84–88
  differentiation and, 95
  eBay example, 91
  employer brand compared
    with, 75, 79, 84–86
  employer brand evolving
    into, 77
  energy and, 87
  filling talent pipeline, 82–83
  IBM example, 78–79
  leadership's influence on,
    195–197
  legacy, 241–242
  as lens for understanding
    culture, 182
  as lens for viewing worker
    experience, 186
  magnet for talent and, 90–92
  marketing, 9
  marketing employer brand
    vs. marketing talent brand,
    111–112
  purpose of, 88

social media impact on,
  212–213, 225–226
  strategy for, 80–82
  tailoring to worker segments,
    74
  time required for building,
    58–59, 122–123
  types of brands, 3, 79–80
  wanting is not enough,
    243–244
  what is needed to support,
    243
  where to start, 102–103
  worker participation in,
    199–200
talent brand hurdles
  believability. see brand belief
  hurdle analogy from track,
    144
  memorability. see brand
    memory
  overview of, 145
  personalization. see
    personalization of brand
  recognition, 145–147
talent brand section, of careers
  site, 153
talent concierge, for brand
  personalization, 159–163
talent marketplace. see also
  marketplace
  changes in, 5
  global competition in, 47
  reputation as benefit in, 59
  targeting segments of,
    237–238
talent pipeline, 103
talent pools, 103
tasks, not sole basis of
  segmentation, 114
Teach for America, 32–33
technology
  caution regarding use for
    building relationships, 209
  connection-orientation of
    new consumer and, 28
  getting scoop on
    companies/work
    opportunities before
    applying, 16
  influencing how people look
    for work, 18
  recruitment tools, 14
  social media and, 219
  worker expectations
    regarding, 3
  Yahoo! careers site organized
    by creative and technical
    needs, 119
telling stories. see
  stories/storytelling
testing marketing approach, 99

TheLadders.com, 224
timing, as basis of talent marketing, 136–137
Total Petrochemicals, 38
Trader Joe's, 102
training, to fill talent pipeline, 83
transactions, vs. relationships, 104–105
transparency
  example of worker's online narration of last day at work, 30–31
  link to integrity, 215
  preparedness of companies for, 210
  privacy vs., 29
  social networking and blogs demanding, 208

U

Ulrich, Dave, 197
unchecked sources, threats posed by social media, 214–215

V

value
  as basis of talent marketing, 134–136
  value added by different types of work, 117
value proposition
  brand categories and, 141
  converting into targeted message, 90–91
  as core of talent brand, 111
  for employees, 100
  employer brand and, 2
  leadership communicating, 189
  recruitment strategies and, 60
  segments balanced with overall unity, 124
  talent brand as extension of, 76–77, 93
vault.com, 208
video feature, on career site, 159
virtual career fairs, 28
virtual recruiting, 14

W

Warrender, Chris, 97
web
  Generation Y reliance on, 3–4
  as reality of new generation, 56
Web 2.0
  as enabling technology for social media, 218
  social media and, 210
  as strategy rather than threat, 217
  Yahoo! strategy for, 81–82
web blogs. *see* blogs/blogosphere
WebEx meetings, 28
webinars, 14
website, in social media strategy, 219–220
Weirick, Kristen
  on authenticity, 32
  on brand reflecting culture, 180
  on demographic and functional perspectives of employer brand, 229
  on differentiated approach to workers, 19–20
  on employee referrals and relationships, 83–84
  on finding quality talent, 58
  on leadership behavior model, 192
  on making company site a "destination", 152–153
  on personalization, 160
  on segmentation, 116
  on storytelling, 151
  on talent brand as a call to action, 98
  on technology for relationship building, 209
welcoming events, for new workers, 200
Whirlpool Corporation
  authenticity at, 32
  brand reflecting culture, 180
  cautions regarding using technology for relationship building, 209
  differentiated approach to workers, 19–20
  finding quality talent, 58
  leadership behavior model, 192
  making company site a "destination", 152–153
  personal approach to candidates, 160
  segmentation approach at, 116
  storytelling on website, 151
  talent branding efforts of, 78
Wikinomics, 211
wonkette, 226
work
  focusing on work instead of jobs, 49–50, 103
  identifying work needed in process of filling talent pipeline, 82–83
  listing types of work available on career sites, 154
  meeting demand for work vs. identifying job candidates, 81
  prioritizing based on value added, 116–117
work application section, of careers site, 155
work availability section, of careers site, 154
worker experience
  as basis of talent marketing, 138–139
  as caring experience, 38
  culture and brand and, 178–179
  demand for authenticity, 31
  description of candidate experience, 155–156
  events celebrating, 200–201
  face-to-face interactions, 199–200
  vs. job, 21
  overview of, 198–199
  recognition of, 201
  social networking for sharing, 62–64
  Southwest Airlines focus on, 45
  talent brand as lens for viewing, 186
  wanting to be part of the action, 27
worker life section, of careers site, 156–157
workers. *see also* employees
  attracting, 1
  brand pressure and, 126–130
  communication of, 204–205
  evaluating demand by segments, 118–119
  expectations of, 17, 20–21
  increasing supply of, 237
  on-boarding experience, 166–168
  participation in talent brand, 199–200
  pipeline of. *see* pipeline of workers
  providing necessary resources, 203
  redefining worker relationships, 241
  role in holding leadership accountable, 190

workers. *see also* employees
  (*Continued*)
  self selection by, 125
  short term outlook of, 23
  what's in it for me, 5
work/life balance
  expectations regarding, 27
  Pitney Bowes website
    emphasizing,
    151–152
  segmentation of brand
    message and, 129

Y

Yahoo!
  career site, 119, 153
  case study regarding, 179
  changing how people look
    for work, 62
  chat rooms, 208
  competition for talent with
    Google and Microsoft, 115
  corporate blog, 208
  cybersurfers, 87
  employees leaking
    confidential information to
    blogs, 215
  employer brand at, 2
  "Hack Day", 112
  leadership toolkit, 197–198
  making use of the yodel in
    job offers, 161–162
  performance ratings at, 170
  recruitment campaign, 205
  reviewing
    strengths/weaknesses of
    culture, 191
  service award program, 139
  social networking for
    checking out employment
    with, 118
  social networking in
    recruitment efforts of, 211
  talent brand strategy, 81–82
  time required for building
    employer and talent
    brands, 58–59
  value creation as first step in
    branding work, 98
  work environment of,
    48–49
Yang, Jerry, 191
year 2000, 89
YouTube
  corporate reputation and the
    web, 16
  corporate uses of social
    media, 223–224
  as preferred destination for
    entertainment, 214
  social media strategy and,
    223–224

About the Authors

For the past twenty years, **Mark Schumann** and **Libby Sartain** have collaborated at such legendary organizations as Southwest Airlines and Yahoo! to create a definitive point of view on the value that an employer brand can bring to any business. In their first book, *Brand from the Inside*, they offered the step-by-step secrets to brand development; in *Brand for Talent* they share their insight into how to market to various talent segments in today's social media world.

Mark Schumann, ABC, is the former global communication practice leader for the consulting firm Towers Perrin. For the past thirty years he has counseled leaders, human resources, and corporate communications on how to recruit, retain, and engage employees; he has also created a range of creative work that has been honored with fifteen Gold Quill Awards from the International Association of Business Communicators.

Libby Sartain is an active business advisor and corporate board member following a distinguished thirty-year career in human resources, including CHRO roles at Southwest and Yahoo! Both companies were listed on the Fortune 100 Best Companies to Work For in America and the Fortune 500 during her tenure. Today, Libby is helping a range of organizations develop employer brand strategies to create magnetic reputations as places to work.